A HISTORY OF
CIVILIZATION
IN**50**
DISASTERS

A HISTORY OF
CIVILIZATION
IN 50
DISASTERS

Tilbury House Publishers
Thomaston, Maine

Tilbury House Publishers

12 Starr Street, Thomaston, Maine 04861

800-582-1899 • www.tilburyhouse.com

First hardcover edition: November 2015

ISBN 978-0-88448-383-0

First paperback edition November 2015

ISBN 978-0-88448-489-9

Library of Congress Cataloging-in-Publication Data

Eaton, Gale.

　A history of civilization in 50 disasters / Gale Eaton.

　　　pages cm— (History in 50)

　　Audience: Ages 12 and up.

　　ISBN 978-0-88448-383-0 (hardcover) — ISBN 0-88448-383-5 (hardcover) —ISBN 978-
0-88448-489-9 (pbk.) — ISBN 0-88448-489-0 (pbk.) 1. Disasters—History—Juvenile literature. 2. Natural disasters—History—Juvenile literature. 3. World history—Juvenile literature.
I. Title. II. Title: History of civilization in fifty disasters.

　D24.E197 2015

　909—dc23   2015031010

Text designed by Janet Robbins, North Wind Design and Production

Cover designed by John Barnett, 4 Eyes Design

Some of the images used in this book are licensed under a Creative Commons commercial-use
license (versions 1 - 4); see http://creativecommons.org/licenses/by/4.0/. Credits are found
next to the images within the text. For images given secondary additional use, refer to the princi-
pal use within the text for credit information.

Printed in China through Four Colour Print Group, Louisville, Kentucky

15 16 17 18 19 20 4CM 5 4 3 2 1

CONTENTS

PRESENTING THE HISTORY IN 50 SERIES
BY PHILLIP HOOSE

The **History in 50** series explores history by telling thematically linked stories. Each book in this series includes 50 illustrated narrative accounts of people and events—some well-known, others often overlooked—that, together, build a rich connect-the-dots mosaic and challenge conventional assumptions about how history unfolds. In *A History of Civilization in 50 Disasters*, for example, Gale Eaton weaves tales of the disasters that happen when civilization and nature collide. Volcanoes, fires, floods, and pandemics have devastated humanity for thousands of years, and human improvements such as molasses holding tanks, insecticides, and deepwater oil rigs have created new, unforeseen hazards—yet civilization has advanced not just in spite of these disasters, but in part because of them.

History in 50 is a canny, fun, and logical way to present history. The stories are brief, lively, and richly detailed. They work as narrative and also as bait to lure readers to well-selected source material. History in these books is not a stuffy parade of generals, tycoons, and industrialists, but rather a collection of brief, heart-pounding non-fiction narratives in which genuine calamities overtake us, genuine athletes leap skyward on feet of clay, and genuine discoverers labor bleary-eyed through the night to take us to the depths of the ocean, explore the vast reaches of space, unlock the genetic code, or develop a vaccine that saves millions of lives. It's history that bellows and shivers and roars.

And who doesn't love lists? Making a list of fifty great episodes of any kind invites—*demands*—debate. Even if the events aren't ranked (they're in chronological sequence), something always gets left out. I just finished reading *A History of Civilization in 50 Disasters*. I paged wide-eyed through plagues, eruptions, famines, microbes, and vaccines that worked or didn't. From my reading chair I took on dust storms, meltdowns, and epidemics at all scales that claimed my unwavering attention. When I closed the book and looked up, blinking, my first thought was, "Unbelievable. How have we ever made it through all this?"

But these feelings quickly gave way to a surge of indignation: *Where was the Tri-State Tornado of March 1925?* It's my favorite disaster—one that hit home. Actually a series of twisters, the Tri-State storm ripped through Missouri and Illinois before closing in on my great-grandparents in southwestern Indiana. Seven hundred people were killed in what is commonly ranked as the worst tornado ever. Contemporary meteorologists agreed that it was surely a category five twister, and yet it didn't make the top fifty disasters? I needed to lodge a protest.

But then I realized that my pique was a good thing. The book had made me care. The stories had swept over me and shaken my certainty like the 1906 San Francisco earthquake. And I realized that many readers will have the very same reaction: *Hey, where's my favorite episode?* It will spur debate. I imagine smart teachers asking students to describe their own favorite historical episodes, backing up findings with research. I imagine readers of all ages heading back to their bookshelves to support their arguments.

History is rewarding, but in my experience most people have to be led to it. So-called Reluctant Readers are mainly reluctant to be bored. They require, and deserve, historical material that meets them partway. History with menacing characters, even if some of them are invisible (germs); history replete with tough decisions; crisp episodes that leave you wondering what you would have done in that situation; history moved by people just like us, often from the humblest of origins, struggling in their daily lives while reaching for greatness—that's the history that works for most readers. And that is the history we have in this brilliant new series. The writing is clear and exciting, punchy stories that are, on average, two pages long. I have high hopes for the **History in Fifty** series, and it gives me pleasure to enthusiastically endorse it. Why? Because it works.

PHILLIP HOOSE is the National Book Award–winning author of *Claudette Colvin: Twice Toward Justice* and *The Boys Who Challenged Hitler: Knud Pedersen and the Churchill Club.*

INTRODUCTION
DISASTERS AND CIVILIZATION

What is a disaster? It comes out of nowhere. It smashes lives. When it's over, things you thought were safe are gone. Houses are burned, forests flattened, sea coasts rearranged. The world is different.

The word *disaster* comes from an ancient word for "bad star." People thought the stars ruled their fates; bad stars, comets, and other evil omens could ruin your horoscope. They may have been right—the disaster that ended the reign of the dinosaurs could well have come from the heavens.

Sixty-five million years ago, many scientists believe, an asteroid with a diameter of 6 to 9 miles (10 to 15 kilometers) collided with the earth. This collision

Dinosaurs witness an asteroid blazing toward impact off the Yucatan Peninsula in this artist's conception. Did this enormous collision 65 million years ago result in mass extinctions and end the age of the dinosaurs? (ESST/Thinkstock)

Pterodactyls fly near the asteroid strike in this alternative view. (Donald E. Davis painting)

would have released a billion times more energy than the atomic bombs dropped on Hiroshima and Nagasaki at the end of World War II. It would have sent ash, debris, and chemicals high into the atmosphere. The cloud would have cut off light from Earth's surface, and plants need light. Hot cinders raining from the sky could have started huge fires, burning vegetation, consuming oxygen, and flooding the atmosphere with carbon dioxide. Herbivores (plant eaters) died, and then so did their predators. The collision marked the end of the Cretaceous period and the Mesozoic Era.

Is that really what happened? There are competing theories (see box, Chapter 28). Whatever cataclysm changed their climate, the great dinosaurs could not adapt; only the smaller winged dinosaurs survived, evolving into the birds we know today. But a disaster for one life form can be a stroke of good fortune for another. Small mammals that had coexisted with dinosaurs for eons—able to survive but not to compete—underwent rapid evolution as the Cenozoic Era began, and 55 million years later, we humans evolved in a world free of dinosaurs. Civilization might never have developed if the dinosaurs had not met with disaster.

What is civilization? It rises from human imagination and ingenuity. It weaves lives together. Like the world itself, a civilization is always changing. And like a disaster, it changes the world.

The word *civilization* comes from an old word for "city." A civilization is a society that has cities, formal gathering places, and a system of writing. Before civilization, hunter-gatherer bands adapted to a variety of climates by creating mini-environments. Think of warm clothes and tents, for instance—portable barriers between human skin and freezing nature.

Civilization is more ambitious. You could see it as a way of making environments easier for humans to live in. Civilized humans don't just adapt ourselves to natural environments; we try to engineer the planet to meet our needs. Ancient Egyptians harnessed the Nile to irrigate their crops; in Yemen, the great Ma'rib Dam captured mountain rains to irrigate dry land; in Peru, farmers terraced the Andes. Civilization is larger than a mini-environment. It surrounds us, blocking out our view of nature.

The most fascinating disasters pit human civilizations against the forces of nature. Even though we've been taming it for millennia, our planet is a wild place.

This book will look at fifty disasters. All of them were caused partly by natural forces: earthquakes and volcanoes; floods and droughts; wind, cold, and

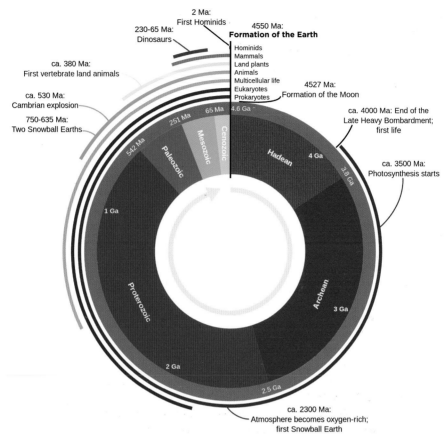

Geologic time can be imagined as a clock face, with the formation of earth 4.55 billion years ago (Ga = billion years; Ma = million years) represented by the stroke of midnight and the present day represented by 12 noon. In this conception, the 2 million years of human existence are a scarcely perceptible few seconds before noon. Some scientists believe that earth's surface was completely or almost completely frozen at three times in geologic time (the "Snowball Earth" theory), most recently 635 million years ago, or 400 million years before dinosaurs evolved. It is both sobering and amazing to reflect that the history of civilization—the subject of this book—is much too short to be visible in this illustration.

microbes. All were caused partly by human actions: where we settled, how we built, and what we carried. Some of the fifty were huge. The Black Death probably killed at least 100 million people in Europe and Asia when the world's total population was 450 million. Others were local. The 1919 Molasses Flood killed 21 people in Boston. All fifty have been chosen because they reveal something interesting about the civilizations they touched.

Hundreds more have been omitted. This book skews toward modern disasters for two reasons. First, reliable information about ancient disasters is hard to come by. We cannot accurately estimate the intensity of earthquakes based on reported damage to pre-modern buildings, even where chronicles agree—and often they don't. The 230,000 deaths that put an 1138 earthquake in Aleppo (in modern-day Syria) high in the most-deadly list may actually belong to an 1139 earthquake somewhere else.[1]

Second, recent disasters may tell us more about what comes next. Today's scientists and policy makers talk about disasters in terms of hazard and vulnerability, risk and resilience. A volcano is a hazard; it has the potential to do harm. Unprepared people living near the volcano are vulnerable; they will be exposed to danger if the volcano erupts. An eruption will have a disastrous impact if vulnerable populations are exposed to it, or if it damages infrastructure and other assets that societies depend on. So the risk of disaster can be thought of as the probability of hazardous events or trends multiplied by the impacts if these events or trends occur.

Disasters and near disasters keep coming. A November 2013 typhoon left more than 6,200 dead and 28,600 injured in the Philippines; more than 4 million people were displaced.[2] In January 2014, a chemical spill left 300,000 people in West Virginia without good tap water. These events made people ask questions about risk and resilience:

> ▷ Typhoons and hurricanes happen every year. As the sea level rises, more people are exposed to storm damage. How should we prepare for these events, and how can we best recover from them? Should we rebuild damaged homes, hospitals, power plants, and subway tunnels on their old sites, or redesign vulnerable communities?
> ▷ Industrial accidents like the one in West Virginia are newer hazards. Humans create them by combining or exploiting our natural resources in new ways. Usually business owners gain the most profit from these activities, but customers benefit as well. Who should pay to guard against damages or to repair them? How can the damages be assessed?

As humans work to manage our risks from natural and environmental disasters, it is not just plate tectonics and changing climates we have to consider. Most of all, it is our own nature. We are the ones who must decide what we value, and figure out how to recover from our own mistakes. We are the ones who must take care of ourselves, our communities, and our world.

37,000 BC
NEANDERTHALS AND THE CAMPANIAN IGNIMBRITE ERUPTION

Forty thousand years ago, humans had no writing, no cities, and no civilization. The Ice Age climate was getting colder. Glaciers spread across Britain, Scandinavia, and the Alps. But hardy Neanderthals hunted the forests of Europe. They had lived there for about 200,000 years, making stone tools, boats, and even cave paintings.

Now they had competition. Their cousins, anatomically modern humans (AMHs), were migrating north from Egypt through Mesopotamia. Soon after AMHs (otherwise known as *Homo sapiens sapiens*) arrived, the Neanderthal disappeared. Could a volcano have helped cause their extinction?[1]

Sulfuric fumes rise from the ground at Solfatara, a crater in the Campi Flegrei. (Fyletto/ Thinkstock)

Volcanoes erupt. The tectonic plates that hold Earth's continents shift and collide. The Pacific grinds against the spine of South America; Africa shoves Italy into Europe. Inch by inch, century by century, pressure builds in the subduction zones where plates drag and overlap each other. It's hardly noticeable, until suddenly the ground quakes or explodes.

Around the world, volcanoes form at hot spots, mid-ocean ridges, and subduction zones. Look at a map, and you can see chains of volcanoes along the edges of continents. Volcanoes erupt where melted rock, called *magma*, squeezes up to the surface of the earth.

In a mild eruption, a volcano leaks heat and gas. Magma near the surface boils water, creating hot springs and geysers. Fumes escape from small vents. This kind of mild activity can go on for centuries. In Campania, a region of Italy, there's a bowl-shaped depression about 8 miles across: the Campi Flegrei ("burning fields"). Romans smelled sulfur there and imagined it was the entrance to the underworld.[2] Sulfur still curls up from the Campi Flegrei, like smoke from chimneys.

A major volcanic eruption is a violent explosion. It crushes magma to small pieces and sends up a miles-high column of dust, ash, and rock (called tephra). Mudslides and liquid magma (called lava) pour down its slopes. Worse, poisonous clouds of ash, fumes, and debris (called pyroclastic flows) may surge downhill at 200 miles per hour (350 km per hour) or more,[3] bulldozing everything in their way. A major eruption can toss rock in every direction, turning a mountain into a valley.

That's what made the Campi Flegrei. Looking down at the area now, you see that 8-mile depression (or caldera), pocked with smaller craters. But it was once a mountain, and the site of Europe's biggest explosion in the past 200,000 years: the Campanian Ignimbrite (CI) eruption. The eruption is named for the distinctive rock it produced, an ignimbrite formed when its unique mix of minerals was shot into the air and pressed across the soil of what is now Campania.

Around 39,000 years ago, it blew 72 cubic miles (300 km³) of ash into the atmosphere. Its tephra column was at least 40 km high[4]—taller than four Mount Everests on top of each other. It spread ash across Europe and western Asia, as far as the Russian plain, the Black Sea,

Most volcanoes are found along the edges of tectonic plates.

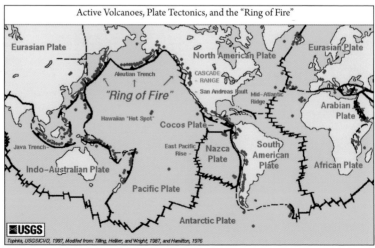

Active Volcanoes, Plate Tectonics, and the "Ring of Fire"

and north Africa. Scientists have found CI tephra a foot deep in Romania.[5] This would be like New Hampshire ash blanketing North Carolina.

The CI eruption was big enough to force climate change—at least temporary cooling in Europe, and maybe over the rest of Earth as well. It came during the Ice Age, and it coincided with the onset of an even colder period (Heinrich Event 4).[6] Some scientists think the cold helped doom the late Neanderthals who still survived in places such as modern Spain.[7] Neanderthals might actually have been better adapted to the cold than modern humans, but they probably needed more food to keep up their energy. Rapid global cooling might have changed their habitat, limiting their forests and forcing them to adopt new hunting strategies and eat different plants. At the same time, the grasslands spread. The new habitat might have been more comfortable for AMHs.[8]

We do not know exactly what happened in that ancient disaster, but even those who argue that it didn't doom the Neanderthals agree that volcanic cooling affected the daily life of a generation of hominids.[9] After the CI eruption, Earth's glaciers kept spreading—they reached a maximum about 22,000 years ago. AMHs pushed north and west into Europe. The Neanderthals gradually disappeared. Researchers still look for clues to their disappearance. Was it because of their pushy AMH cousins, or because the biggest explosion in 200,000 years made their lifestyle unsustainable?

How Do Scientists Study Prehistoric Disasters?

First, they date eruptions and trace their fallout. One way to do this is by studying core samples of ice and sediment. An exploding volcano throws out its own unique blend of rocks and minerals. Wherever its ash settles, scientists can find its geochemical fingerprints. They can identify Campanian Ignimbrite (CI) in polar ice and underwater sediments, and figure out when it happened by studying the layers (or *strata*) above and below it.[10]

To estimate the effects of eruptions on climate, scientists can use tree rings. In bad years, trees grow slowly and their rings are narrower. Events deeper in the past have to be guessed from trickier clues, such as ancient layers of pollen. When the climate cools too much, forests die off and there will be less tree pollen in the mix.

Using sophisticated instruments and models to test their hypotheses, scientists still cannot agree about just how prehistoric eruptions affected human life. But one thing is clear from archaeological records—humans have always liked to live near volcanoes. When we started making stone tools, we used volcanic rock: first lava, and later obsidian. The ancient Romans made cement from volcanic ash and lime. The Greeks used sulfur from volcanoes to repel insects, and the Egyptians used it in medicine.

Volcanic ash breaks down to make wonderfully fertile soil; farming around the world has benefited from volcanoes.[11] A look at the map shows that volcanoes, like humans, are most numerous along the earth's coastlines. As long as we want rich soil and easy access to the sea, we will probably keep settling next to volcanoes.

Scientists obtaining an ice core. (Photograph by Peter Rejcek, National Science Foundation)

The Youngest Toba Tuff Eruption

Around 73,500 years ago, the Youngest Toba Tuff eruption in Indonesia—the largest eruption anywhere on earth in the past 2.5 million years—may have spewed 480 to 720 cubic miles (2,000 to 3,000 km³) of ash and cooled the earth by 3–5° C for several years.[12]

Supervolcanoes cut off light and warmth, kill vegetation, and wreak havoc with ecosystems around the globe. Scientists hypothesize that they have affected the fate of the human race. Some genetic studies suggest that *Homo sapiens* experienced a bottleneck—a dramatic population drop—at around the time of the Toba eruption. Although our numbers more than recovered, our diversity was affected; each group of survivors grew from a smaller, more local gene pool. But did Toba really cause such a bottleneck? The theory is contested.[13]

Sixty miles long by 18 miles wide (100 km by 30 km), Toba Lake, on the Indonesian island of Sumatra, fills the caldera of the Toba supervolcano and is the world's largest volcanic lake. (Rafal Cichawa/Thinkstock)

Anatomically Modern Humans and Neanderthals

Evolution happens over millions of years, as new families and species diverge from older ones. Some of the new lines flourish; others die out. Anatomically Modern Humans (AMH, or *Homo sapiens sapiens*) are now the only surviving species of genus Homo, which emerged 2.3 million years ago, but we once shared the earth with close cousins. Neanderthals (*Homo sapiens neanderthalensis*) lived in Europe and Asia from 400,000 to 30,000 years ago.[14] AMH evolved from archaic *Homo sapiens* 200,000 years ago[15] and headed north from Africa 60,000 years ago.[16] Neanderthals have often been portrayed as brutish and stupid, but recent studies show that the genetic distance between AMH and Neanderthal was very slight. Interbreeding took place, and today most people of Asian and European descent carry some Neanderthal genes. Neanderthal traits such as paler skin may have helped the newcomers adapt to colder northern climates,[17] but there were fitness costs to hybridization as well.[18]

A bust of a male Neanderthal who lived 70,000 years ago, reconstructed from fossil remains found in a cave in Iraqi Kurdistan and on display display in the Hall of Human Origins in the Smithsonian Museum of Natural History in Washington, D.C. (Tim Evanson)

2

1600 BC
ERUPTION AT SANTORINI UNDERMINES MINOAN CIVILIZATION

Thousands of years after the CI eruption, the world got warmer and the glaciers began to shrink. In six places around the world—China, Egypt, India, Mesopotamia, Mexico, and Peru—Stone Age humans began creating civilizations. They domesticated animals, planted crops, and established farms. They built temples and government buildings, and moved into cities. They learned how to use metal. Copper alloys, such as bronze, made better tools and weapons than stone, and around 3300 BC, the Bronze Age began.

One of the great Bronze Age civilizations centered on Crete. Its people, the Minoans, traded actively all around the Aegean Sea. The city of Akrotiri, a day's sail north of Crete on the island of Thera, was a regional hub in the Minoan network.[1] It had a fine harbor and easy access to several other important towns. It was a good place to break a journey—until it was destroyed.

This fresco, found on a wall in buried Akrotiri, shows what the busy Minoan town was like in its heyday.

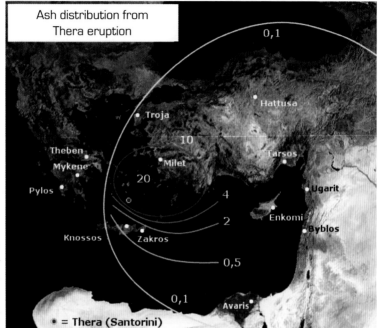

Ash distribution from Thera eruption

0,1

Hattusa

Troja

10

Theben

Mykene

Milet

Tarsos

20

Pylos

4

Ugarit

2

Enkomi

Byblos

Knossos   Zakros

0,5

0,1

Avaris

• = Thera (Santorini)

Thera's ash was carried throughout the eastern Mediterranean region, from Turkey to Egypt.
(Al Mare)

Sometime between 1700 and 1500 BC, the largest European eruption since the CI cataclysm 35,000 years earlier rocked Thera. Its plume rose 22 miles (36 km); its traces still show up in the Black Sea, Turkey, and Egypt. An estimated 10 cubic miles (40 km³) of rock from under the island either blew sky high or poured into the sea, where it set tsunamis ricocheting around the Mediterranean. Akrotiri was buried, and the volcano caved in on itself, leaving sections of its rim as smaller islands curled around an underwater caldera.[2]

Somehow, people must have known the eruption was coming. They had been repairing earthquake damage; probably fresh earthquakes and explosions warned them of danger.[3] They abandoned Akrotiri before the eruption, leaving empty houses behind: tall buildings with stone staircases, bright frescoes painted on the walls, and hot and cold running water.

Some scholars link Thera to the myth of Atlantis, a rich empire that sank beneath the sea.[4] The Greek philosopher Plato (427–347 BC) placed Atlantis some 9,000 years before Solon led Athens (about 600 BC). It lay beyond "the pillars of Hercules"—that is, beyond the Strait of Gibraltar. But people since then have argued that Plato's "pillars of Hercules" might have been somewhere else, and that Atlantis was in Turkey, or Sweden, or the Canary Islands. Some think Atlantis was really Minoan Crete, destroyed by the sea 900 years instead of 9,000 years before Solon.

That would make the timing right. Minoan civilization peaked around 1600 BC and declined soon after. Archaeologists have hypothesized that its end was connected with the eruption on Thera.[5] Testing that hypothesis requires careful dating of both the eruption and the Minoan collapse. The eruption probably did happen around 1600 BC. According to radiocarbon dating, that's when two olive trees died under the ash in Akrotiri.[6] On the other hand, historians and archaeologists think a broken bowl from Cyprus—also found under the ash—was made after 1560 BC.[7] If they are right, the eruption must have come later.

Archaeological site at Akrotiri.
(Norbert Nagel)

The volcano did affect the Minoans. Falling ash may have contaminated their water supply and damaged harvests. The loss of Akrotiri, a central hub, would have increased their trading costs over time.[8] But the most immediate damage came from tsunamis, which wrecked ships and harbors. The coasts of Crete were battered and undefended. Minoan culture lasted another 50 or 100 years, but the eruption fatally weakened it, and soon it was conquered by the Greeks.[9]

Thera's volcano is not extinct. Its violent eruptions occur every 20,000 years or so, with moderate to vigorous episodes at 5,000-year intervals.[10] It erupted in 1950, and the island suffered a large earthquake in 1956. Building codes have been tightened since then, and local seismic activity is carefully monitored.

3

AD 64
EMPEROR NERO BLAMES GREAT FIRE ON UNPOPULAR CULT

Nero was the popular young emperor of Rome, but he would rather have been a singer. The saying goes that Nero fiddled while Rome burned, but actually he was at a singing contest in the nearby town of Antium when the fire broke out. Still, he could have had the fire set. Was he monster enough to torch his city, leaving hundreds of thousands homeless? Why would anybody believe such a thing?

Rome had more than a million inhabitants at the time—about as many as San Jose, California, has today. Its race track, the Circus Maximus, was over five times the size of Boston's Fenway Park; 200,000 fans could gather to bet on their favorite charioteers. Wealthy Romans lived in mansions on fashionable hills, while the less wealthy crowded into 47,000 apartment blocks. Bakeries, pharmacies, shops, and taverns lined crooked streets. Upper stories jutted out and nearly touched, so the roads were like tunnels. Owners lived above shops, climbing up from the back doors on ladders. Rome had 55 miles of streets, but only two roads in the walled central city were wide enough for one cart to pass another.[1]

Romans cooked and heated their homes with open flames, and house fires were common. Major fires in AD 6, 22, 26, and 36 leveled entire neigh-

borhoods. Rome's first responders were the Vigiles, or Night Watch. They served as both policemen and firefighters but had no fire hoses, pumps, or reliable access to the nine aqueducts that delivered the city's water. Instead they had to lug bronze or leather buckets from water basins, reservoirs, or the Tiber River.

In the night of July 19, AD 64, the Circus Maximus went up in flames. Did a cooking fire run out of control? Did somebody set the blaze deliberately? The historian Tacitus, nine years old at the time of the fire, heard both explanations. Shops under the Circus walls sold flammable goods including lamp oil. Wooden stands burned quickly, and strong winds drove the fire into adjoining tenement blocks. The flames moved faster than men with battering rams could make fire breaks, spreading in

Nero was a teenager when he became Emperor of Rome.

8

The Fire of Rome, as imagined by French artist Hubert Robert in 1785.

all directions, not just downwind. Many suspected arson, but a firestorm can act as its own arsonist, shooting sparks everywhere.[2]

On July 20, word reached Nero in Antium. He hurried back to Rome on July 21 and saw imperial palaces and private mansions ablaze on the Palatine Hill. People struggled to rescue books and golden treasures. Nero stared. Someone heard him say the flames had a certain beauty. Then he whipped into action. He ordered a new fire break, had camps set up for the homeless, and organized relief supplies.

Before July 26, fire consumed three of Rome's fourteen districts and littered seven others with ash and rubble. Only four districts were mostly undamaged. Charred corpses lay in the ruins, but many bodies were incinerated. Nobody could count the dead.

Nero's enemies claimed he'd engineered the fire. On July 19, his song for the contest was about the destruction of Troy. People said this proved it: he'd been thinking of Rome, not Troy. Later he used burned land to expand his palace, and people said that was what he'd planned all along. And while he supported the rebuilding, he established Rome's first building regulations: wider streets, lower buildings, and stone walls. Grumblers claimed dark, narrow streets had been healthier.

Evidence against Nero was circumstantial, but people believed it. Historians Suetonius (fifty years later) and Cassius Dio (later still) believed it. Tacitus said Nero tried to shift blame to "a class hated for their abominations," and surviving manuscripts identify this hated group as Christians. Modern historian Stephen Dando-Collins argues that forgers altered the record, substituting Christians for Nero's intended scapegoat, the cult of Isis.[3] In any case, the scapegoating failed. Romans—at least a vocal faction of the Roman elite—believed Nero himself was guilty. Everyone knew he had murdered his foster brother and his mother, and such a man was capable of anything.

After the fire, Nero's enemies pushed their advantage. Imperial politics grew ever more dangerous and paranoid. When Nero uncovered a plot against him, he gave suspects a choice: suicide or decapitation. Deaths mounted, and so did the plots. In June AD 68, the Senate ordered Nero's execution, and he committed suicide instead. His death triggered a civil war among rivals to succeed him, and there were four emperors in the year 69 alone. If it hadn't been for the fire, would Nero have had a long and prosperous reign? If so, history might have unfolded differently for the most powerful empire of the era.

Anthropogenic Disasters

Volcanoes, floods, and other natural hazards cause disasters when they affect humans, but we humans don't cause them. We simply expose ourselves to them by settling where they are likely to occur. Fire, too, is a natural hazard. It can be kindled by lightning. But the Great Fire of Rome was at least partly anthropogenic—caused by humans. Even if there were no arsonists, humans contributed both fuel and a spark to the conflagration.

4

AD 79
VESUVIUS BURIES POMPEII
AND HERCULANEUM

The Romans knew about volcanoes. Mt. Etna, on Sicily, erupted often. But in AD 79, Mt. Vesuvius had been dormant so long nobody remembered what it could do. The most significant event there in generations had been an encampment of escaped gladiators and slaves in the crater during the Spartacus Revolt in 73 BC. The crater looked cindery, like remains of a great fire, but vineyards flourished on the lower slopes and sheep grazed higher up.[1]

Most people stayed even after an earthquake in AD 62 leveled Pompeii, parts of Herculaneum, and private dwellings in Naples. Hundreds of sheep died; with their noses close to the ground, Roman philosopher Seneca said, they were poisoned by fumes from the depths.[2] He may have been right. Leaks of carbon dioxide before modern eruptions have killed people and livestock.[3]

But Pompeii residents rebuilt. The town was still a regional center in AD 79, with about 20,000 people, 8,000 of them slaves. Its streets were paved with lava blocks; its low brick houses had interior courtyards and gardens. Pompeii had at least 35 bakeries, 89 taverns, a large gymnasium, three public baths, schools, cockfight booths, and two theaters. A rowdy audience of 12,000 could watch gladiators in its amphitheater. Herculaneum, with

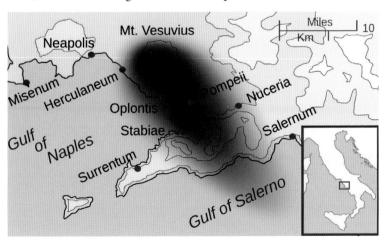

Ash covered Oplontis, Pompeii, and Stabia. Not shown on this map is the pyroclastic flow (carried by gravity rather than wind), which reached Herculaneum. (MapMaster)

At the Hercula-neum excavation a row of arched entrances marks the boathouses where skeletons were found.
Norbert Nagel/ Wikimedia Commons/ License: CC BY-SA 3.

about 5,000 residents, was artsy and upscale, home to weavers, mosaicists, marble workers, and fishermen.[4]

The August 24 eruption buried both towns. A small explosion, proba-bly hours before noon, would have alerted the population but perhaps didn't alarm them unduly. The widow Rectina, who lived at the foot of Vesuvius and could escape only by water, asked her friend Pliny the Elder to cross the Bay of

Ash buried people as they fled Pompeii, and molded itself to their bodies. In 1864, Giuseppe Fiorelli discovered that by filling the empty cavities with plaster, excavators could capture the forms of the dead.[5] (Edella/Thinkstock)

Naples and rescue her. (If she was terrified, why did she not go with her messenger? Maybe she did not want to leave her possessions and her retainers behind.) Pliny, a naturalist, had already noticed the volcanic plume and decided to investigate. But he also had command of the Roman fleet at Misenum, and now he launched the warships in hopes of evacuating the thickly populated coast.

Vesuvius exploded again at noon, sending ash and pumice 9 to 16 miles (15 to 25 kilometers) high. Pumice snowed down, collapsing roofs in Pompeii; people could not run but had to wade through debris. Falling ash and stones blocked the fleet's approach to the coast. Pliny detoured to Stabiae, beyond Pompeii. We do not know where the fleet turned, or how many people they managed to rescue along the shore. Pliny spent the night with a friend and died the next morning, probably choked by dense fumes. His sister and nephew stayed behind in Misenum, but fled that morning because of an earthquake. They saw the sea rush out and back before the volcanic cloud sank to earth and cut off their view, surrounding them in darkness.[6] The nephew, Pliny the Younger, described it years later in two letters to Tacitus, the first detailed eyewitness account we have of an eruption.

Volcanologists and archaeologists have put together the rest. Vesuvius let loose six pyroclastic flows of superheated gas and molten rock. The first raced through Herculaneum around midnight. Hundreds of fleeing people died on the beach, burned and asphyxiated; the flow buried them in a deposit up to 75 feet (23 meters) thick. The fourth surge overran Pompeii, already blanketed under 13 feet (4 meters) of pumice.[7] The sixth reached the outskirts of Stabiae.

Emperor Titus treated the eruption as a national emergency. He visited the area to begin relief efforts, appointed two former consuls to head ongoing operations, and used his own resources as well as public funds to help survivors. The region's agriculture suffered for centuries, however, until volcanic debris weathered into fertile soil. Pompeii and Herculaneum were rediscovered in the 1700s—time capsules from the Roman Empire—and their ancient tragedy was a gift for modern scholars. Ash buried the towns and preserved them so they could be studied.

Vesuvius erupted at least 27 times between 1631 and 1944. Its 1872 and 1906 eruptions may have helped decide millions of Calabrians to move to the United States. Today, millions visit Pompeii and Herculaneum each year and learn about their history, but the volcano may still contribute to human history in new ways.

Carbon Dioxide from Volcanoes

Carbon dioxide (CO_2) is a "greenhouse gas," one of the ingredients that warms Earth's atmosphere. It is also a natural part of the life cycle. Plants take it in through their leaves during photosynthesis, and give off oxygen. Animals breathe oxygen and give off CO_2. It is not toxic, but if there is too much of it in the air, it will suffocate humans and animals. In 1986, Lake Nyos—which lies over an inactive volcano in Cameroon—suddenly "exploded" and released a cloud of CO_2 into the area. It suffocated 1,700 people and 3,500 farm animals.[8]

Volcanoes give off CO_2 and other gases when they erupt. But even when a volcano is not erupting, CO_2 can escape from magma beneath the surface. After a series of small earthquakes in 1989, trees began to die at Mammoth Mountain in California because there was too much CO_2 in the soil.[9] And because CO_2 is heavier than air, it tends to be most concentrated near the ground. Seneca was almost right. Sheep grazing on the slopes of Mount Vesuvius would have been suffocated—not poisoned—by fumes from the depths.

CO_2 warms the atmosphere, but it is not the only thing a volcano emits. A large eruption may send a tall column of ash and sulfur compounds into the stratosphere. There they circulate, blocking some of the sun's energy and reflecting it back into space. So, in spite of its CO_2 emissions, a large eruption can cause a volcanic winter.

Fumaroles like this one—fissures in the earth, often associated with volcanoes—emit steam and noxious gases including carbon dioxide.
(Fyletto/Thinkstock)

5

536
THE CASE OF THE MYSTERIOUS ASH

The sixth century was catastrophic for civilizations around the world. The western part of the old Roman Empire had fallen to barbarians in the fifth century: Britain to the Anglo-Saxons, Spain to the Visigoths, North Africa to the Vandals, and even Italy itself—the original seat of the empire—to the Ostrogoths. The great sixth-century emperor Justinian reconquered much of the lost ground, but a series of unfortunate events undid many of his accomplishments. Europe turned a historical corner from classical antiquity to the Middle Ages, and what was left of the Roman Empire became the Byzantine Empire.

Other ancient powers fell at about the same time. The Sassanid Empire in Persia peaked and began its decline. In Yemen the Great Dam of Ma'rib had irrigated the land for over a thousand years, but in the sixth century it crum-

Volcanic ash prevents much of the sun's light and warmth from reaching the ground. The 536 event dwarfed this recent eruption of the Sakurajima volcano in Japan. (IPGGutenberg UKLtd/Thinkstock)

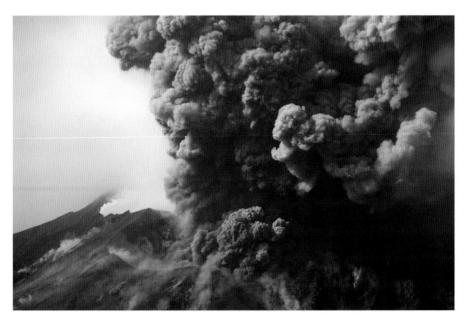

15

Near East, 565 AD

The European and Near bled and went unrepaired, probably for lack of manpower. Without it, crops
Eastern world in 565. failed. Italians reported worldwide famine in 537.[1] In Mongolia, fierce Avar
(Thomas Lessman) horse lords were weakened by famine and overcome by their Turkic under-
lings. The Avar survivors migrated to the Balkans, where they created a new
empire and exacted tribute from Byzantium. Crops failed in China, and hunger worsened ethnic and religious unrest; the government had to give repeated
tax amnesties between 538 and 551. Great cities and cultures in Mexico, Guatemala, and Peru all collapsed.[2]

Why all this tumult in the sixth century? Tree ring samples from around
the world point to a period of unusual cold beginning around 535, and historical evidence agrees. European writers said the sun was dimmed for months in
536. Heavy snow killed birds in Mesopotamia that year, while drought caused
15,000 Saracens to leave Persia.[3] A worldwide drop in temperature could be
caused by a layer of dust in the stratosphere, filtering out light and warmth
from the sun, but what could have made such a great layer of dust? A comet
hitting the earth? Ancient astronomers would have mentioned it. A meteor-
oid? Even if unseen, a meteor that large falling on land would have left a crater;
falling in the ocean, it would have kicked up a huge tsunami. Somebody would
have mentioned it.[4]

A volcano is the likeliest culprit, and ice cores in Greenland and Ant-
arctica show a concentration of sulfuric acid at about the right time. But
which volcano? One near the equator seems likeliest, because it would have
influenced the weather in both hemispheres. Two mysterious bangs were
heard southwest of China in 535. Could it have been Krakatoa, in Indonesia? The volcano that exploded there in 1883 rose from the huge underwater caldera left by an earlier eruption.[5] A 1999 expedition by Haraldur

Sigurdsson could not date that eruption conclusively, but datable charcoal above and beneath its deposits suggested a date between 6600 BC and AD 1300—probably after AD 1.[6] More recent investigators have concluded that there must have been a major volcanic event in 535, but it could not have been Krakatoa.[7]

Whatever caused it, was a global cold snap enough to shake the world? The ecological crisis led to famine and disease. Distressed populations rebelled or migrated; old powers (like the Romans, the Yemenis, and the Avars) eroded, while new ones (like the Turks) gained traction.[8] It appears that even a short-term climate change can affect political and economic conditions around the world.

The Mystery Eruption of 1257

Studying sulfate deposits in glacial ice, scientists long suspected that a huge eruption in 1257 affected northern Europe's weather in 1258. Violets, strawberries, and apple trees bloomed in January that year, but the summer was cold and harvests failed. Recent investigators believe another Indonesian volcano, Samalas, was responsible. Its geochemical profile matches glass shards in the ice cores, and the timing matches. Old Javanese histories written on palm leaves say the eruption destroyed Pamatan, the capital of the Lombok kingdom. Archaeologists hope they will one day find a city buried in the ashes, as well preserved as Pompeii.[9]

6

541
JUSTINIAN'S PLAGUE
WEAKENS THE
BYZANTINE EMPIRE

When Emperor Justinian began his rule (527–565), Constantinople was probably the largest city in the world, with nearly half a million people. It was the capital of the Roman Empire, and even after losing Rome, the Roman Empire was still huge. Justinian's territories included modern Greece, Turkey, Syria, and Egypt. His armies conquered much of northern Africa, Italy, and southern Spain. The empire ringed the Mediterranean Sea, where merchant ships carried silks from China, ivory from Africa, and grain from Egypt.

Then in 541, half the population of Constantinople died of plague. The poor died first, according to John of Ephesus, who was there. Sometimes as many as 16,000 of them died "in a single day." Government officials kept count at first, but they gave up counting and even burying the dead after the first 230,000, and "corpses were heaped up in the streets."[1]

Emperor Justinian, flanked by soldiers and church leaders. Mosaic in the Basilica of San Vitale, Ravenna, Italy, 547.

Some people took days to die; others would seem fine one moment and die the next. People fell in the streets with swollen bellies and open mouths, "throwing up pus like torrents, their eyes inflamed and their hands stretched out upward," said John.

Another witness, Evagrius, survived plague as a child but lost most of his family. He wrote, "With some people it began in the head, made the eyes bloody and the face swollen, descended to the throat and then [killed them]. With others, there was a flowing of the bowels. Some came out in buboes [pus-filled swellings] which gave rise to great fevers, and they would die two or three days later. . . . Others lost their senses before dying. Malignant pustules erupted and did away with them."[2]

The plague didn't just happen in Constantinople. It entered the empire through Egypt and emptied cities around the Mediterranean. And it didn't just happen once. It might leave a city for a year or a decade, and then come swooping back. By 602, four major plague epidemics had wiped out a third of the empire's population.

By 543 the economy suffered. Wages and prices doubled, then tripled.[3] Tax income shrank; there were not enough taxpayers. The army shrank, too; emperors could no longer pay soldiers. The Persians attacked from the east, and Avars from the northwest. The pandemic that began in 541 weakened the Roman Empire.

This humble animal may have sealed the fate of the Roman Empire. Rats infected with bubonic plague stowed away on ships and spread the plague around the empire.
(Peter O'Connor)

Who knew what caused it? Evagrius thought it was sometimes caused by contact and "living together," and sometimes spread by healthy migrants from infected areas. In 549, Justinian enacted "a law meant to hinder and isolate people arriving from plague-infested regions"—a quarantine.[4]

We now believe the pandemic was caused by *Yersinia pestis*, the plague bacillus. (There are other theories, but *Y. pestis* DNA has been found in the teeth of ancient and medieval plague victims.)[5,6] *Y. pestis* occurs naturally in wild rodent populations, and hungry fleas carry it from creature to creature. Justinian's Plague probably began in China. Infected rats stowed away on ships and hitched rides with traders and soldiers up the east coast of Africa (where several important trading centers vanished at about this time). They spread plague as far west as the British Isles. Rats and fleas are always hungry. In 541, their hunger changed history.

The Decline of the Byzantine Empire after Justinian

Perhaps the Byzantine Empire never fully recovered from the plague and the upheavals that followed. In 614, the Sassanids captured Jerusalem and carried home one of Christianity's most famous relics, the True Cross. In 626, with the Avars and Slavs, they besieged Constantinople itself. Emperor Heraclius (610–641) fought off the siege, defeated the Sassanids at Nineveh in 627, and triumphantly restored the True Cross to Jerusalem.

But his problems were just beginning. By 632 the Arabs—united by a vital new religion, Islam—began conquering the old Sassanid territories. By 661 they had taken Egypt and Syria from the Byzantine Empire; by 750 their holdings stretched from Portugal to Pakistan, by way of northern Africa. Yet the Romans held Constantinople against two Arab sieges (674–78 and 717–18). Europe north of the Pyrenees remained Christian territory throughout the Middle Ages, and the remains of the old Roman Empire stood until 1453.[7]

By 650, the Byzantine Empire had lost much of its territory to Arabs in the east and Visigoths in Spain. By 750, the Arab empire would stretch across North Africa and include Spain and Portugal, wrested from the Visigoths. (Justinian43)

7

1287
ST. LUCIA'S FLOOD CREATES A NEW SEA

On December 14, 1287, a massive storm killed an estimated 500 people in England and rearranged the coastline. The country lost important harbors at Hastings, Romney, and Winchelsea.[1] Merchants and fishermen had to find and develop new infrastructure.

Across the North Sea, wind piled the waves higher and drove them against the dikes that guarded the Netherlands. The storm surged over embankments, flooded wide areas, and reportedly drowned at least 50,000 people.[2] There, too, the coast was reshaped. A freshwater lake became an inland sea—the Zuiderzee, or Southern Sea.

The 1287 St. Lucia's Flood wasn't the first to open new channels and create permanent lakes in the Netherlands. There had been a dozen serious floods in the previous two centuries, including seven between 1212 and 1282. When

Three major European rivers carry sediment through the Netherlands to the North Sea. Pliny the Elder described the shore as one great mudflat, and this view of the Wadden Sea (the southeastern portion of the North Sea) from the Netherlands island of Schiermonnikoog shows that the description is still apt today. (Photo by Bert Kaufmann)

A 1421 flooding at the Netherlands town of Dordrecht is shown in two altar paintings by an unknown master.

land sinks or sea levels rise, flooding follows. The cause can be tectonic shifts or severe climate change—or human activity. The St. Lucia's Flood was a natural disaster, but humans helped engineer the conditions that made it a disaster.

"Netherlands" means "low lands." The deltas of three rivers—the Rhine, the Meuse, and the Scheldt—tangle there on their way to the North Sea. Pliny the Elder described the place as one great mudflat with no clear line between land and water. In ancient times, raised peat bogs grew on the coastal plains—mounds of partially decayed moss, shrubs, and sedge that accumulated over the ages to form a useful fuel. Tides washed in and out around them, and early inhabitants built villages on artificial mounds above flood level.

About 800, people took up more active forms of water management. Europe's climate became milder at about this time, and the next four or five centuries are called the Medieval Warm Period. Growing seasons lengthened, harvests improved, and Europe's population grew from an estimated 38.5 million in the year 1000 to 73.5 million in 1340.[3] To feed more people, Europeans farmed more and more land. They cut down forests to make room for more farms. In Flanders and the Netherlands, they even pushed back the sea, using dikes and drainage canals to make farmland from bogs. They called such land "polders,"[4] and for centuries they grew enough grain there to feed Holland. But draining the peat bogs made the land sink about 3 feet per century,[5] and so the new farms could easily be flooded when storm surges topped the dikes. And around 1300, as the Medieval Warm Period ended, violent storms became more frequent.

By 1350, farming in the Netherlands was less profitable. The soil was too wet and salty for grain or cattle. Maintaining dikes, canals, sluices, and dams was labor-intensive, and the plague made labor scarce and expensive. As old dikes failed, new lakes (such as the Haarlem Lake) formed.[6]

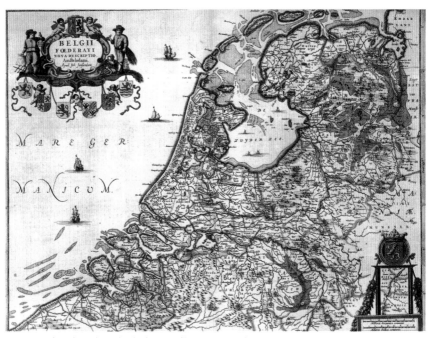

A 1658 map shows the Zuiderzee, the inland sea created by St. Lucia's Flood.

Accidental lakes proved useful for fishermen, peat sellers, and merchants. New waterways provided cheap transport to the interior, and cities grew.[7] The Dutch became urban. They also became increasingly inventive. By 1408 they started using windmills to drain fields. Knowledge of water management techniques began to be written down, and by 1584 inventor Simon Stevin had several patents on drainage devices.[8] New crops included hemp, to make rope for nets and rigging.[9]

A Dutch polder landscape. (CreativeNature/ Thinnkstock)

To keep living in their country, the Dutch had to develop more than levees, sluices, and other water management technology. They had to develop regional water boards, institutions to "compel individuals and communities to pay the taxes and perform the public works that kept the drainage and flood control system functioning."[10] To this day, the water boards guide long-term planning.[11]

So the floods of the Middle Ages affected the political and economic geography of the Netherlands as much as the landscape. The 1287 disaster was one episode in a long negotiation between natural forces and technology. All that water helped make the Dutch a democracy and a great sea power.

Peat

Peat is a useful substance. Gardeners use it to enrich soil, and industries use it to filter out toxic materials from waste water. After an oil spill, dry peat helps soak up the mess.[12] (One of the major ingredients of peat is sphagnum moss, which can hold up to 20 times its dry weight in water.)

Peatland covers about 3% of Earth's surface and serves as a natural "carbon sink"—that is, it absorbs and holds more carbon than it releases into the air.[13] Peat buried under heavy sediment eventually becomes coal,[14] which is mostly carbon and an important fuel.

But peat itself is a fuel, usually closer to the surface and easier to get at than coal, and humans have been burning it for centuries. The Romans extracted it from English moors two thousand years ago. More recently, the British government encouraged farmers to root out the sphagnum moss from fields on the Somerset Levels and plant maize (corn) instead. The soil produced more food, but the region became more vulnerable to flooding. Disastrous storms in the winter of 2013–2014 flooded homes and farms for weeks.[15] The government encouraged farmers to replant sphagnum moss and restore the bogs—and the Netherlands sent flood control equipment.

Another problem is that peat, like coal and other fossil fuels, releases carbon dioxide (CO_2) into the air when burned. CO_2 is a "greenhouse gas," and the more CO_2 we release into the air, the warmer Earth's average surface temperature becomes.

Peat harvest. (arrfoto/Thinkstock)

8

1315-1317
GREAT FAMINE STARVES
NORTHWESTERN EUROPE

The rain began in May, seven weeks after Easter, and kept falling. Northwestern Europe was flooded. Fields turned to muddy wallows. Plowing
was impossible—oxen sank in the mud. The king of France tried to invade
Flanders, but his army could not march through the mud. Horses sank to their
saddle girths; wagons mired. King Louis retreated, but the rain did not. In central Europe, whole villages washed away, and their people drowned. And still
it kept raining, through July and a cold August, beating unripe grain flat in the
fields. In the autumn of 1315 there was little to eat.[1]

The floods of 1315 were followed by the floods of 1316. Grains rotted;
wet hay rotted; and valuable topsoil was carried away.[2] Recovery took years,
because people had less uneaten grain to plant the next year and less farmland
to plant it in.

The economy of Europe at the time depended on subsistence farming—
farming that yielded the bare necessities of life. Peasant farmers lived harvest
to harvest. Most were serfs, and that meant they belonged to the land. They
did not own it; it owned them. Legally, they could not move to the city or look
for work in another country. They owed labor and crops to landlords, and in
return the lords owed justice and protection to their serfs. But when famine
hit, lords could not protect their serfs from hunger.

In the 1200s—the last century of the Medieval Warm Period—one
estate's farms in southern England yielded about three bushels of grain for
every bushel sown. Farmers could set aside one third of their grain for the next

*Subsistence farming, ca. 1310: A
reeve oversees serfs as they harvest
wheat with reaping hooks*

year's planting and use two thirds to feed people and animals until the next year's harvest. There was little left over in the best of years. But 1315 was a very bad year. There was not enough bread to feed the people nor enough hay to feed farm animals.

And 1316 was worse yet. The same farms yielded less than two bushels for every one sown. It was too cold to shear lambs that summer, so there was no wool to trade. Grain was not ground, so the mills turned no profit. Oats, peas, beans, and barley did little better than wheat. In England, King Edward tried to cap the price of ale at a farthing per gallon—less than brewers had to pay for the grain to make it.[3] (Everybody drank ale; it was safer than water. Edward was never popular, and his efforts at price control didn't help.) Europe was even low on salt. Making it took fuel, and all the fuel was wet.[4]

The famine lasted until 1322. People starved all over northern Europe. Sheep froze to death. In 1319, a rinderpest epidemic killed hungry cattle and oxen. In 1320 an epidemic of glanders struck, killing nearly half of Europe's horses by 1322. When the weather finally improved, peasants had few strong beasts to pull the plows and little manure to use as fertilizer. Pigs managed to thrive, but people ate most of them.

People in the country ate what they could find—nuts, roots, even bark. People in the cities could find even less. Many lay moaning in the streets, their stomachs swollen with hunger. Others turned to robbery. They stole food and anything that could be sold for food—even the lead from church roofs. They pirated fish and grain from boats, and they plundered graves. There were rumors of cannibalism, like today's urban myths—hard to pin down, but people believed them.[5]

Beggars foraged for food in refuse heaps and spread disease. Bodies lay stinking in streets and fields. Cattle and humans, rich and poor, were buried in mass graves; towns opened new

"Hunters in the Snow," a painting by Pieter Bruegel the Elder (1526/30–1569), shows a slice of life during the Little Ice Age.

cemeteries. Probably five or ten percent of the urban population of Flanders died in these famine years. Meanwhile, the warriors of England and Scotland did their best to starve each other out by destroying any food they could find along the borders.

Europe's food supply didn't recover until the 1320s. The Medieval Warm Period was over, and the new normal was colder, stormier, and less predictable.[6]

Medieval Drinking Water

Medieval water was often unsafe to drink. The germs that cause disease had not been discovered, and people did not know that boiling water makes it safer. Nobody had indoor plumbing; water might come from a well in the same yard where people and animals relieved themselves. Alcoholic beverages—ale, beer, hard cider, and wine—were safer than most water because alcohol kills germs.

Medieval Climate Change

Earth's climate has changed often in the past 600 million years. There have been ages hot enough for tropical plants to live in Europe and crocodiles in the far north of Canada. There have been ages when glaciers the size of continents spread from the poles.[7] We are currently living in the Holocene Epoch, an interglacial period that began about 11,700 years ago.[8] The Holocene climate has been relatively mild and stable for the past 6,000 years,[9] conducive to civilization as we know it. Over the past 6,000 years we have developed alphabets, cities, clipper ships, baseball, microbiology, and e-commerce.

But even Holocene weather varies. Summer and winter come every year; the El Niño cycle repeats on average every five years; and deep in the ocean, the "global conveyor belt"—a worldwide system of currents with long-term effects on climate—may complete a cycle every thousand years.[10] The sun has cycles, too. Sometimes it gives off more heat, sometimes less. Earth's orbit varies a little; sometimes it is closer to the sun, sometimes farther away. Major vol-

canic eruptions can fill the atmosphere with ash and debris, blocking the sun's energy before the ground can absorb it. And some scientists argue that human farming began to warm the climate as long as 8,000 years ago.[11]

In the Medieval Warm Period (which has been variously dated anywhere from 800–1200[12] to 1000–1300[13]), conditions in northwestern Europe were comfortable, with temperatures close to the 1960–1990 average. The English harvested grapes for wine, and the Vikings settled Greenland. Then came the Little Ice Age. Some geologists date it by the increase of glaciers in the Swiss Alps (1300–1950) and others by low summer temperatures in the Northern Hemisphere (1570–1900).[14] They know it affected Europe; they search peat bogs and coral reefs to learn if and how it affected other parts of the world.

The medieval climate change probably depressed average temperatures by little more than 1° F and less than 1° C.[15] Even that modest difference shortened growing seasons and changed the way people lived.

9

1348–1353
THE BLACK DEATH
DEPOPULATES EUROPE

The Mongol Empire once stretched from Korea to Russia, but by 1330 it had splintered into four smaller empires. One was China, where plague killed up to 90% of the province of Hubei in 1334—an estimated 5 million people. The disease then followed ancient trade routes west by land and sea. In 1335, it killed about 30% of the Persian Mongols, who were at war with the Mongols of Russia and eastern Europe—the Golden Horde.

The Golden Horde swept off to besiege the Italian colony of Caffa, in present-day Crimea, taking the plague along. Soon the Mongols were too sick to fight, but rumor says they catapulted their dead over the Italian walls before leaving. Biological warfare! Soon the plague reached Italy.[1] Between 1347 and 1350, probably one of every three Europeans died. The continent's population as of 1340 was as high as 73.5 million; a century later, it was only 50 million.[2]

"God for the sins of man has struck this great punishment of sudden death," said the King of Sweden,[3] and most people agreed. Some joined groups of "flagellants" and roved from town to town, beating themselves to atone for their sins. Others blamed the planets, or foul air, or tainted food, or the gaze of dying victims—or the Jews. Nonsense, said the pope, pointing out that the plague took people where there were no Jews, and it took Jews, too. But in 1349, people who believed the lies burned hundreds of Jews.[4]

Twe y tego Dziecka Zarly
Zapieniądz teraz nie Warty
Tu to Sęń się Wydworować
Zeby z Smiercią nie tańcować

As deaths mounted, artists imagined Death dancing off with people of every degree—judges and thieves, children and grandparents, rich and poor alike.

The real villain was *Yersinia pestis*, a new strain of the bacillus that caused Justinian's plague in 541.[5] Wild rodents harbor the disease, and their fleas spread it. As rats swarmed ashore in ports across Eurasia, their fleas feasted in crowded city neighborhoods. They bit more poor folks than rich. But young or old, rich or poor, merchant or peasant, the plague spared nobody. Doctors had no idea how to ease the pain. From England to Syria, whole villages became ghost towns. Everybody either died or ran away.

After so many deaths, people had to change how they did things. Labor shortages drove wages up, while reduced

Jews, blamed for spreading plague, were burned to death in Strasbourg, 14 February 1349.

Spread of Bubonic Plague in Europe

1347		1350	
mid-1348		1351	
early 1349		after 1351	
late 1349		minor outbreak	
● Centre of uprisings		● City for orientation	

Copenhagen
Lubeck
London Brunswick ● Magdeburg Warsaw
Rouen Bruges
Frankfurt Prague
Paris
Vienna
Bucharest
Milan ●
Ravenna
Marseilles Florence
Toledo Rome Thessalonika
Barcelona
Athens

The spread of plague through Europe, 1347–51.

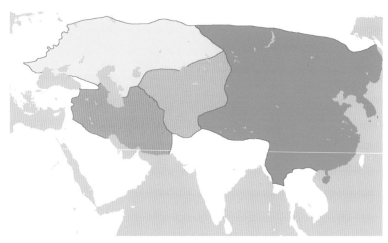

After 1300, the Mongol Empire split into four realms: The Golden Horde (yellow), the Chagatai Khanate (gray), the Yuan Dynasty (green) and the Ilkhanate (purple).

demand drove the price of grain down. The English found that tending sheep took fewer people than raising wheat and brought more profit.[6] Feudalism, the old system that tied serfs to the land, declined. Many escaped to the cities, where professional guilds had lost members and needed new apprentices.[7] Europe began to develop a middle class, a capitalist economy, and a medical bureaucracy. Venice appointed three men to a public health committee in 1348.[8]

Modern languages got a boost. Doctors, lawyers, clergymen, and scholars had used Latin for hundreds of years, and now fewer people knew it. In England, the nobility spoke French, and now common English-speakers rose into the educated classes. Maybe the Black Death helped save the English language from extinction.[9] Maybe it stimulated the invention of the printing press and other labor-saving devices.

What was it like to live right after the Black Death? Terrifying, but also exciting. The Mongol Empire never recovered, and the world's population took centuries to rebound. The first wave of plague died down after 1350, but every few years it struck again. Many died young. But the new social mobility meant those who survived could live in ways their parents never imagined.

The Black Death Gets Its Name

How did the "Black Death" get its name? It's true that bubonic plague can blacken victims' skin with gangrene and necrosis. Plague also fills whole populations with dark fear and sorrow. But people in the Middle Ages just called it the "Great Pestilence" or "Great Plague." The English did not begin to call it the "Black Death" until long afterward, in 1832.[10] The Greeks and Romans may have used the phrase "Black Death" for other diseases. But wherever it came from, the name now identifies the fourteenth-century plague—not other *Y. pestis* pandemics. It is a convenience.

1665: Bubonic Plague Takes a Last Swipe at London

After killing so much of Europe in 1347–50, the plague returned at irregular intervals. To contain it, authorities quarantined travelers from suspected plague hot spots; banned crowds at weddings, funerals, theaters, and markets; killed dogs and cats at the beginning of outbreaks; and even improved sanitation by paving streets and enforcing cleanliness.[11] Venice built an isolation hospital in 1403, and Tuscany set up a special "pest-house" for fumigating silks in 1631. Still, another epidemic hit Turkey in 1661, the Netherlands in 1663, and London in 1665. Theaters and schools closed, noblemen retreated to country estates, and streets fell silent. Individuals wore masks to block contagion, or smoked pipes and carried sweet flowers, as if better smells could purify the air. Doctors wore early hazmat suits: long waxed robes, gloves, and beaked masks. In spite of all precautions, at least 70,000 Londoners died of plague in 1665: roughly 15 percent of the population, or 17 percent of those who stayed in town.

Three hundred years had passed, and Europeans still could not stop the Black Death. But there were signs of modern thinking. Authorities collected data and published weekly *Bills of Mortality* in Bristol, Cambridge, Leicester, London, Norwich, and York. There were printing presses and readers to spread news of the epidemic. People were even doing cost-benefit analyses. Sir William Petty calculated that if each plague victim had a value of £7 and the next great plague killed 120,000, evacuating the city of London

A plague doctor's hazmat suit, 1656, with ankles conveniently exposed to flea bites.

in advance would cost £50,000 and not evacuating would cost £840,000. Fortunately for London, this never happened; 1665–66 was the last bubonic plague epidemic in Britain. Before 1894, when the third international pandemic began, modern thinking would lead to bacteriology.

1450
LITTLE ICE AGE EMPTIES
A VIKING COLONY

Beginning in 870, Vikings from Norway colonized Iceland. Their timing was good. An era of warmer-than-average climate around the North Atlantic was beginning, and this so-called Medieval Warm Period created three centuries of better than usual farming conditions in Iceland. (See Chapter 8.) By 970 the population there rose to an estimated 35,000.[1]

In 986 Erik the Red, a hotheaded exile from Iceland, started a new settlement by a Greenland fjord. The terrain looked familiar, with grasslands for farming and herding and good access to fishing. Ancestors of today's Inuits lived in northern Greenland, but the south was empty. The Norse established

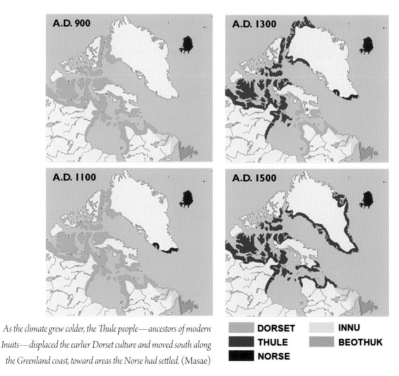

As the climate grew colder, the Thule people—ancestors of modern Inuits—displaced the earlier Dorset culture and moved south along the Greenland coast, toward areas the Norse had settled. (Masae)

DORSET   INNU
THULE   BEOTHUK
NORSE

about 280 farms there, some of them in a smaller settlement to the west. They built churches, and by 1124 the Eastern Settlement had a bishop.

But Greenland straddles the Arctic Circle. The environment was fragile, and the Little Ice Age began around 1300.[2] The Inuits migrated southward. They met and traded with the Norse, although contact was probably limited.

The Norse abandoned the Western Settlement by 1360. The Eastern Settlement may have lasted another century, though our last written word of it dates from 1408. In 1494, when Pope Alexander VI divided the New World between Spain and Portugal, he wasn't worried about a Norse claim. The colony had disappeared.[3]

What happened? Were the people attacked by pirates or Inuits? Did they fall victim to an epidemic? Their bones give no clear evidence of battle or plague.[4] Archaeologists have sifted abandoned Norse farms down to the last housefly in the kitchen[5] and bit of fecal DNA in the farmyard.[6] At one western farm, occupants may have been snowed in for a hungry winter. Across the fjord, there may have been a landslide; sand and permafrost preserved a ruined farm for centuries.

Most scholars believe that climate change played a major role in the colony's collapse. Growing seasons were short in Greenland, and even shorter after 1300. A medieval European lifestyle depended on hay for livestock and grain to make bread and ale. The Norse Greenlanders kept up with medieval European fashions in clothing and architecture, but not in cooking. They had to do without grain,[7] and they stopped keeping cows.[8]

The first church at Erik the Red's settlement was a small chapel that might have looked like this reproduction. (Photo by Claire Rowland)

Europeans also needed wood for building, cooking, and smelting. Trees are sparse near the Arctic.[9] Even if the early settlers had not cut them down, the local birch and willows could not have met the farmers' needs. They had to import lumber from Europe, but pack ice between Greenland and Iceland blocked the ships that could have brought it. Also, the Black Death took half of Norway's population in 1349 and a third of Iceland's in 1402. Demand for Greenland's exports (polar bear skins and walrus ivory) fell, so the Greenlanders had less cash to buy lumber and other European goods.[10]

The Norse inhabited Greenland for more than 400 years. They adapted to their environment, up to a point. They ate seal and caribou instead of beef. But they kept living on farms, and they did not use seal oil for heating and cooking. They hunted, but they did not copy successful Inuit hunting techniques.[11]

In the end, maybe the population simply dipped below a sustainable level. Young people moved away, looking for better opportunities. Perhaps there were too few men to marry the women, and too few children to carry on.[12] The remaining colonists may have staged an orderly exodus, packing their valuables for a reverse migration to Iceland or Norway.[13] As one scholar puts it, "All available evidence indicates that the Norse simply died out, maintaining ethnic purity to the end rather than merging with the Inuit either biologically or culturally."[14]

The Roanoke Colony

In 1587, a small English colony settled on Roanoke Island, off North Carolina. But in 1588, England needed all its ships to fight off the Spanish Armada. When a supply ship finally reached North Carolina in 1590, the only sign of the colonists was the word "Croatoan," carved on a fence post. That Lost Colony is also a mystery.

The Norse in North America

The Greenlanders established an outpost in Newfoundland around 1000. They called it Vinland, and they liked its long growing seasons, mild winters, tall trees, and plentiful game. So did the Native Americans—Beothuks and Dorsets—who lived there already. They were short by Viking standards and made their weapons of ivory and stone, not iron. The Norse killed the first ones they met, but the Norse were vastly outnumbered. The Greenland colony, with only about 500 people, wasn't large enough to invade a thickly settled continent.[15] It might have been more interesting if they had been able to set up a friendly exchange of goods and ideas. Could friendly neighbors in Vinland have helped the Norse survive the Little Ice Age? Could the Norse have gone on to establish colonies in Nova Scotia and lands west and south? The odds were always against it.

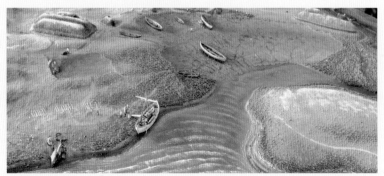

A model of Leif Eriksson's outpost in Newfoundland. He called it Vinland; archaeologists have located it at L'Anse aux Meadows. (Torben Brinker)

11

1507-1537
SMALLPOX CONQUERS
THE WESTERN HEMISPHERE

Columbus discovered the New World in 1492. Vikings and other Europeans had visited the shores of North America before him, but their visits had little effect on life there. Columbus triggered a major disaster for the American Indians. He thought he'd found a shortcut to Asia (he was wrong) and great wealth for the rulers of Spain (that part was right).

The New World wasn't Asia, but like Asia, it had rich, sophisticated empires. The Spanish and Portuguese sent out small bands of soldiers to conquer them. It shouldn't have worked.

We do not know for sure how many people lived in the Western Hemisphere—or in Europe or Asia—in 1500. Nobody kept statistics. But researchers have estimated the population of central Mexico at 25.2 million people in 1518.[1] Mexico's greatest power was the Aztec empire. It may have had more citizens than France at the time; its capital was larger than Paris, which was then Europe's biggest city.[2] Yet in 1519, the Spanish conquistador Hernán Cortés arrived in Mexico with approximately 500 men and marched inland, losing soldiers along the way. In 1521, he conquered the Aztecs.

In the Andes Mountains of South America, the Incan empire covered more territory than any other country on earth. It had roads and aqueducts to rival Rome's. It had state factories and storehouses, and a unique form of writing. Yet Francisco Pizarro and 168 Spanish soldiers overcame five or six thousand Inca troops one day in 1532 and seized control of the empire.

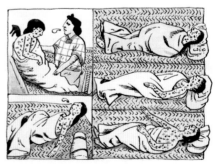

How could this have happened? The people of Mexico and Peru scorned Europeans as short, hairy men who never bathed and smelled no better than you'd expect. Guns, armor, and horses seemed to give the Europeans a military advantage, but the Americans could have turned it around. The Incas, for instance, had archers with better aim than Spanish gunners, armor that was lighter and

A sixteenth-century Aztec illustration shows smallpox victims.
(Dorling Kindersley/Thinkstock)

35

At Machu Picchu, ruins of the advanced Inca civilization. (Martin St-Amant - Wikipedia - CC-BY-SA-3.0)

more flexible than Spanish armor, and steep mountains where Spanish horses stumbled. How could a small band of Spanish conquistadors have conquered Peru so fast?

The Europeans' most lethal weapon was one they didn't even know they'd brought along: smallpox. The smallpox virus was endemic—common—in Asia, Africa, and around the Mediterranean. It killed a large percentage of its victims, especially when it struck new territories. But Europeans often had smallpox as children, and survivors were immune for life. Native Americans had never met smallpox before. None of them had immunity, and more of them died.

By 1532, after two smallpox epidemics, the estimated population of central Mexico had dropped by a third. A Spanish friar wrote that "in most provinces more than half the population died"—many "of starvation, because, as they were all taken sick at once, they could not care for each other."[3] By 1623, there may have been only 700,000 souls left in Mexico. In Peru, the Inca population may have fallen by half.[4]

An Incan sculpture of hammered gold. (Karel Jakubec)

Survivors must have been demoralized. Most were left with ugly scars on their faces and bodies; some were blind. Those who had not been sick themselves had lost family, friends, and key players in their local governments and economies—not to mention their armies. Unable to defend themselves, they yielded not just to the Spanish soldiers but to the Spanish religion, Christianity.[5]

Smallpox, plague, influenza, and measles: a succession of Old World diseases depopulated Central and South America over the next century. European settlers moved into the emptied space. A few respected the rights of Native Americans; the Dominican friar Bartolomé de las Casas fought to defend them against abuse.[6] But many Europeans cared more about getting rich. Native Americans did not make satisfactory slaves, partly because too many of them died in epidemics. So Europeans imported slaves from Africa, who already had some immunity, to do the heavy work in their mines and plantations. (The Africans carried another virus to the New World: yellow fever.)[7]

That smallpox epidemic five centuries ago made the world a different place. It affected who lives where and how people treat each other to this day. We live in a world that smallpox made possible.

12

1556
DEADLIEST EARTHQUAKE
EVER LEVELS SHAANXI

The most lethal earthquake on record hit China's Shaanxi Province on January 23, 1556. In "only seconds," it killed 830,000 people, "leveled mountains, altered the path of rivers, caused massive flooding, and ignited fires that burned for days."[1] It was felt up to 500 miles (800 km) away and caused damage 270 miles (435 km) from its epicenter in the lower Wei River valley.

Many towns were ruined. City walls tumbled; temples, offices, and houses collapsed; the ground gaped open. In Huaxian, near the epicenter, water gushed from the earth and formed canals; 60% of the people were killed. Fifteen miles away in Weinan, the ground sank more than 10 feet and 50% of the inhabitants were killed.[2]

We know this much thanks to China's chronicles, which go back more than 4,000 years. But it can be difficult to understand the records, because languages, place names, and even geological features have changed over the centuries.[3]

Also, modern seismologists have questions that the old records cannot answer. Why, for example, has northern China had so many disastrous earthquakes? It sits on a craton—in the middle of a continental plate, not where one plate moves under another and may get caught.[4] Cratons are supposed to be old, stable ground, yet several active faults cross northern China. The 1556 quake probably struck on the Huashan fault and ruptured others along the northern front of the Qinling Mountains.[5] Its intensity was high—estimated at between 7.9 and 8.3 on the Richter scale—but not the greatest in geological terms. Chinese earthquakes are lethal hazards partly because so many people live in China.

Another factor is that since prehistoric times, many people in Shaanxi and surrounding provinces have lived in yaodongs: cave houses hollowed out of hillsides. The region's "yellow earth" is loess, a sediment made largely of wind-blown silt. It is easy to burrow into and comfortable to live in. Loess caves stay warm in winter and cool in summer, and Shaanxi is a place with extreme temperatures and few trees or other building materials. Cave houses make sense.[6]

Unfortunately, loess is slippery.[7] Earthquakes trigger landslides in hilly loess areas, even on gentle slopes, and these slides spread great distances.

Traditional yaodongs (cave houses in Shaanxi loess) contributed to the 830,000 deaths in 1556; they are still popular. (Meier & Poehlmann)

Living in yaodongs increases a population's vulnerability to these hazards to this day. In 1920, the Haiyuan Earthquake (magnitude 8.5) was felt over most of China and took 234,117 lives. About 500,000 houses and cave dwellings collapsed. Landslides in hilly loess areas caused the worst problems. Buried villages, destroyed farmlands, and clogged rivers all led to economic loss and casualties.[8]

Measuring Earthquakes

Scientists have used more than one scale to measure the severity of earthquakes. Examples:

▷ The Modified Mercalli Intensity Scale is based on observable effects of a quake. It uses Roman numerals from I (barely perceptible) to XII (damage total).[9] It can be used to describe and compare earthquakes before the invention of seismographs.

▷ The Richter magnitude scale is based on the largest seismic wave recorded on a seismograph 100 km from the epicenter. It is a logarithmic scale, and each whole number step represents a tenfold increase: a 6.7 quake is ten times greater (and releases 31 times more energy) than a 5.7 quake.[10] A microearthquake of magnitude 2.0 is usually imperceptible to people and picked up only on local seismographs. Thousands of earthquakes 4.5 or higher occur every year. A magnitude 4.5 quake can be detected by instruments around the world but usually does little damage. In an average year, there will be just one great earthquake of magnitude 8.0 or higher.[11]

▷ The moment magnitude scale is a better measure for giant earthquakes, which roar through faults the length of a mountain range.[12] It measures quake size based on the area of fault ruptured, the average amount of slip, and the force required to overcome friction sticking rocks together.[13]

Thomas C. Hanks and Hiroo Kanamori developed the moment magnitude scale after the Great Chilean Earthquake of 1960 showed problems with the Richter scale. At magnitude 9.5, the Chile quake is still the largest on record. It caused thousands of deaths, spurred nations around the Pacific to develop a tsunami warning system, and provided evidence for the theory of plate tectonics.[14] It also drove the development of a new scale.

13

1600

HUAYNAPUTINA
ERUPTS IN PERU

Along the Pacific coast of South America, the Nazca tectonic plate grinds under the South American plate, pushing up steep mountains. The Andes rise 10,000 feet (3,000 meters) and more above sea level. Every fold of the land holds its own microclimate, and the land has more folds than origami. This gave ancient Peruvians a varied diet. Allied villages along a single river traded seafood and coastal squash and beans, potatoes and grains from the foothills, and the meat and wool of llamas herded in the mountains. Variety helped them survive droughts, landslides, earthquakes, and other hazards.[1]

For people along the Rio Tambo, Huaynaputina changed this in 1600. It was just a low hill in a mountain valley, its last eruption long forgotten.[2] Nobody realized it was a volcano. Then the earth began to quake and "a scary fog" appeared. Peruvian religious leaders in the village of Quinistacas called for "sacrifice of the nicest young girls, the best animals, and the prettiest flowers" to the mountain. Forty miles away, in Arequipa, a Roman Catholic priest told his flock to expect divine punishment.[3]

Earthquakes intensified. On the morning of February 19, 1600, there were three or four quakes every 15 minutes; by late afternoon they felt continuous. The mountain exploded, plunging the region into darkness. Ash and pumice fell. Lightning flashed.[4] People heard the explosions in Lima, more than 500 miles (800 km) away. The eruption lasted at least until March 6 and sent up a column of tephra 20–22 miles (33–35 km) high.[5]

The cover of a 1615 book describing the devastation at Arequipa.

Pyroclastic flows surged down the Rio Tambo. "The river got covered by another river of fire and all the fish died," said one witness. "Also the animals that ran for their lives all died later because of nothing to eat."[6] At least ten villages around Huaynaputina were destroyed by earthquakes and falling ash, and the river carried fire and destruction across all the farms it passed on its way to the sea. Ash fell on Cuzco and Lima to the northwest and La Paz to the east. In Arequipa the cathedral collapsed under its weight. Some residents prayed, while others lost all faith in the church and cast spells instead.[7]

Arequipa, Peru's second largest city, spreads out beneath the inactive volcano Misti in this recent photo. Huaynaputina is 43 miles (72 km) southeast of Misti. (jirivondrous/Thinkstock)

Huaynaputina, the worst South American eruption in recorded history, had a VEI (volcanic explosivity index) of 6. It strained the economy of Peru. Rebuilding Arequipa took years. (It is now called the "white city" after the volcanic rock used to rebuild it.) Crops and livestock were destroyed; fertile land became a desert, and agriculture didn't recover for 150 years.[8]

Did Huaynaputina damage crops on the other side of the world? The year 1601 was unusually cold even by Little Ice Age standards. French grapes ripened late, Japanese lakes froze early, and famine in Russia killed as many as two million people. In hindsight, maybe Huaynaputina's estimated thousand-person death toll needs to be revised upward.[9]

A New Response to Volcanoes: Engineering

In 1600, European colonists and native Peruvians reacted to a volcanic eruption much the same way: they appealed to higher powers. But Europeans were beginning to think differently. In 1669, an eruption of Mt. Etna destroyed several villages in Italy. Mt. Etna erupts often. But this time, when residents of Catania saw the lava flowing toward them, they tried to stop it. They thought a wall could shunt it away from their town. People in the neighboring town of Paterno objected—Catania's wall would send the lava pouring down over Paterno. So there was a battle, and that stopped the first documented effort to control a volcano's damage by means of engineering.[10] Yet something had changed. After centuries of exposure to a familiar hazard, people had taken action to reduce their vulnerability to risk.

14

1616–1619
EPIDEMIC READIES MASSACHUSETTS FOR ENGLISH SETTLEMENT

Smallpox moved more slowly in North America than in Mexico and Peru. The Native American population was sparser there, for one thing, and the smallpox virus, *Variola,* spread faster in dense populations. Unlike many viral diseases, it did not infect other animals and could only pass from human to human.

But epidemic disease struck New England between 1616 and 1619, spreading south from a French settlement in Nova Scotia. Indians suffered fever, headache, nosebleeds, and skin lesions; they turned yellow. Nearby European fishermen and traders escaped, but between 30% and 90% of the Native American population of New England may have died.[1] In 1620, when the Pilgrims arrived, once busy villages were empty; the coast from Maine to Massachusetts was a graveyard. The Wampanoag confederacy had dropped from 20,000 to fewer than 1,000 people.

John Winthrop, the first governor of Massachusetts, welcomed this sign that God favored European settlement. "The natives, they are neere all dead of the small Poxe, so as the Lord hath cleared out our title to what we possess," he wrote.[2] Modern researchers have speculated that the disease was not smallpox but plague, yellow fever, influenza, chickenpox, typhus, typhoid fever, trichinosis, meningitis, or hepatitis. Another possibility is leptospirosis, a bacterial disease that causes fever, headache, nosebleeds, skin lesions, and jaundice. Rats on European ships could have brought it to the Canadian Maritimes and shared it with native rodents. Indians would have been more exposed to the disease than Europeans, who usually wore boots and rarely bathed.[3]

Whatever the disease was, it helped the English. Fearing their traditional Narragansett enemies, the Wampanoag

In 1606, French explorer Samuel de Champlain drew a thriving community at Plymouth, Massachusetts; it was more of a ghost town when the Pilgrims landed 14 years later.

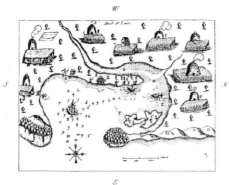

British Captain Simeon Ecuyer, portrayed by Ken Treese, second from right, offered blankets infected with smallpox to the Indians besieging Fort Pitt. From left, interpreters Christopher Jones, Ted Boscana, Treese, and Patrick Andrews
(The Colonial Williamsburg Foundation)

formed a cautious alliance with the Pilgrims, who probably would not have survived otherwise.

Another epidemic helped the Plymouth settlers in 1633. Smallpox swept away whole native towns, said Increase Mather, "in some of them not so much as one Soul escaping the destruction."[4] Moving inland, it devastated the Huron and the Iroquois. Later epidemics killed half the Cherokees, nearly half the Catawbas, two-thirds of the Omahas, and "perhaps half the population between the Missouri River and New Mexico." Smallpox "cleared out" the land for English occupation, and at least once, the English tried to spread it deliberately. In 1763, during the French and Indian War, Sir Jeffrey Amherst and his officers plotted to send infected blankets and handkerchiefs from Fort Pitt to their Indian enemies.[5]

European treatments for smallpox included herbs and noxious chemicals, bleeding, sweating, and even wrapping victims in red flannel. None of these treatments worked. Then in Constantinople, in 1717, Lady Mary Wortley Montague learned about something new: inoculation. "The small-pox, so fatal, and so general amongst us, is here entirely harmless," she told a friend.[6] Well, it wasn't *entirely* harmless. Inoculation involved rubbing pus or ground scabs from a smallpox victim into superficial scratches on a healthy person's arm. This induced a mild case of smallpox. The inoculated patients were contagious, and had to be quarantined until they recovered. Up to two percent of them died. But if they survived they would be immune to smallpox, which normally killed thirty percent of its victims.

News reached Boston, and in 1721, so did the worst smallpox epidemic yet. The new treatment was controversial, but doctors inoculated 280 patients, and only six died. Meanwhile, 5,800 of Boston's 11,000 people fell ill, and 844 died. Charleston, New York City, and Philadelphia began inoculating their citizens. During the American Revolution (1776–1783), George Washington had his soldiers inoculated against smallpox.

The United States won its freedom from the British in 1783. Freedom from smallpox took longer, but inoculation was a great weapon in the struggle. In 1796, Edward Jenner showed that inoculation with cowpox made people immune to smallpox as well. The cowpox virus was related to the smallpox virus but much less dangerous.

15

1666
THE GREAT FIRE OF
LONDON—PAPIST PLOT
BURNS OUT THE PLAGUE?

London's last bubonic plague epidemic ravaged the population in 1665. It ebbed in 1666, claiming fewer than 2,000 victims in the city. People who had fled to the country came back, and newcomers poured in. There were some 300,000 residents,[1] and as many as 100,000 of them lived within the ancient walls that circled the heart of the city.[2] Like Romans 1600 years before, Londoners built their upper stories out over narrow streets. They needed every inch of living space. Ten families squeezed into one ten-room house; some of them took in lodgers. Tinkers and courtiers, merchants and chimney sweeps, street vendors and actors and coachmen, Puritans and pickpockets, they all jostled up together.

Everybody knew London could burn. Building regulations had improved matters—no more thatched roofs, no more wooden chimneys—but still there were timber houses with shared walls, fireplaces for heat, and candles for light. There were "storehouses of oils, pitch, tar, rosin, wax, butter, brimstone, hemp, cordage, cheese, wine, etc."[3] to fuel a fire. Romans would have recognized most of the fire-fighting equipment, too: wooden ladders, leather buckets, and squirts to douse the flames; firehooks, chains, and axes to demolish buildings around the blaze.

The summer of 1666 was hot and dry. Streams ran low. And at 1 A.M. on Sunday, September 2, fire broke out in a bakery on Pudding Lane. Baker Thomas Farriner and his neighbors tried to contain it. The Lord Mayor came by in a coach too broad for the street, and said, "Pish. A woman might piss it out."[4] But a gale-force wind seized control, and for the next five days, London burned.

Booksellers sealed their wares into the crypt of St. Paul's for safety, but the cathedral's lead roof melted. Molten lead rolled down the cobblestones to the Thames, filling the air with poisonous fumes. Books burned for days. Their ashes fell miles away. Meanwhile the Guildhall glowed like "a palace of gold or a great building of brass."[5] Fire heated it to over 1,200° Celsius. The firestorm's own winds eddied through the city, carrying sparks against the gale. People suspected arson.

Who would burn London? The French or the Dutch might; they were at war with England. Some thought Catholics might; some thought Puritans. King Charles II told homeless crowds that "the hand of God and no plots" had started the fire,[6] but people wanted a scapegoat. The baker must have been drunk, said some. And just as in Nero's Rome, some said the king himself might have started the fire to clear ground for new development.

In this painting done in 1797 by Philippe-Jacques de Loutherbourg, people have taken shelter under a bridge during the Great Fire.

Relations between king, parliament, and city officials were touchy. During the English Civil Wars (1642–1651), parliament forces led by Oliver Cromwell had established a Commonwealth in England, and in 1649 they beheaded King Charles I. His son Charles II was restored to the throne only in 1660. People could easily imagine that he might want revenge on the families who had made his own family suffer.

But Charles fought the flames along with his subjects. A dimwitted French watchmaker confessed to arson and was hanged. (There's evidence he didn't do it.) The wind escaped punishment.

Fire destroyed about 400 acres within the walls and another 60 outside them: over 13,000 houses, 87 churches, and the headquarters of 52 trade associations. Courts, jails, wharves, printing presses, and the Royal Exchange burned. To this day, it's said only a handful of people died. More likely hundreds died, but their bodies were never found, and reporting was interrupted.[7] It's true that many survived—and between 65,000 and 80,000 of them were left homeless.[8]

Six months later, the ruins still smoked. Thieves and murderers prowled there. Rebuilding took years. So many workers were needed that many

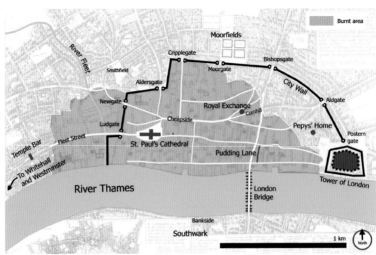

non-guild members found work, and guilds lost much of their old control over the labor force. Royal and city officials negotiated street plans and new building requirements. (Brick and stone replaced wood, and new streets were wider.) Sir Christopher Wren designed a beautiful new St. Paul's Cathedral. The plague never came back, and a false belief took root. Hundreds of years later, people still believed you could cure a city of plague by burning it to its foundations.

1755

EARTHQUAKE IN LISBON SHAKES EUROPE'S PHILOSOPHERS

All Saints' Day fell on a Sunday in 1755, and in Lisbon, the pious went to church. So did the cautious; in Portugal, the Inquisition still burned people for offenses against the Catholic faith. Medieval as it seemed, the city was the hub of a modern empire, rich with Brazilian gold and African slaves.[1] Lisbon had between 150,000 and 260,000 people,[2] and at 9:30 A.M. on November 1 that year they crammed its many churches.[3]

Around 9:40, the earth moved. Candles, statues, and pillars fell; churchgoers stampeded toward the doors. Two minutes later, a more intense shock lasted ten minutes. Churches pitched like boats in a storm; houses fell; dust roiled up and hid the sun. Before the air cleared, a third shock toppled what was left standing.[4] Flames broke out, and wind fanned a fire that would last for days. People ran to the river and begged for space on boats, hoping to escape. At about 11:00 A.M., three tsunamis wrecked ships, warehouses, and docks in the harbor. Hundreds drowned.

King José I watched in horror. Some members of his court urged him to move the capital inland, or maybe even to Brazil. But his secretary of state gave more practical advice: "Bury the dead and feed the living."[5] The secretary of state proved so helpful that José made him a nobleman: the Marquês de Pombal.

Nobody knows how many died. Pombal estimated between 6,000 to 8,000; a church estimate put it at 40,000. Earthquake, fire, tsunamis, and crime together probably took between 10,000 and 20,000 lives,[6] and that was just in Lisbon. The earthquake ruined cities all along Portugal's southern coast and toppled minarets and aqueducts in Morocco. The tsunami killed people in Martinique, over 3,000 miles (4,800 km) across the Atlantic.[7]

Scientists still debate the cause. Suggestions include an earthquake affecting more than one fault, or two simultaneous earthquakes, or a major slip on a subduction zone in the Gulf of Cadiz.[8] In 1755, the first debate was not about seismology but about divine justice. What had

The earthquake was followed by tsunami and fire.

The earthquake at Lisbon. (Photos.com/Thinkstock)

humans done to deserve such punishment? Some preachers said God was showing the error of Deists and other modern thinkers who "tried to explain the world in natural terms alone."[9] Deists said that if anybody deserved God's punishment, it might be the Inquisition—for cruelty to nonbelievers.

Earthquakes had always been seen as divine punishment, but 1755 came in the Age of Enlightenment, a time when European intellectuals turned from tradition to reason as a guide to truth. So after the Lisbon quake, international discussion took some new directions. Optimistic philosophers at the time

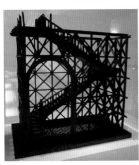

A model of the pombaline cage, a wooden structure designed to make more earth-quake-resistant buildings in a reconstructed downtown Lisbon. (Galin Hola)

believed that we live in "the best of all possible worlds," but the tragedy raised doubts. It moved the French writer Voltaire to mock shallow optimism in *Candide*, his most influential work. Other thinkers, anticipating modern science, concentrated less on the moral implications than on the mechanics of the earthquake. In 1760 John Michell, a Cambridge geology professor, had an insight that marked the beginning of modern seismology: earthquakes can move in waves.[10]

Meanwhile the efficient Pombal took charge of relief efforts and reconstruction. He had looters hanged, commandeered food from incoming ships, got church permission to bury the dead at sea, and organized temporary housing. There was unprecedented foreign aid; Great Britain alone sent £100,000, half in gold and half in supplies (food, shoes, and even pickaxes). The nations of Europe had become interdependent, and news traveled faster than it used to.[11]

For the rebuilding effort Pombal and his architect, General Manuel da Maia, established an earthquake code, possibly the first ever. They set minimum street widths and maximum building heights, and called for fire breaks between buildings. A wooden framework called the "pombaline cage" (gaiola pombalina) reinforced masonry structures.[12] Pombal was a low-born newcomer to the nobility, but in the process of saving Lisbon he became the virtual ruler of Portugal for 22 years. He did his best to drag the nation into the Enlightenment.

1755 Cape Ann Earthquake

Did the Lisbon event shake colonial Boston? On November 18, 1755, a 6.0 earthquake off Cape Ann, Massachusetts knocked down chimneys from Maine to Connecticut. Seismologists don't know why. Contemporaries thought it might be divine punishment.

Travel times of the tsunami from the 1755 Lisbon earthquake, calculated by NOAA with the Tsunami Travel Times (TTT) software. Red contours denote 1- to 4-hour arrival times; yellow is for 5 to 6 hours; green is 7 to 14 hours; and blue is 15 to 21 hours.

1815
MT. TAMBORA TAKES MORE LIVES THAN THE BATTLE OF WATERLOO

In the spring of 1815, two dangerous powers burst out. Napoleon, Emperor of France (1804–1814), escaped from exile on the Mediterranean island of Elba and won back control of the French army. His old enemies Great Britain, Prussia, Austria, and Russia declared him an outlaw and raised armies to fight him again. On the other side of the world, an estimated 36 cubic miles (150 km³) of molten rock escaped from a supposedly extinct Indonesian volcano. The greatest eruption of the past 2,000 years began on April 5. For a while its plume shot more than 25 miles (40 km) into the air.[1] Its explosions were heard hundreds of miles away. European listeners thought they heard a battle at sea or a ship in distress; they mobilized soldiers and readied lifeboats. Sumatrans thought they heard their ancestors fighting demons on the way to paradise; Javans thought a sea spirit was celebrating her child's marriage. On April 10 the eruption intensified. Soon Mt. Tambora had ejected enough ash to cover the ground 40 inches deep within 20 miles (32 km) of the volcano, and eight or ten inches deep even a hundred miles away.[2]

The Battle of Waterloo, June 1815, as painted by William Sadler II.

Red areas show thickness of ashfall.

Cannon fire was a logical explanation for the racket. All Europe had been embroiled in the Napoleonic Wars (1803–1815), and the fighting had affected European colonies around the world. Napoleon's France had seized Indonesia from the Dutch, and in 1811 Britain had seized it from France. In June, Napoleon was defeated at the Battle of Waterloo, with 75,000 casualties. Indonesia's colonial fate would be negotiated at the 1815 peace conference in Paris.

But Tambora's casualties outnumbered Waterloo's. About 12,000 people lived too close to escape the fire and lava that poured over their villages or the tsunamis that tossed their fishing boats ashore. In the weeks and months that followed, another 70,000 or 80,000 people died of hunger and disease.[3] Crops were buried. People ate the tops of palm trees and the stalks of plantains. Even a princess—a daughter of the Rajah of Sang'ir—starved to death.[4] Ash poisoned the air and the drinking water, killing people and livestock.[5] By July, Tambora was topped with a caldera instead of a cone,[6] but like Napoleon, it cast a long shadow.

High in the stratosphere, Tambora's ash cooled Earth for over a year, reducing the amount of sunlight that reached the surface. In New England and the Canadian Maritimes, 1816 was called Eighteen Hundred and Froze to Death or The Year Without a Summer. Mary Godwin Shelley, to amuse her friends on a cold summer vacation in Switzerland, wrote *Frankenstein*.

But cold weather spoiled more than summer vacations. In parts of Europe, the price of wheat doubled between 1815 and 1817. French wine harvests failed. Hungry Germans rioted, and many emigrated to America and Russia. One German professor of medicine published a helpful *Introduction to the Baking of Bread from Sawdust*. (He recommended birch wood, because his dog gained weight on it.)[7] In parts of China, too, summer frosts in 1816 led to crop failures, famine, "a massive death toll, displaced refugees," and "social unrest."[8]

People around the world fell ill. Malnutrition lowers resistance to disease, and migrations help spread it. Typhus and dysentery epidemics broke out.[9]

A few scholars wonder if Tambora chilled the political climate as well. By making life harder in post-Napoleonic Europe, did it contribute to "a climate of mistrust and fear" that stalled liberal movements?[10] In China, where the Qing dynasty already had to contend with rapid population growth and Western imperialism, did the hardships of a volcanic winter contribute to the empire's decline?[11]

The caldera (kettle-like crater) of Mt. Tambora, where a tall cone once stood as a landmark to sailors (Jialiang Gao)

In 1816, some guessed the epic cold was caused by a new human technology: lightning conductors.[12] Others suspected volcanic ash. (Benjamin Franklin, as ambassador to France in 1784, observed that dust from a 1783 eruption in Iceland reduced the amount of sunlight reaching the ground.[13]) After Krakatoa erupted in 1883, scientists identified Tambora as the earlier culprit. Volcanologists study it to this day for what it can teach us about the relationship between volcanism and the Earth's tectonic system—and its implications for risk management.

18

1817
COLONIALISM HELPS
CHOLERA GO GLOBAL

In November 1817, cholera attacked British troops in India. The disease was endemic in Bengal, and Bengalis had at least some resistance to it.[1] The British, who had ruled there since 1757, had none. Now Lord Hastings mustered his troops for a campaign in northern India, taking cholera along. A contemporary wrote that hundreds "dropt down" every day as the army moved forward, "and covered the roads with dead and dying; the ground of encampments and line of march, presented the appearance of a field of battle, and of the track of an army retreating under every circumstance of discomfiture and distress."[2]

Hindu villagers believed the epidemic had begun when the British violated sacred laws. They camped in a grove sacred to Hurdoul Lal, they killed cattle, and they ate beef. The epidemic was a sign of the gods' displeasure. From 1817 on, when cholera threatened, people in northern India sought the favor of Hurdoul Lal.[3]

And from 1817 on, cholera threatened the world. It spread in seven pandemics: 1817–23, 1829–51, 1852–59, 1863–79, 1881–96, 1899–1923, and 1961 to the present.[4] Like smallpox and plague, it spread with armies and refugees, trade caravans and pilgrimages; it spread where people crowded together without clean water. Cholera hit in times of famine. In Europe it flared up at times of crisis, such as the revolutions of 1848, the Crimean War, and the Franco-Prussian War.[5]

The symptoms are disgusting: uncontrollable diarrhea and vomiting. This helps cholera spread rapidly, but it is less helpful to humans. Untreated, dehydration causes kidney failure, electrolyte imbalances, coma, and shock.[6] Tens of

Treatment of victims during the 1832 cholera epidemic in Paris; engraving by J. Roze.

Cholera dead awaiting burial in Zaire, July 1994. (© Jenny Matthews / Alamy)

millions died of cholera in the nineteenth century, and its stench appalled the middle classes. Cholera made it harder to ignore dirt and poverty.[7]

Europeans associated the disease with other races. British colonists thought Hindu religious practices "obscene,"[8] and Russian colonists thought central Asians were "dirty."[9] Worried about disease caused by filth, bad smells, or newly discovered germs, colonists widened the physical and social barriers that separated them from their subjugated peoples.

The long struggle to control cholera led to medical progress on several fronts:

▷ Epidemiology: John Snow's maps showed the disease was spread by tainted water.

▷ Treatment: O'Shannessy and Latta rehydrated victims with intravenous saline as early as 1832; it was reintroduced in the 1890s.

▷ Bacteriology: Filippo Pacini discovered the *Vibrio cholerae* bacillus around 1854; Robert Koch discovered it again in 1884.[10]

By 1917, an American public health official touted the conquest of plague and cholera: "The security which civilized countries may enjoy against their attacks is a brilliant demonstration of the triumphs of modern sanitary science."[11]

But we cannot be so sure. Even though we know how to control it with clean water and treat it with cheap rehydration therapy, cholera still takes lives. The cholera vibrio now lives in warm, moderately salty waters around the world[12]—not just in the Ganges estuary, but even in the Chesapeake

Bay.[13] It attaches itself to plankton and shellfish.[14] Warmer ocean temperatures may help it spread.[15]

Unsanitary living conditions definitely help it spread. In temporary shelters for disaster survivors or war refugees, or in underdeveloped countries around the world, "more than a billion of the poorest and most marginalized people" are still "at risk of ingesting feces with their food and water."[16] In 2011, 58 countries reported 589,854 cholera cases and 7,816 cholera deaths.[17] The World Health Organization (WHO) argues that we have an ethical obligation to make safe water and sanitation available to everyone, but we are not there yet.

Cholera Riots and the Burke and Hare Murders

To fight cholera in the nineteenth century, governments "dusted off their files on bubonic plague and put what were by now fairly traditional policing measures into operation: military cordons sanitaires, quarantine, fumigation, disinfection, isolation."[18] These led to bitter strife between British and Bengalis, Russians and Uzbeks—and between rich and poor. Many European rioters attacked noblemen. The English attacked doctors.

Cholera hit Britain in 1832, just four years after a gruesome series of murders. The murderers, William Burke and William Hare, killed at least 16 people and sold their victims' bodies to a doctor at the University of Edinburgh for dissection. In Britain at the time, the only bodies legally available for medical research were those of executed criminals—and the British were no longer

executing hundreds of criminals each year for petty crimes. One illegal way to get bodies was to dig up recent graves. Burke and Hare didn't bother with burial, and the doctor paid them between £7 and £10 for each fresh body.[19] (This may not sound like much, but an average male farm worker in 1832 earned about £29 a year.[20])

Britain was shocked by the Burke and Hare murders, and Parliament took action. The 1832 Anatomy Act authorized persons with legal custody of a dead body to donate it for medical research. This eliminated the motive to imitate Burke and Hare.

But British crowds were still suspicious. Cholera hit so fast; it killed healthy people in next to no time. Rioters believed that doctors were killing off the poor to supply corpses for anatomy classes.[21]

19

1845-1852
THE IRISH POTATO FAMINE SOWS BITTERNESS AND DISTRUST

A cold autumn rain falls, and falls, and falls. It can't wash away the sickening smell from the potato fields. A fungus destroyed American potatoes in 1843 and reached Europe in June 1845. Now it spoils the Irish crop. Overnight, healthy potatoes rot in the earth. Black and oozing, they smell of death.

The Little Ice Age wasn't over, but after 1700 Europe's farms fed more people and the population rose. One reason was the enclosure movement, consolidating land under the management of landlords instead of allowing tenants to work small patches. Another reason was the potato. An acre of potatoes yielded two to four times as many calories as an acre of grain.

In richer countries, potatoes helped feed the city workers needed for the Industrial Revolution.[1] In Ireland, they fed the poor. The Protestant English ruled Catholic Ireland, and in the 1600s they imposed Penal Laws to prevent Catholics from owning land, horses, or firearms. By 1750, English and Scots controlled 95% of Irish land. Some of the Irish moved abroad; some turned Protestant. Most became tenant farmers. An Irish family needed just one acre of potatoes and the milk of one cow. They had no money, their clothes were rags, but their children grew tall and strong. Then the potatoes failed. Landlords exported beef and grain to England; peasants went hungry.

Experts debated the blight. What caused it? Some blamed the rain; some thought potato stocks had degenerated. Few believed in the fungus.

Debates on how to relieve the famine were even more benighted. By February 1846, the Irish were dying fast. They boiled seaweed; they ate grass; some even sucked the blood of

Population Fall in Ireland 1841-1851

- Over 30%
- 20 to 30%
- 10 to 20%
- 0 to 10%
- Population Rise

Source: Edwards, RD, Williams, TD; "The Great Famine: Studies in Irish History 1845-1852"; Lilliput Press, 1956. Reprinted 1997. Figure 20, p260 Produced for www.irelandtheisland.com

Ireland's population shrank drastically in the 1840s.

56

A starving family seems to straggle through modern Dublin in this sidewalk memorial.

their cows. Some turned to robbery. But they died of starvation and fever while government officials in London debated relief measures. Any acceptable solution had to address the Corn Laws—tariffs on grain imports that had been contested since 1815. More important, the solution had to help end "dependency on government"[2] and work as "a penal instrument for forcing modernization against the resistance of the irresponsible classes in Ireland."[3] It had to improve the Irish national character. (Policy makers were sure the Irish character needed improvement.)

While London debated, landlords in Ireland evicted their poorest tenants. Why? Under an 1843 law, owners had to pay "poor rates"—taxes to relieve the poor—for every tenant who held land valued at £4 or less. Evictions saved the landlord taxes and at the same time cleared land for more profitable uses.

EJECTMENT OF IRISH TENANTRY.

Irish peasants being evicted from their cottage, which is already being destroyed. (Photos.com/Thinkstock)

The enclosure movement had been going on since the 1500s. It was a painful process, and like the potato blight, it had reached Ireland. In March 1846, one landlady sent soldiers, constables, and bailiffs to evict 270 residents from Ballinglass. By nightfall only one of the village's 61 cottages was left standing; bailiffs drove villagers away from the ruined walls. It was a trend. In early 1847, Mayo landowners filed between 5,000 and 6,000 eviction notices and impossible demands for rent payments. Homeless families and ruined houses dotted the landscape.

In 1845, Ireland had almost 8.2 million people. By 1855, 1.1 million had died of starvation and disease; 2 million had emigrated, mostly to Canada and the United States. Many died on ships; many ended up in poorhouses. In America as in England, there was vocal opposition to "public welfare for paupers," and comfortable people tended to believe that the poor "had only themselves to blame."[4]

The potato blight affected many countries. But in Ireland, where peasants had no alternative crops, harsh policies deepened the suffering. The famine's legacy of bitterness is still felt.

Ridiculous Tip for Starving Peasants

One suggestion for salvaging the good bits from infected potatoes: use a grater. The helpful pamphlet admitted this would be "a great deal of trouble," but expected that "all true Irishmen will exert themselves."[5] The average Irish peasant could probably buy a grater for less than two weeks' pay. Eating infected potatoes didn't usually kill people—it just made them very sick.

1871
IRISH POOR BLAMED FOR BURNING OF DRY, WINDY CHICAGO

Chicago grew from a muddy swamp. In 1833, it had fewer than one hundred inhabitants. By 1870 it was the fourth largest city in the U.S.—about the size of London in 1666. With 298,977 people[1] and 59,500 buildings,[2] it was a tinderbox.

Working-class people crowded their tiny lots with wooden buildings: not just cottages and outhouses, but barns and sheds. Scattered among the homes were flammable businesses, factories, and warehouses full of paint, alcohol, lumber, and coal. In wealthier neighborhoods, shade trees surrounded wood buildings. Even public buildings with stone or brick exteriors had flammable tar and shingle roofs. And to control mud in the streets, Chicago used pine-block roadways and wooden sidewalks.

This 1872 print shows Chicago in flames while throngs of refugees flee. (Courtesy Northern Illinois University)

CHICAGO IN FLAMES.

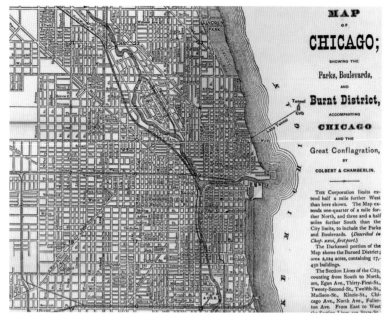

In 1870, firefighters averaged more than eleven calls a week. Little rain fell in the summer of 1871—scarcely an inch between July and October—and there were so many fires that people got used to them and stopped paying attention.

The great fire of 1871 began on the evening of Sunday, October 8, in the O'Leary barn. The O'Learys' whole property was just 25 by 100 feet, but they had five cows, a calf, a horse, and three tons of newly delivered timothy grass in that barn; in their shed was kindling wood and two tons of coal. They were ready for winter.

A neighbor ran three blocks to call in the fire alarm—but the call failed to reach the watchmen. Fanned by a dry wind and fed by dry wood, the fire destroyed 17,500 buildings and 73 miles of street in the heart of Chicago. Even the waterworks had a wooden roof; when it burned, hoses went dry. Families ran through the streets, herding children, dropping possessions, and losing track of each other in the crowds. A child who stopped to brush a burning cinder from her eye became hopelessly separated from her family.[3]

On Tuesday, it began to rain. The fire ended. Only 120 bodies could be found, but another 180 must have been incinerated or fallen into the river.

Chicago after the fire, as shown in a panoramic series by photographer George N. Barnard.

Nearly 100,000 people were left homeless. (One was Mary Harris Jones, an Irish-American schoolteacher and dressmaker. After losing her husband and four children to yellow fever in Memphis, she had started over in Chicago. Now she had lost everything again.)[4]

The U.S. army helped set up tents and distribute supplies. Trainloads of relief began to arrive on Tuesday; financial contributions came from as far away as Europe. Businessmen found temporary quarters. City leaders talked of rebuilding. It took years, but the new "Chicago School" of architecture featured steel girders, stone facades, and clean lines—little to burn. Meanwhile, lower-middle class families had no fire insurance, no funds for rebuilding, and no access to loans.

Far from helping the poor, Chicago tended to blame them for the fire. Maybe the real culprit was the weather: the long dry spell and the strong wind. Maybe it was hasty building with flammable materials, or an understaffed fire department with inadequate equipment. But many blamed the shiftless poor, represented by the O'Learys and those overworked firemen. It was a period when social classes were increasingly segregated, and Chicago zoning after the fire made it harder for the working poor to live near their work.

A broadside calling for a meeting at Haymarket Square in 1886 following the Haymarket Riot.

Nine years later there were 503,185 people living in Chicago, and the gulf between rich and poor was wider than ever. In 1886, a Haymarket Square demonstration for the eight-hour workday became a riot when police fired into the crowd. Anarchists and labor unions were blamed. (Mary Harris Jones became a labor organizer. As Mother Jones, she would be called "the most dangerous woman in America.") Did festering resentments from those days of fire help fuel class warfare?

Other Fires on October 8, 1871

The October 8 wind fanned fires across the Midwest. The Great Michigan Fire consumed forests and several towns. In Wisconsin, the Peshtigo Fire burned an area about twice the size of Rhode Island and generated a fire tornado. (Seventy years later, the U. S. military imitated that fire tornado to destroy enemy cities in World War II.[5]) The exact death toll is unknown, as the fire also took town records, but estimates range from 1,200 to 2,500, making it the deadliest fire in American history. With no survivors to identify them, many were buried in a mass grave. Could all these fires have been started by fragments of the dying Comet Biela as some have suggested? This doesn't seem likely; meteorites are cold to the touch. A summer drought, a number of barely contained fires already burning, and a sudden strong wind are explanation enough.

A fire tornado. (Photo by Tech. Sgt. Matt Hecht, U.S. Air National Guard)

21

1878
YELLOW FEVER IN
THE AMERICAN SOUTH

"The atmosphere was heavy with poison," said an 1878 refugee from Grenada, Mississippi. Nearly half the 2,200 townspeople had fled; officials even flung open the jail so prisoners could escape. Yellow fever had arrived in town on August 12, and before leaving it sickened approximately 1,050 residents and killed 350. It happened fast. People were buried in whatever clothes they were wearing when they died, and if no graves were ready, the hearses left bodies on the ground.[1]

Yellow fever is caused by a virus and spread by mosquitoes. In most people, it causes only mild symptoms or none at all. But 3 to 6 days after infection, some people are seized by fever, chills, severe headache, back pain, body aches, nausea, vomiting, and weakness.[2] Then they get better—some for good, others only for hours. The unlucky ones get sicker. Their skin and eyes turn yellow with jaundice. Their fever soars, they bleed, they go into shock, and their organs fail.[3]

The disease originated in Africa and spread to South America with the slave trade.[4] The 1878 epidemic came to the U.S. by way of Cuba, where the Spanish government had just put down a revolution. Rebels fled from Havana to New Orleans, where fever appeared by May.

By July, the Louisiana State Board of Health knew of fourteen cases, with seven deaths. Most early victims were children in a fairly clean part of New Orleans. Residents were shocked. While the city council spent $8,000 on disinfectant, 40,000 of the city's 211,000 people fled. The runaways—many of them already sick without knowing it—spread the disease.

The Grenada refugee said she could practically taste poison in the air, "and it was impossible to remove it with disinfectants." Many people at the time believed that contagious diseases were caused by breathing "miasma," infected air that rose from humid, swampy ground.[5] Another theory was that poor sanitation caused epidemics, so carbolic acid and other disinfectants could protect streets and houses.

The miasma theory was reasonable. Mosquitos breed in swamps, so living near swamps could be a risk factor for yellow fever and other mosquito-borne diseases. And who would blame mosquitoes? Usually bites only made people itch. In 1881, when Carlos Finlay hypothesized that mosquito bites might spread yellow fever, everybody made fun of him.[6]

Running away was even more reasonable. Even George Washington yanked his government out of Philadelphia during the 1793 epidemic.

On August 13, 1878, yellow fever killed a Memphis woman. Four days later, an estimated 25,000 people had stampeded out of Memphis. Nearby communities drove them back at

The Memphis Safety Patrol arrests yellow fever refugees in the woods. (Courtesy Tennesse State Library and Archives)

TENNESSEE.—ARREST OF YELLOW-FEVER REFUGEES BY THE SAFETY-PATROL OF MEMPHIS.—FROM A SKETCH BY OUR SPECIAL ARTIST.

gunpoint; nobody wanted the fever. Some refugees sheltered in the woods; others made their way to Missouri, Kentucky, Ohio, and Georgia.

About 20,000 stayed in Memphis: 14,000 African Americans and 6,000 whites. People believed African Americans were immune to yellow fever. Some may have survived asymptomatic cases as children in Africa or the American South, but they were not all safe. At least 11,000 of the 14,000 fell sick, and 946 died. Meanwhile, almost all the 6,000 whites were sick, and 4,204 died.

While the epidemic raged, the South endured hunger, unemployment, and civic unrest. Quarantines cut food supplies and idled transportation workers. Many people abandoned the "ordinary courtesies of life," and racial hostility and distrust broke out. Yet there was also heroic selflessness. Doctors, nurses, and relief workers hardly rested; five of six doctors in one small town died of fever themselves.

The 1878 yellow fever epidemic was the worst disaster to hit the American South since the War Between the States, and it pushed the nation's public health movement forward. New Orleans improved its quarantine measures. In 1880, working on the sanitation theory of disease prevention, Memphis became the first American city with a sewer system built "on correct principles."[7] In 1900, U.S. Army researchers visited Carlos Finlay in Cuba and found that he was right: mosquitoes carry yellow fever. Since then nets, insecticides, and vaccines have helped control the disease. The last U.S. yellow fever epidemic hit New Orleans in 1905, but it still takes an average of 30,000 lives yearly in Africa and South America.[8]

1883
ERUPTION OF KRAKATOA
DRIVES SCIENTIFIC ADVANCE
AND COLONIAL DISCORD

Indonesia is a diverse place, with hundreds of ethnic groups: Javanese and Sundanese, Malay and more.[1] Volcanoes make fertile soil, and Indonesia has more active volcanoes than any other country. Its rich crops have drawn traders and invaders for centuries. Pepper! Cloves! Nutmeg! Indian and Arab merchants sold them to the ancient Romans. The Portuguese sailed around Africa for them. In 1602 the Dutch East India Company sent its ships out from the Netherlands to exploit the rich crops of Indonesia's Spice Islands (the Maluku Islands or Moluccas), and in the nineteenth century the Netherlands claimed Indonesia.

Coffee! Sugar! Rubber! Opium! Tobacco! The Dutch planted new cash crops and grew richer. Other Europeans did profitable business in Indonesia as well. Indonesian farmers provided most of the labor, and Dutch landlords got most of the rewards. Some Indonesians resisted; there was war in Aceh. But colonial ports seemed peaceful. Colonists' wives hired Indonesian women as amahs to nurse their children. Ships came and went in the busy Sunda Strait between Java and Sumatra, past the

Krakatoa. Rep. Roy. Soc. Com.   Plate 1.

View of Krakatoa during the Earlier Stage of the Eruption.
from a Photograph taken on Sunday the 27ᵗʰ of May, 1883.

On a night in 2008, Krakatoa's small eruption and tracks of lava are reflected in the water. (Thomas Schiet)

uninhabited island where the volcano Krakatoa stood. Technology advanced. Lighthouse keepers tended their lamps; telegraph operators sent messages to newspapers and insurance agents in London. A European woman left a small elephant unattended in her hotel room, where it ran amok. People wondered later if the elephant was upset by the impending eruption.[2]

In May 1883, Krakatoa belched. It frightened people, but they soon got used to its rumblings and bangs. The steamship *Loudon* took tourists to the island for twenty-five guilders.

On August 26, Krakatoa sent a stream of ash 17 miles (27 km) into the air. The captain of the *Loudon,* passing 30 miles (48 km) north of Krakatoa en route to the town of Telok Betong on the east shore of Lampong Bay, reported "enormous columns of smoke." The *Loudon* reached Telok Betong at 7:30 P.M., but steamed some way offshore during the night, anchoring in 30 feet (10 meters) of water. This probably saved the ship the following morning when, at 6:30 A.M., four "colossal waves" rolled in. According to a passenger:

"Suddenly we saw a gigantic wave of prodigious height advancing toward the seashore with considerable speed. Immediately, the crew ... managed to set sail in face of the imminent danger. . . . The ship met the wave head on and the Loudon *was lifted up with a dizzying rapidity and made a formidable leap. . . . The ship rode at a high angle over the crest of the wave and down the other side. The wave continued on its journey toward land, and the benumbed crew watched as the sea in a single sweeping motion consumed the town. There, where an instant before had lain the town of Telok Betong, nothing remained but the open sea."*

"We saw the lighthouse collapse and the houses disappear," wrote another passenger, and the place where the town had been "turned into ocean."[3] The tsunami had been generated by the destruction of the island of Krakatoa, some two-thirds of which (9 square miles or 23 square kilometers) collapsed into the sea from heights up to 1,500 feet (450 meters).

The *Loudon* headed for Java with the news. But at 8:00 A.M. "daylight began to fade," and by 10:00 A.M. "it was pitch-black." The darkness lasted for eighteen hours, pierced only by occasional lightning. The crew could see nothing, and the compass deviated wildly. They anchored. Thick mud fell. It covered the deck and clogged everyone's eyes, ears, and noses. It smelled dreadful, as a "hellish sulfuric acid spread through the air." They nearly suffocated. Violent winds tossed their ship; the sea floor quaked and sent monstrous new waves through the dark.[4] One tsunami carried the steamship *Berouw* a mile inland, killing all twenty-eight people aboard, but the *Loudon* rode out the disaster.

Almost 3,000 miles (4,800 km) west and south, on Rodriguez Island, people heard Krakatoa explode; it sounded like heavy guns. In Indonesia, the tsunamis destroyed 165 villages and towns, seriously damaged 132 more, and killed over 36,000 people. Floating pumice carried human bones as far as South Africa.[5]

Never before had news of an eruption been covered so quickly by newspapers on the other side of the world. Not all Krakatoa's aftereffects were negative. Science advanced. New instruments traced variations in atmospheric pressure around the earth, and variations in tides as far as the English Channel. Volcanic ash, high in the atmosphere, cooled temperatures around the world; some believe it lowered sea levels for decades. Sunsets were brilliant. Artists painted the afterglow of Krakatoa in England, and firefighters in upstate New York thought there was a massive blaze to their west. Scientists mapped the ash and began to learn about the jet stream.

But Krakatoa's most significant legacy may be political and religious. Indonesians lost homes and loved ones, and their Dutch governors could do little to ease their suffering. Some turned to religion for explanations and comfort, and for many of them religion meant Islam. By the time of the 1888 Banten Peasants' Revolt, anti-Dutch feeling was mixing with Islamic fervor. The revolt failed, but Indonesian commitment to Islam has only deepened since.

A restive Krakatoa.
(Byelikova
Oksana/
Thinkstock)

23

1887
THE YELLOW RIVER FLOODS

They call it China's Sorrow. The Huang He (Yellow River) pours down from loess plains full of rich yellow silt and snakes through China to the Bohai Sea. The river nourished ancient Chinese civilization with some of the world's best farmlands, and lashed it with legendary floods.

"Just before harvest, the five dikes were opened . . . thousands of families were crying and screaming amidst the flood,"[1] wrote a poet. In September 1887, the Huang He burst its lower dikes and created a vast lake, about the size of Lake Ontario.[2] An estimated 900,000 people drowned.[3] Starvation and disease killed hundreds of thousands more.

How did this happen? Silt kept raising the riverbed. In ancient times, when it rose higher than the plains around it, the river simply changed course. As early as the fifth century BC, the Chinese built embankments to protect fields and cities. Waterworks improved over time but needed constant dredging. In the Northern Song Dynasty (960–1128), the river broke its levees 74 times and shifted course 8 times. It was "half water and half silt," and after 30 years of neglect, the level in one canal topped surrounding plains by 13 feet.[4]

Nomads attacked China's northern borders, and military objectives often dictated water policies. In 1128, in a last-ditch effort to stop Jurchen invaders, Song troops broke the levees. The Huang He moved south and drained into the Yellow Sea,[5] devastating the once-rich Huaibei region.

In 1411, the Ming Dynasty (1368–1644) opened the Grand Canal. Ming policy for the Huang He protected two key resources: a memorial to the emperor's ancestors, and grain ships on the canal. Farmlands were not a priority. The memorial was not even a grave, but a cenotaph, where the ancestors' caps and clothing were buried. An official wrote in 1604, "If both the imperial cenotaph and the Grand Canal remain unaffected, we do not need to worry about where the Yellow River flows."[6]

By 1850 China's population reached 430 million. To feed them all, farmers adopted more

High water on the Yellow River. This photograph was taken during the 1887 flood.

intense irrigation, higher-yield strains of rice, and New World crops that grew on marginal lands. This led to hillside erosion and increased flooding.[7] The Qing emperors (1644–1912) faced an ecological crisis.

China faced political and fiscal challenges as well. From 1841 to 1851, it cost about a third of one year's revenue to repair four major levee breaks. Then the Taiping Rebellion (1850-1865) drained resources. In 1855, when the Huang He broke its northern levees and flowed back to its pre-1128 outlet on the Bohai, the state could not prevent it.[8]

Floods in 1887 and 1931 killed millions. In 1938, more died when the Nationalist government deliberately broke dikes to stop Japanese invaders. (The Japanese attacked from a different direction.)

Since 1956, industrial engineering has limited flooding, but the river's sediment conditions have worsened. Its channel is 33 feet (11 meters) above the level of surrounding plains.[9] Its delta has become more fragile and susceptible to natural hazards.[10] Climate change and rising sea levels threaten to renew China's Sorrow.

Conflicts of Interest

Shen Baozhen, governor-general of Liangjiang, summed up a problem in the late nineteenth century: "Conflicts of interest between civilian farmland and the canal are irreconcilable. After a dozen days without rain, the farmers desire to open the sluices for irrigation, but the officials close them in order to maintain the water level for passing ships. When the canal overflows, the officials open the sluices and dams in order to protect the embankments, thereby turning the peasants' farmlands into one huge lake."[11]

24

1889
THE HONOLULU BOARD
OF HEALTH BURNS OUT
BUBONIC PLAGUE

Plague again! The third pandemic broke out in south-central China before 1870, killed tens of thousands in Canton in 1893, and reached the port of Hong Kong in 1894. Health authorities from Bombay to Buenos Aires braced for disaster. Would a medieval disease kill millions of people at the dawn of the twentieth century?

Yes. Between 1899 and 1950, plague took an estimated 15 million lives: as many as 12 million in India, but only 7,000 in Europe and 500 in the U.S. There were probably unreported cases, however. Imagine somebody on your block dies a "suspicious death," and doctors say it's bubonic plague. Then your brother gets a fever. He can't move. He curls up like a baby and moans and vomits. He can't talk straight. He has open sores on his skin and painful swollen glands. Should you call for a doctor?

Honolulu's Chinatown aflame. (Courtesy Hawai'i State Archives)

If you live in Honolulu's Chinatown in 1899, here are some reasons you might not:

1. Quarantine. White doctors will take your brother to the quarantine hospital. They won't let you see him, even for a last good-bye. Instead, they will quarantine you and everybody else in your house at a detention camp, in case you are already carrying the disease.
2. Cremation. If your brother dies of plague, white doctors will cremate his body to keep the plague germs from hiding in the soil and killing again later. You will not be able to send your brother's bones home to China. What will become of his spirit?
3. Cleansing. White doctors believe that plague bacteria hide everywhere—in your clothes, under your floorboards, behind your walls. They will fumigate your possessions and burn down your house. When you finally get out of the detention camp, where will you go?

Public health authorities in Honolulu did their best. Bacteriologists could recognize the plague bacillus under their microscopes, but they didn't know how fleas spread it from rats to people. What if it spread through the air, like diphtheria, or survived underground like anthrax? They didn't know, and it was their job to be careful.

But how could Asians trust them? A white minority had ousted Hawaiian Queen Liliuokalani in 1893 and declared the Republic of Hawaii instead; they wanted the United States to annex the islands. White landowners ran sugar plantations, importing labor from China, Japan, and the Azores. White legislators proposed laws to keep those workers in the fields. White doctors had fought an 1895 cholera epidemic with quarantine and disinfectants. The people of Chinatown knew that Western medicine would invade their privacy, hurt their business, and disrupt their lives. In 1887, King David Kalakaua tried to replace the Western-dominated Honolulu Board of Health with a Hawaiian board of kahunas—traditional healers.

Nobody knew the fire department would burn most of Chinatown flat on January 20, 1900. The authorities said it was an accident. They were burning infected premises and the wind came up. The Chinese believed the fire was set on purpose to destroy Chinese. Eight or ten thousand Hawaiians, Chinese, and Japanese were left homeless and held in the detention camp. Two years after the epidemic, hundreds of refugees still lived in the camp. Their homes, property, and even their jobs had gone up in smoke. In 1902 Congress ratified the annexation of Hawaii, and eventually the federal government compensated victims for part of what they had lost.

Residents of Honolulu's Chinatown quarantined in 1899. (Courtesy Hawai'i State Archives)

Honolulu reported 71 cases of plague and 61 deaths that year: an 86% fatality rate. Authorities liked to believe that the accidental burning of Chinatown had "done away with most of the danger."[1] It had not: twenty victims died after the fire, and a few more every year until 1910. But the Board of Health kept quiet about the situation; they wanted to protect commercial interests.

Plague in San Francisco, 1900

Plague reached San Francisco the next year. Public health authorities there would have liked to imitate Honolulu and burn Chinatown. They thought it was full of gambling, opium, crime, dirt, and disease.[2] They quarantined it twice, and they planned to move the Chinese to Mission Rock. But the Chinese won a lawsuit against the Board of Health. Judge William Morrow of the U.S. Circuit Court ruled that it was wrong to quarantine an entire neighborhood based on culture and ethnicity. He ordered the quarantine lifted.[3] Meanwhile, scientists discovered how rat fleas spread plague.

There were just 39 known cases of plague in San Francisco in 1900: 35 Chinese and 4 whites. They all died. Fleas escaped quarantine and bit California ground squirrels, so there's been plague in North America ever since. And Chinatown survived to become one of San Francisco's greatest assets.

1902
MT. PELÉE BURIES A CITY

On a map, the islands of the Lesser Antilles look like a string of beads, curving between the Caribbean and the Atlantic. Up close, they're volcanic. They outline a subduction zone, where the South American plate drives under the Caribbean plate and pressure builds. Martinique's Mount Pelée was not the only volcano to erupt there in 1902. About 100 miles (160 km) south, on St. Vincent, La Soufrière erupted on May 5, destroying the largest surviving remnant of Carib culture. Still farther south, on May 7, an underwater volcano known as Kick 'em Jenny may also have erupted.

Pelée gave warning. It started belching sulfur in 1901. Professor Gaston Landes noticed mild ground tremors in February 1902. By April, there was

After Pelée destroyed St. Pierre, Fort-de-France, the capital, was Martinique's largest remaining city. Refugees crowded in. (William H. Rau/ Courtesy LOC)

A 1902 photograph of pyroclastic surge from Mt. Pelée. New technology, the high-speed camera, allowed geologists to document this terrifying phenomenon. (Alfred Lacroix)

enough sulfur in the air to tarnish silver overnight in St. Pierre. Then came eruptions, and residents thought of leaving.

The authorities weighed risks. Evacuating St. Pierre's 26,500 people looked impossible. The one coastal road was too narrow, and available ships too few. The capital, Fort-de-France, was too small to absorb the refugees. And was the trouble really necessary? Lava flows would run down ravines and bypass the city, they thought. Evacuation would disrupt lives for nothing, and expose property to looters and fire. Besides, there was an important run-off election scheduled for May 11. The local newspaper editor soothed "timid"[1] readers who wanted to go. Instead, he wrote on May 3, it was citizens' duty to help refugees from villages closer to the crater. Hundreds poured into the city.

Dutifully, people stayed. Animals got skittish. Insects fled the upper slopes, and found a rum and sugar factory in nearby Precheur. The ants loved it, and on May 5 the factory owner asked Landes how to get rid of them.

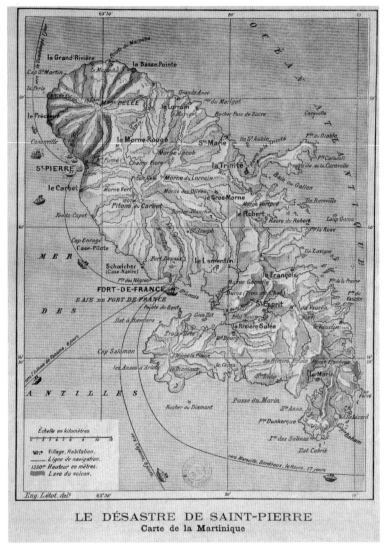

LE DÉSASTRE DE SAINT-PIERRE
Carte de la Martinique

Later that day a lahar—a mudflow—destroyed his factory, killing about 150 people.

On May 7, the French governor of Martinique and his volcano commission concluded that St. Pierre was in no danger. The next day, Pelée destroyed the city, killing the governor, the newspaper editor, the American consul, and an estimated 30,000 other people. The only survivors were a prisoner in solitary confinement, a cobbler at the edge of town, and a girl hiding in a seaside cave. All three were badly burned.

Pelée was a serial killer. Volcanoes kill by collapsing roofs under the weight of ash or hurling debris at people's heads. They let loose poison gases, fires, floods, lightning, and tsunamis. They kill indirectly, through famine.[2] Pelée's weapon on May 8 was a pyroclastic surge, a massive cloud of burning rock, gas, and debris that raced into town at 120 miles (190 km) per hour. It buried people under flattened buildings, seared their lungs when they breathed, and charred their flesh. It started a firestorm that raged for three days.

The eruptions lasted for months. Geologist Alfred Lacroix arrived from Paris and documented a pyroclastic surge with new technology: the high-speed camera. Then there was a lull. In July, a typhoid epidemic broke loose in Fort-de-France. To limit contagion, the government ordered refugees home to their villages—just as Pelée began rumbling again. Terrified residents begged the new governor to evacuate the town of Morne-Rouge, but he refused. (Their emissaries were described, scornfully, as a "racially mixed delegation of semiliterate natives.") On August 30, another pyroclastic surge killed 2,600 people—over half of them in Morne-Rouge; the governor at last changed his mind and organized more effective relief.[3]

Pelée continued to erupt into 1903. Meanwhile, the prisoner who survived St. Pierre's firestorm made headlines for the Barnum and Bailey Circus, and in October 1902, Santa Maria erupted in Guatemala, killing about 6,000 people. The Guatemalan eruption was larger and more explosive, but Pelée took more lives. With its human interest stories and scientific discoveries, lethal politics and pyroclastic surges, Pelée is famous to this day.

26

1906
SAN FRANCISCO SHAKES
AND BURNS

The United States seized San Francisco in 1846 during the Mexican-American War. Gold was discovered nearby in 1848, and fortune hunters mobbed the neighborhood. Miners and merchants alike fueled the city's adolescent growth spurt. By 1906, San Francisco looked more like a proper, grown-up city. Wooden houses with brick chimneys stood on filled land where brooks had once streamed down hillsides. A three-foot water main ran into the city from its reservoirs, and a maze of smaller pipes carried water to bathtubs and fire hydrants. Fire chief Dennis Sullivan called for a more powerful saltwater hydrant system. At risk were fishermen and artists and millionaires, swimming pools and Chinatown, grand hotels and an even grander $6,000,000 city hall.[1] In 1900 San Francisco was the ninth largest city in the U.S., with 342,782 people—more than three times the size of Los Angeles.[2]

In the aftermath,
a shell of a city.
(Courtesy
LOC)

But San Francisco sits right on the San Andreas Fault, where two of Earth's tectonic plates—the North American plate and the Pacific plate—rub past each other at a rate of about one and a half inches a year. Normally. Once in a while something sticks, as something might stick in an escalator, and the plates lock together. Pressure builds, and builds, and finally releases.

San Francisco in flames after the 1906 earthquake. (Courtesy LOC)

At 5:12 the morning of April 18, 1906, something broke loose under San Francisco Bay, and the pent-up energy of years burst out at speeds of up to two miles a second. City streets bulged and sank. Filled land liquefied. Buildings lurched and leaned. Telegraph cables broke. Gas mains and water mains ruptured. The brick chimneys of the California Hotel pitched down into the fire station. (Sullivan was killed.) Fire broke out and raged for three days. Sullivan had been right.

Why do we still remember the San Francisco Earthquake? Partly for the harm it did. At 7.9 or 8.3 on the Richter scale, it was not the greatest earthquake in magnitude. Others have had far higher death tolls. Officially, only

Snarled traffic in a shaken city. Soldiers from the local army base helped with the disaster response. (National Archives)

428 people died as a direct result of the San Francisco quake and fire. But the real number may have topped three thousand, and with 28,188 buildings destroyed, 225,000 people—over half the city's population—were left homeless.

We should also remember the disaster response. Officials reacted quickly. Soldiers from the U.S. army base in San Francisco helped city workers control the fires, discourage lootings, and set up camps for the homeless. Famous restaurants fed people on long wooden tables in the streets. Things were soon under control, more or less.

A Cincinnati Post headline the day after the quake.

Still, disasters spread confusion, and there's a reason we don't know the exact death toll. Some people found confusion helpful in 1906. Insurance companies tried to limit their losses by blaming everything on the earthquake. If a building was ruined before it was burned, that was the owner's bad luck and not the insurance company's. Investors and city boosters, on the other hand, wanted to blame the fire. Fire, caused by human error, can be prevented by human foresight: new building codes and better equipment would make San Francisco safe from fire. Nobody knew how to make a city safe from earthquakes, and nobody wanted to discourage this city's growth.

These two San Francisco earthquake photos—one from 1906 and one from 1989—show eerily similar effects. (Courtesy LOC(t), USGS(b)).

One class of immigrants the authorities did try to discourage: the Chinese. The fire leveled Chinatown, but the Chinese insisted on rebuilding right where they'd been. And in spite of the 1882 Chinese Exclusion Act, immigration rose. One loophole in the act allowed the Chinese relatives of legal residents to join them in the U.S. The fire destroyed Chinese immigration records, and this made it easy for would-be immigrants to claim they were joining husbands or fathers or brothers in San Francisco. The Chinese, like the insurance companies and the investors, found some benefit in confusion.

27

1908
TUNGUSKA ASTEROID LEVELS FOREST IN SIBERIA

I f a tree falls in the forest and nobody hears, does it make a noise? If a meteor explodes over a remote forest in Siberia, is it a disaster?

A little after 7 A.M. on June 30, 1908, peasants in Nizhne-Karelinsk saw a bright blue-white light in the sky. A glowing cylinder met the northwest horizon, and a "forked tongue of flames" streaked up. A mighty crash, six hundred miles away, made villagers think "the end of the world was approaching."[1] The explosion had "the energy of a large hydrogen bomb."[2] It flattened trees for hundreds of square miles. At a trading post forty miles from ground zero, a man was hurled from his chair and felt as if his shirt were on fire.[3] The atmospheric shockwave circled Earth twice, and for the next two nights skies were eerily bright in Europe and Asia.

Trees felled by the Tunguska explosion. (Courtesy the Leonid Kulik Expedition)

Asteroid fragment explodes over Chelyabinsk in 2013. (Photo by Marat Ahmetvaleev)

What was it? The Evenks, who herded reindeer in the area, thought the fire-god Ogda had come to strike them down.[4] Other guesses involve aliens, a black hole, anti-matter, and even time travel.[5] Scientists consider it more likely that either a comet or an asteroid entered Earth's atmosphere and exploded 3 to 6 miles above the ground. It left no crater—or is Lake Cheko the crater? The matter is debated.[6]

Tunguska is so remote we don't know if the lake existed before 1908. Russian geologist Leonid Kulik looked for the meteor in 1921 and led a scientific expedition in 1927, but getting there wasn't easy. He had to rely on reindeer-drawn sledges. Evenki guides wouldn't go near the place,[7] and it didn't yield the hoped-for bonanza of useful minerals. In 1939, World War II began. Kulik died of typhus in a German POW camp, and the Tunguska site was neglected until the 1950s.

Recent scientists test their hypotheses about the event using every tool from soil analysis to computer modeling. They want to know how often impact events occur, how much damage they are likely to do, and how soon we can see them coming. The amount of energy released over Tunguska could have destroyed a city like London. A 1- or 2-kilometer meteor, landing in the right place and at the right angle, might set a continent aflame or send mega-tsunamis around the ocean rims; a 10-kilometer one might blacken the sky for years, plunging Earth into cosmic winter.[8] But rocks that size hit the earth, on average, once every 89 million years.[9]

What does fall usually does little damage. According to NASA, "about one hundred tons of interplanetary material drifts down to Earth's surface" every day.[10] We don't even notice it. Even larger objects—like the 3-meter-wide Asteroid 2014 AA, which was discovered on January 1 and hit Earth on January 2, 2014[11]—may strike our planet unnoticed.

In February 2013, a 19-meter (62-foot) asteroid fragment exploded over Chelyabinsk, home to more than 1.3 million Russians. Nobody saw it coming. Windows shattered in 7,000 buildings, and over 1,000 people suffered minor injuries—glass cuts, flash burns, and temporary blindness.[12] Drivers took viral videos of a speeding object brighter than the sun. Defense satellites recorded its path; so did a worldwide infrasound network. Researchers can reconstruct its trajectory. But like the Tunguska object, the Chelyabinsk asteroid left surprisingly little debris. Most of it was vaporized.

The Chelyabinsk explosion did leave at least one observable effect: Congress doubled the annual budget for NASA's Near Earth Object Program to $40 million. The program's astronomers keep an eye on about 1,500 "potentially hazardous" asteroids—objects as big as an Egyptian pyramid that come within 4.65 million miles of earth.[13] Close observation will give us warning, so we can launch spacecraft to deflect any asteroid that might collide with Earth. But the best reason to study asteroids may be positive. They could hold clues to the origins of life on earth.[14]

Impact Events and the End of the Dinosaurs

One or more meteor impacts probably caused mass extinctions about 65 million years ago—or so most scientists have come to believe since 1980.[15] One struck Mexico's Yucatan Peninsula, leaving a crater 93 to 120 miles (150 to 180 km) in diameter: Chicxulub. Around 40,000 years later an even larger meteorite made a crater three times as wide off the west coast of India: Shiva.[16] When debris from these collisions fell to earth, it created a layer of what's called the Cretaceous-Tertiary Boundary Clay (KTBC).[17] Geologists have recovered this clay around the world, from Montana to Hokkaido. The clay contains iridium and other elements that are rare on Earth but more common in asteroids. Dinosaur footprints and other fossils from the Cretaceous Period lie below the KTBC. Above the KTBC, diversity plummets. An estimated 75% of all Earth's plant and animal species died off at the end of the Cretaceous Era.

The extinction happened. But was it really caused by meteor impact? Other enormous collisions have left their marks on Earth—one of them created Chesapeake Bay 35 million years ago—but those impacts don't coincide with breaks in the fossil record. Another theory is that the end-Cretaceous extinctions were caused by volcanic activity, like mass extinctions at the end of the Permian (see Chapter 50) and Triassic Eras. Geoscientist Gerta Keller proposes that the eruption of the Deccan Traps, a huge volcanic event in what is now India, released massive lava flows that could have raised climate temperatures by at least 7° F in less than 10,000 years and acidified the oceans, killing "all but the hardiest life-forms."[18]

28

1918
INFLUENZA KILLS MORE THAN WORLD WAR I

In 1918 World War I drew to its close. After four long years of trench warfare Great Britain, France, Russia, and their allies (including Italy, Japan, and the United States) had beaten Germany, Austria-Hungary, and the other Central Powers. More than 8.5 million soldiers from 16 nations had died; another 28.9 million were wounded, taken prisoner, or missing in action.[1] Europe had lost a generation of men.

But as troops returned home, they spread an even greater disaster. In September, American military hospitals began to fill with blood. Soldiers bled from their noses; some bled from their ears; some coughed up blood. Their heads ached. They hurt all over. There was no known cure for the agony, and young men died, drowned in their own bodily fluids.

In the U.S. influenza claimed 675,000 lives—roughly 0.65% of the population. Many countries suffered more. Mexico lost up to 4% of its population and over 5% of its young adults. Most flu epidemics kill children and the elderly; in 1918, young adults were twice as likely to die.[2] The 1918 pandemic infected an estimated 500 million people (one third of the world's population at the time), and may have killed 50 million.[3] Figures are still debated.

What caused it? The world had seen other influenza pandemics, but the flu virus is a shapeshifter. It mutates constantly, and populations with some immunity to one strain of flu can be overcome by another.

Where did it start? Probably not in Spain, although it was called "Spanish flu" at the time. A wave of flu-like disease early in 1918 targeted young adults in New York City.[4] A Kansas outbreak affected farms and army bases at about the same time. Maybe American soldiers carried it to Europe. Wherever it came from,

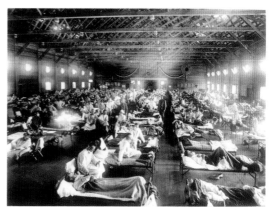

Soldiers stricken with influenza crowd a hospital ward at Camp Funston, Kansas.

Red Cross litter carriers in Washington, D.C. (Courtesy LOC)

it gained strength in an extreme environment. Soldiers from five continents met on French soil. Men fought in cold, muddy trenches; they were worn down by fear, wounds, and mustard gas; they were in contact with birds, pigs, and other animals that could have spread a mutated virus.[5]

Quarantine kept the flu out of Australia until December 1918, and death rates there were lower. But Australians called it the Bubonic Plague,[5] after another recent pandemic (see Chapter 25). Like plague in 1900, flu in 1918 focused the efforts of medical detectives and public health experts around the world. And as they had blamed poor immigrants for plague outbreaks in 1900, some now blamed them for flu. Town authorities in Norwood, Massachusetts, searched immigrant neighborhoods for cases of flu and coerced victims into treatment and isolation;[6] the same thing happened in other towns as well. These tactics allowed local elites to feel they were taking appropriate measures to control disease and limit risk—and to see the poor as responsible for their own suffering, thus reducing society's obligation to care for them.

Meanwhile, in Paris, flu deaths mounted again in 1919 while American president Woodrow Wilson was there for the peace talks. Wilson was internationally admired for his "Fourteen Points" statement calling for free trade, democracy, self-determination, and the formation of a League of Nations to guarantee the sovereign rights of nations, but many of his ideals conflicted with the national interests of other leaders at the table. He succumbed to the flu in April, and though he struggled back to the peace talks within days, he never fully recovered.[7] The Treaty of Versailles, negotiated at those talks, might have been very different if Wilson had not been ill. The conditions and reparations imposed on Germany were fiercely resented by Germans, and many believe the treaty sowed the seeds of World War II.

Most people recovered from the flu, but hardly any family escaped its effects. Some who lived through the disease never regained their health. Orphans lived with weakened or grief-stricken relatives. The full impact is unknown, but one effect has been lab-tested: our flu epidemics are still caused by descendants of that 1918 mutant virus.[8]

29

1919
THE GREAT MOLASSES
FLOOD BLAMED ON
ANARCHISTS

O n January 15, 1919, a wave of molasses—dark, sweet, and sticky as honey—killed 21 people and injured 150 more. It burst from a holding tank and surged into Boston's North End like a tsunami, 15 feet high and moving at 35 miles per hour. It crushed a wooden house, shifted a brick fire station from its foundation, and smashed elevated train tracks. Horses still mingled with cars on Boston's streets in those days, and dozens of horses, stuck in molasses, had to be shot. Rescuers waded through chest-high molasses, and hospital staff had to begin treatment by clearing molasses from

Boston's North End waterfront, slick with molasses after the explosion. (Courtesy Boston Public Library/ Boston Globe)

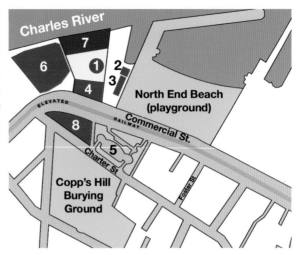

Detail of the molasses flood area. **1.** Purity Distilling molasses tank **2.** Firehouse 31 (heavy damage) **3.** Paving department and police station **4.** Purity offices (flattened) **5.** Copps Hill Terrace **6.** Boston Gas Light building (damaged) **7.** Purity warehouse (mostly intact) **8.** Residential area (site of flattened Clougherty house)

victims' noses and mouths. Before the dead could be identified, they had to be washed in hot water.

How could this be a natural disaster? The owner's attorney said anarchists must have bombed the holding tank,[1] and people could easily believe that. The U.S. was enduring a Red Scare, and if any political group was scarier than the socialists, it was the anarchists. Socialists had revolted against the Russian tsars in 1917, toppling the Romanov dynasty after 300 years of rule and setting up a new Marxist government. That was scary. But anarchists did not believe in laws and governments at all. That was scarier. People associated anarchists with labor strikes, terrorist bombs, and immigrants. The North End was one of Boston's poorest neighborhoods, densely packed with immigrants—especially Italians. In 1917, an anonymous caller had even threatened to blow up the molasses tank.

Enemies might indeed have wanted to blow up the tank in 1917. Molasses was not just a sweetener; it was an ingredient for war. Distilled into alcohol, it helped make dynamite and other explosives. The tank's owner, United States Industrial Alcohol (USIA), upped production even before the U.S. entered World War I. Now the war was over, but the Red Scare was not.

No anarchist was seen, however. Weather was a likelier culprit. Boston temperatures plunged to 8° F on January 10.[2] Bitter cold over the next few days congealed molasses in the tank. Then, on January 12–13, the steamer *Miliero* pumped in another 600,000 gallons of molasses that had traveled from sunny Cuba up the warm Gulf Stream to Boston. In the nearly full tank, warm molasses pushed against cold molasses and began to ferment. Gas pushed outward, and workers in the area heard loud, groaning noises.[3] By noon on January 15, Boston's temperature was an unseasonably warm 40.5° F.[4] Heat makes things expand.

The weather had an accomplice: human negligence. USIA had built the tank hastily in 1915. Because it was only a receptacle, it was not as thoroughly inspected as a building. Its steel walls were too thin, and too few rivets held them together. It leaked molasses from the beginning. The company camouflaged drips with paint, but hungry neighborhood children stood under the tank and caught molasses in pails. The explosion killed two 10-year-old children.

Cleaning up the mess took weeks. Crews scrubbed and steamed, pumped seawater over the street, siphoned goo out of basements, and did their best to clear out sewers.[5]

Wreckage under the elevated tracks, with firemen in the foreground.

The legal mess took longer, as 119 claims were consolidated into a single proceeding. Hearings went through September 1923. The well-publicized anarchist bombing of Wall Street in 1920 helped the USIA case, heightening the Red Scare. So did the case of Boston-area anarchists Nicola Sacco and Bartolomeo Vanzetti, who were convicted of a 1920 Braintree payroll robbery and murder. Maybe they actually did it; the case is still argued. But there was no evidence of a bomb in the molasses tank. Plaintiffs argued that USIA was criminally negligent. Its substandard tank had endangered homes, commercial structures, and even a playground. In April 1925, the court auditor awarded damages to the plaintiffs.

The tank was never rebuilt. The war's end and Prohibition—a 1920–1933 national ban on liquor sales—cut the demand for alcohol. But years later, people still claimed to smell molasses on hot days in the North End.

Molasses Spill in Honolulu Harbor

In September 2013, 223,000 gallons of molasses leaked into Honolulu Harbor, depriving sea life of oxygen[6] and killing a thousand colonies of coral.[7] The molasses was in transit from Hawaii's last sugar plantation to California when it leaked from a faulty pipeline, disrupting the marine ecosystem. Transport of hazardous substances like oil and gasoline is regulated; transport of molasses is not, and the company had no plan for dealing with molasses spills.[8]

30

1923
KANTO EARTHQUAKE FLATTENS TOKYO AND YOKOHAMA; KOREANS MASSACRED

Japan in 1923 was as contradictory as the U.S. It was moving toward liberal democracy; it had luxurious shops and restaurants and a labor movement.[1] But the economy was weak, and some thought the nation's morals were weak.[2] Rice riots in 1918 raised fears of civil unrest. Socialists were considered dangerous—and so were Koreans. Japan had annexed Korea in 1910 and suppressed the Korean Independence Movement in 1919. Anger remained. Ethnic Koreans working in Japan faced distrust and discrimination.

On September 1, 1923, a magnitude 7.9 earthquake ravaged two great Japanese cities: Yokohama, a westernized metropolis of almost half a million, and the capital, Tokyo. The quake destroyed about 45% of Tokyo's buildings and 90% of Yokohama's.[3] It pushed land north of Sagami Bay nearly 6 feet higher, and destroyed Tokyo's water mains. It generated a tsunami with wave heights up to 39 feet (12 meters).[4]

Within half an hour, fires broke out in more than 130 places. People fled to the river; bridges collapsed. People ran to open ground; a 300-foot-tall "fire tornado" burned 44,000. In all about 140,000 died,[5] and 2.5 million were left homeless.

The homeless were insecure. Up to 1,000 aftershocks jolted them in following weeks. They lacked food, water, and shelter. They lacked reliable news, *In the aftermath,* so rumors spread. (A larger earthquake was on the way, people heard. Bigger *victims in the streets.* tsunamis. Mt. Fuji would erupt.) Martial law was declared on September 2, as

new rumors pointed at human threats. (Koreans were setting fires and poisoning well water, people said. They were looting. Rioting.[6] Some of these lies were even printed in newspapers.[7]) An estimated 20,000 Koreans lived in and around Tokyo. Japanese citizens became vigilantes, taking the law into their own hands. That week they killed 6,000 people who seemed alien—mostly Koreans, but also ethnic Chinese and even northern Japanese.

The urge to find a scapegoat, so common after any disaster, led to a massacre.

Did authorities start the rumors themselves? Did they hope to contain civil unrest by giving people a target?[8] Whatever started it, the lawlessness alarmed the government. On September 5, Prime Minister Yamamoto condemned the violence and called for the nation to "exercise strong self-control and endeavor to live up to the principle of peace."[9]

The Ministry of Education sent Boy Scouts through Tokyo and Yokohama to collect stories of miraculous escapes, tragic loss, and (especially) ideal

Ginza after the earthquake: Broken cables above add to chaos on the ground. (Yoshikawa Kobunkan)

Japanese virtues. By October 20 they published two volumes of these tales for use in elementary schools. They emphasized "loyalty to the Emperor, filial piety, benevolence and charity, sacrifice, courage and bravery, and, obedience, respect and advancing public good."[10]

News of the quake reached the outside world by radio: "CONFLAGRATION SUBSEQUENT TO SEVERE EARTHQUAKE AT YOKOHAMA AT NOON TODAY. WHOLE CITY ABLAZE WITH NUMEROUS CASUALTIES. ALL TRAFFIC STOPPED." International relief saved thousands. U.S. warships hurried rice, canned roast beef, reed mats, gasoline, and other supplies to Yokohama, and the American Red Cross raised $12 million for victims.[11] Still, economic damages were four times higher than Japan's 1923 budget.[12] Plans to rebuild Tokyo cost too much; the legislature debated endlessly. Reconstruction took until 1930.[13]

For many, moral reconstruction was more important. The disaster was a divine punishment, they said, or a warning against new Western values, or an opportunity for reform. One even suggested that the burning of Tokyo was "a form of purification." (He wrongly believed the 1666 fire of London had ended plague there.)[14] Right-wing opposition to liberal tendencies was mounting before the quake. Afterward, a less optimistic Japan moved faster toward militarism and war.[15]

Refugees pack the square in front of Ueno Station, one of Tokyo's main railway stations. (Osaka Mainichi)

31

1938
UNPREDICTED HURRICANE
BATTERS NEW ENGLAND

Storm surges flooded low-lying coastal communities, while heavy rainfall flooded rivers. This photograph shows the Merrimack River pounding a Manchester, New Hampshire mill. (NOAA)

We get the word "hurricane" from Juracán, a Carib god of chaos and disorder. Hurricanes are common in the Caribbean, but few hit the Northeast with much power. The Great Colonial Hurricane of 1635 punched Massachusetts, killing an estimated 46 (including 8 Native Americans)[1] when Boston was only five years old. The Great September Gale of 1815 struck Connecticut and Rhode Island, destroying at least 500 homes, 35 ships, and 38 lives,[2] before Yankees used the word "hurricane." Generations passed between such storms. Our system of naming them didn't begin until 1953.[3]

So it's not surprising that Leray Davis, a doctor in Long Island's Westhampton Village, thought his barometer was broken at 2:40 P.M. on September 21, 1938. He shook it and shook it, and still it read "hurricane." He drove off to

Storm surge pushed Norman Caswell's school bus off the road in Jamestown, Rhode Island. (Jamestown Historical Society)

make house calls. Minutes later his family fled on foot as a hurricane obliterated Westhampton Village.[4]

Professional weather forecasters did no better. Florida and the Carolinas had braced for this hurricane, but it missed them. Experienced analysts at the Washington Weather Bureau thought the storm would veer out to sea. A young substitute, Charles Pierce, calculated that a trough of low pressure would cause it to head straight north, moving fast enough to maintain its strength and making landfall at Long Island. He was right, but experience and precedent blinded his supervisors to the evidence. The storm caught the Northeast unprepared.[5]

Once it hit, the storm imposed its own news blackout. It knocked out communications—and as people struggled to escape flooded or upturned houses in Connecticut, they had no way to warn Rhode Island and Massachusetts of what was coming.[6] Would warning have helped? The storm's landfall registered on seismographs in Alaska.[7] The Blue Hill Observatory at Milton, Massachusetts, recorded a sustained wind of 121 miles per hour and gusts up to 186 miles per hour. (Maybe it went higher, but at that point the anemometer broke.)[8] The Connecticut River flooded. Narragansett Bay flooded. Hartford, Providence, and many other cities were awash. The storm killed at least 564 people and injured at least 1,700 more. It destroyed 8,900 buildings and damaged another 15,000. It destroyed mills and fishing fleets,[9] depriving some workers of their livelihoods at the end of the Great Depression; but on the other hand, clean-up efforts created work.

The storm left Long Island and southern New England dazed. Some never recovered. Norman Caswell was driving a Rhode Island school bus when the storm swept it off the road. Seven of the eight children aboard drowned, and Caswell, broken by the experience, died not long after.[10] But World War II was coming, and it would bring massive social change to America. What replaced the storm's ruins would be completely different.

What Makes a Storm a Disaster?

How much damage a storm does depends on many factors: its area, its forward momentum, and the size and readiness of the population it strikes can matter more than whether it is a Category 1 or 5 storm on the Saffir-Simpson Hurricane Scale. The tight, fast-moving 1938 hurricane was still a Category 3 storm when it reached Massachusetts. In 2012, Superstorm Sandy was no longer even a hurricane when it reached New Jersey and New York, but it sprawled over 1,100 miles of the Atlantic and then merged with a nor'easter. Sandy caused fewer deaths; is that because people were ready? Better forecasts and speedier communications gave residents more warning than in 1938. But Sandy caused more than ten times as much property damage, even adjusting for inflation; is that because it covered a wider area, or a wealthier one?

Tropical cyclones in the North Atlantic are called hurricanes. In the Pacific, they are called typhoons, and some are deadlier than Atlantic hurricanes. As sea levels rise, the urban poor are especially vulnerable to cyclones. The Bhola cyclone of 1970 drove a powerful storm surge across the Bay of Bengal and over the Ganges delta, killing half a million people.[11] In 2013, Typhoon Haiyan (otherwise known as Yolanda) killed 6,201 people in the Philippines—especially in the city of Tacloban, where the poorest residents squatted in low-lying shanty towns by the coast.

1952
KILLER SMOG
SHROUDS LONDON

On December 5, 1952, a London fog set in. It killed thousands of people and left many more gasping for breath. Elderly people died. Police, checking up on people whose neighbors hadn't seen them lately, would find them dead in their rooms. Babies died. Even healthy adults died, especially if their work kept them outside too long. A garage mechanic died after a morning of car repairs.

The call for garage mechanics was high. Car batteries were dying all over London. Visibility was so bad that many drivers left their cars by the roadsides—with the lights on, so other drivers could see them. Nobody imagined the fog would last long enough to wear down the batteries.[1]

But it kept getting thicker. People got lost on their own property. One doctor, called to a patient's bedside in the middle of the night, tried for hours to walk three blocks. He finally woke up a blind neighbor to help him navigate.[2] The weather didn't clear until December 9.

London fogs were nothing new. In 1306, Edward I banned the commercial use of coal fires while Parliament was in session.[3] The ban had little effect. Londoners had to burn something, and coal was what they could get. They used it for heating, for cooking, and for business, and its smoke filled the air.[4] Edward's noblemen coughed and hacked as they debated laws and taxes.

Masked policeman watches traffic through the December 1952 fog. (© Hulton-Deutsch Collection/ CORBIS)

The Houses of Parliament and Big Ben seen across the Thames on a cold London day. (Richard Ashcroft/Thinkstock)

The Industrial Revolution began around 1760, and more coal was burned as machinery and chemical processes replaced old-fashioned ways of making things by hand. The new factories were efficient but dirty—"dark Satanic mills," the poet William Blake called them. Increasingly, smoke mixed with fog to make something worse. In the twentieth century it was named "smog," but it wasn't new. London smogs took lives in 1873, 1880, 1882, 1891, 1892, and 1948.[5]

Other countries had their own lethal smogs. In 1930, coal-polluted air took 60 in Belgium's Meuse River valley.[6] In 1948, it killed nearly 40 and made 7,000 ill in Donora, Pennsylvania,[7] another industrial town in a river valley. People in Donora thought air pollution meant jobs, so they had to put up with it. It was the price they paid for economic progress.[8]

A killer smog is a collaboration between humans and nature. Human industry turns natural resources into pollutants. Throughout the 1952 smog, Londoners kept emitting chemicals from houses, factories, and cars. Thousands of pounds of carbon dioxide, hydrochloric acid, fluorine compounds, and sulfur dioxide filled the air.[9] No wonder people felt sick. They were breathing sulfuric acid.

And they were breathing more of it because a stalled high-pressure system had caused a temperature inversion in the Thames valley. Warm air overhead prevented the cooler city air from rising, and hills trapped it in the valley. The smog raised London's death rate higher than even the 1866 cholera epidemic.[10] The city ran out of hospital beds for the sick and shrouds to wrap the dead.[11]

The public health emergency galvanized British opinion. In spite of strong opposition to air pollution control,[12] Parliament finally passed a Clean Air Act in 1956.[13] The United States passed a similar law in 1970, establishing the Environmental Protection Agency (EPA). The U.S. has cut emissions of six common pollutants by 72% since 1970, while population has risen by 53%, energy consumption by 47%, and gross domestic product by 219%.

Environmentalists and industry still disagree about regulations. In the state of Maine, for instance, paper mill officials said in 2013 that looser smog rules would make more jobs.[14] But air, polluted or not, crosses boundaries. Multilateral treaties like the United Nations Economic Commission for Europe (UNECE) Convention on Long-Range Transboundary Air Pollution try to control smog.[15]

Clean air regulations in Europe and North America are only the beginning. Today's worst air pollution comes from fast-developing economies elsewhere in the world. But in 2014, President Obama used his authority under the Clean Air Act to tighten EPA restrictions on carbon emissions.[16] The U.S. should set an example, he said. Maybe we can have jobs, economic progress—and cleaner air.

The Trouble with Burning Coal

Coal is a fossil fuel. Millions of years ago, soil buried dense wetland forests. More and more weight compacted the dead trees and plants. The temperature around them rose. Surrounded by mud and acidic water, they did not decay. Slowly they became coal—a sedimentary rock made mostly of carbon from carbon-based life forms.[17]

Coal has helped fuel civilization for thousands of years. The Chinese used it to smelt copper 3,000 years ago, and nations around the world now use it to generate electricity. (It powers 37% of U.S. electricity generation[18] and 40% worldwide.[19]) This involves mining the coal, transporting it to power plants, and burning it.[20]

The costs of using coal are significant. Some have always been obvious. Coal miners die underground (a 2014 explosion and fire killed nearly 300 miners in Turkey), or they die of respiratory diseases like Black Lung. And coal smoke obviously pollutes the air, as Parliament complained in 1306.

Scientists now worry about the more hidden costs of burning coal. Some of its emissions—like sulfur dioxide and mercury compounds—are toxic. Others—like carbon dioxide (CO_2)—are greenhouse gases and contribute to global warming.

We need greenhouse gases. Earth's average surface temperature is now about 15° Celsius, or 59° Fahrenheit. Deep in the Ice Age, it may have been about 8° Celsius cooler.[21] But without greenhouse gases, it would have been about -19° Celsius,[22] or -2° Fahrenheit. Greenhouse gases let the sun's warmth reach Earth's surface, but then they keep much of it from escaping. Like a good blanket on a cold night, they conserve heat and help create an environment that enables life as we know it.

So why all the concern about greenhouse gas emissions from burning coal and other fossil fuels? If CO_2 is a natural part of the atmosphere, why are we worried?

It doesn't take much of a temperature anomaly to change the balance of nature in ways that affect our lives. A dip of less than 1° Celsius can make a Little Ice Age or a volcanic winter. An equally small rise can cause widespread drought and famine.

Most of the CO_2 and other greenhouse gases in our atmosphere are natural. But a growing percentage was put there by humans. And Earth's average surface temperature is now rising twenty times faster than it normally rises after an ice age. Human activity appears to be tipping a delicate balance, and the result could be very uncomfortable for life as we know it.

1968-1985
DROUGHT IN THE SAHEL STARVES SUB-SAHARAN AFRICA

The Sahel is a semiarid strip of Africa extending from Senegal and the Gambia on the Atlantic coast to Sudan and Eritrea on the Red Sea. North of it lies the great Sahara Desert; south of it, rain forests and savannahs.

Fabled empires like Timbuktu once flourished in the Sahel. Now its inhabitants live in a dozen different countries. They speak different languages and follow different religions. But they have much in common. Several nations—Burkina Faso, Cape Verde, Chad, the Gambia, Guinea Bissau, Mali, Mauritania, Niger, and Senegal—formed the Permanent Interstates Committee for Drought Control (CILSS) in 1973. They estimate that over half the population depends on agriculture, growing crops such as millet, sorghum, cowpea, groundnut, and cotton.[1] Other people of the Sahel, like the Tuareg and the Fulani, are semi-nomadic cattle herders. This can lead to conflict when farmers and herders need to use the same land for competing purposes.

The climate of the Sahel swings. After decades of good rainfall, it will suddenly shift to decades of drought and famine. A period of severe drought began

Tuareg herders in Mali, 1974.
(H. Grobe)

Young men fish by hand in a natural spring in Niger in 2013. (©FAO/Giulio Napolitano)

around 1968, and by 1985 approximately 100,000 people had died of famine and disease.[2] The cattle-based economy collapsed in 1973 and again in 1984; Tuareg herds starved, and people crowded into relief camps for grain.[3]

What triggered the drought? In the 1970s, scientists pointed to human activities like deforestation and overgrazing. Treeless, overgrazed ground is a lighter color, so it absorbs less sunlight and reflects more energy away from the earth. That could affect rainfall.[4] But according to evidence from stream deposits, lake beds, and fossil sands, the Sahel has had periodic droughts for thousands of years, even before deforestation.[5] A leading hypothesis is that Sahel rainfall depends at least partly on sea surface temperatures.[6] Drought in Africa could be related to the El Niño / Southern Oscillation (ENSO) cycle.[7] Complicating the picture is dust. The less rain falls on the Sahel, the more African dust will blow across the Atlantic—and dust itself can affect climate.[8]

Drought leads to famine when people do not have other resources and opportunities. Even without drought conditions, people may starve because of locust invasions, epidemics, or the seizure of their harvests.[9] By 2005, the Sahel had partially recovered, but the ecosystem remained fragile. Climatologists predicted that human release of aerosols and greenhouse gases into the atmosphere would cause dryer conditions in the twenty-first-century Sahel.[10] Sadly, the prediction may come true. Three major droughts in the past decade have put 20 million people at risk of hunger and acute malnutrition.

The Dust Bowl

The most famous U.S. drought hit during the Great Depression, beginning in 1930. Like the Sahel, America's semiarid Great Plains average fewer than 20 inches of rain a year and are subject to extended droughts. The 1862 Homestead Act encouraged settlement there. Grazing and farming destroyed native grasses that once held soil in place. Then rain stopped, and crops failed. Wind blew dried topsoil from the fields in great dust storms. In May 1934 a powerful "black blizzard" dropped 12 million pounds of dust on Chicago. The next winter's snow in New England was red with Great Plains dust. April 14, 1935—"Black Sunday"—was even worse. A region that had been America's breadbasket now had a bleak new name: the Dust Bowl. People died of malnutrition and "dust pneumonia," but the greatest tragedy may have been displacement. Houses and tractors were buried in dust; banks foreclosed on farms; half a million Americans were made homeless. Parents gathered their children, packed the few things they could fit into their cars, and left Texas, Oklahoma, and Kansas behind them. The search for work took many of them to Bakersfield, in California's San Joaquin Valley—the salad bowl of the world.

In 2014, worsening drought threatened the San Joaquin Valley.[11] Was it caused by human activity?[12]

Dust storms like this one in South Dakota helped bury hope in the depths of the Great Depression. (USDA)

El Niño

Over the tropical Pacific, the trade winds usually blow from the east, pushing the ocean's surface waters westward, toward Indonesia. This causes colder water to well up from the ocean depths along the coast of Peru. The upwelling carries nutrients from the ocean floor into sun-lit surface waters, spurring the growth of phytoplankton that form the foundation of the ocean food chain. Zooplankton eat the phytoplankton, and fish eat the zooplankton. Peruvian fisheries are among the world's richest.

But once every 3 to 5 years on average, the flow changes and there is an El Niño event. The trade winds weaken or reverse. For a few months or even two years, Peru's ocean waters stay warmer and its fishing isn't so good. Fishermen in the 1800s would notice this change around Christmas, so they called it "El Niño," after the Christ Child.[13]

El Niño is more than a local phenomenon. It is related to the Southern Oscillation, a see-saw pattern of reversing surface air pressure between the eastern and western equatorial Pacific. Between El Niño years, there are normal years and sometimes La Niña years, when ocean temperatures in the equatorial Pacific are cooler than normal. Scientists call the El Niño/Southern Oscillation pattern "ENSO" for short.

continued on p. 99

El Niño

continued from p. 98

El Niño affects weather around the world in different ways. It has been associated with flooding in the southern U.S. and Peru; drought in the West Pacific; and devastating brush fires in Australia.[14] Forecasters track the ENSO cycle to predict global weather, but the pattern is complicated by climate change. Since 2000, the average temperature during cool La Niña years is warmer than in any warm El Niño year before 1996.

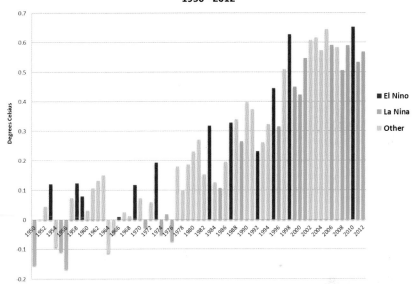

**Annual Global Temperature Anomalies
1950 - 2012**

El Niño years have been warmer than the normal years around them—but recently, even cool La Niña years are hotter than El Niño years used to be. (NOAA)

34

1970-1975
SMALLPOX ERADICATED
IN BANGLADESH

I n 1967, the World Health Organization (WHO) formed a Smallpox Eradication Unit. The disease had been killing, blinding, and disfiguring humans for thousands of years (see Chapters 11 and 14). Vaccination gave individuals and populations immunity, but smallpox was still endemic in many parts of the world. In Africa and South America, the more lethal form—*Variola major*—had been supplanted by *Variola minor*, which was only a little worse than chicken pox. It only killed one or two percent of its victims. In Asia, however, *Variola major* kept coming back in one epidemic after another.

Victims died horribly. A doctor remembered the "ugly, penetrating odor of decaying flesh" in the smallpox ward, and "the hands, covered with pustules, reaching out, as people begged for help."[1] There was no help. Even water was no comfort, because the insides of victims' mouths were lined with sores. Smallpox fevers reached 107 degrees. Victims hallucinated, and typically died on the eighth or ninth day.

Mass vaccinations had failed to eradicate smallpox. The WHO campaign relied on surveillance and containment: global surveillance and regular reporting to identify new cases as soon as they occurred, and prompt identification and treatment of all the victim's contacts to contain the threat before it could spread. Smallpox spread only from human to human and was not harbored by other animals. It could be destroyed—couldn't it?

Not easily. A few of the hurdles:

> ▷ The supply of vaccine: It had to be potent, pure, and stable over time, even in hot climates. Global quality control was a political and bureaucratic challenge.
> ▷ The vaccinating techniques: One system often led to infected wounds; another used equipment that broke down. Bifurcated (forked) needles worked best.
> ▷ Reporting: WHO surveillance could only be effective with good, timely data.
> ▷ Negotiating cultural priorities: In some countries, traditional practitioners inoculated villages—and accidentally spread the

disease. For some ethnic groups, vaccination was taboo. Others, when sick, would go home from the city to their villages, spreading the disease along their way.

▷ Access: In some parts of the world, maps were as bad as the roads, and open warfare endangered the WHO workers. Ethiopian villagers destroyed one WHO helicopter with a grenade, fearing the return of Italian occupiers from World War II.[2]

And even when smallpox was eradicated in a whole country, it could come back. Bangladesh (East Pakistan until 1971) wiped out smallpox in 1970 and went for months with no new cases. But there were other disasters, including a cholera epidemic and a cyclone that killed half a million people in Bhola. The Bangladesh Liberation War began in March 1971, lasted nine months, and brought famine along with freedom.

It also brought smallpox back. Ten thousand Bangladeshis had taken refuge in India, and epidemics spread in camps. In January 1972 the exiles began to return, and by May 1973 there were nearly 6,000 cases of smallpox in Bangladesh. WHO operatives fought back, but it seemed that every time the number of infected villages dipped below 100, some other disaster compounded the problem. In 1974, heavy monsoon rains destroyed crops, starving refugees swarmed into camps and slums around Dhaka, and the government decided to bulldoze the slums—leaving over 100,000 people homeless. Many had smallpox. By April 1975, there were 1,300 infected villages.

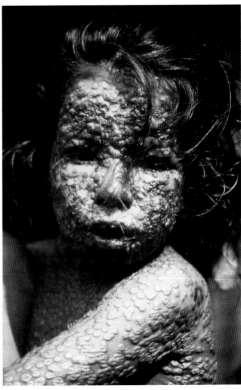

Yet in November 1975, medical staff were treating their last case of *Variola major*: Rahima Banu, on Bhola Island. They inoculated and isolated him; they vaccinated 18,000 people who lived within a mile of his house; they searched markets and schools and offered rewards for detecting new cases. By January 1976, WHO had interrupted transmission of smallpox throughout Asia. In 1977 they reported the last naturally occurring case of *Variola minor*, a popular hospital cook in Somalia. The smallpox virus survived only in laboratory samples. The new question was not, "Can we eradicate smallpox?" but "Should we keep the remaining supplies of this virus, or destroy it?"

This young girl in Bangladesh was infected with smallpox in 1973. In December 1977, a WHO International Commission officially certified that smallpox had been eradicated from Bangladesh. (CDC/James Hicks)

35

1976
EARTHQUAKE WIPES OUT CHINESE CITY OF TANGSHAN AS MAO LIES DYING

n 1976, a magnitude 7.8 earthquake destroyed Tangshan, an industrial city of about 1.06 million in China's Hebei Province. Land masses on either side of the Jiyunhe Fault had been slipping past each other for years, pressing on other faults.[1] At 3:42.53 A.M. on July 28, a 23-second quake released enough energy to kill 242,000 Tangshanese and injure or disable another 164,000.[2] Some thought an atomic bomb had hit. "Did we win the war?" asked one man as they dragged him from the rubble.[3] He thought there must have been one.

China knew war. The Revolution of 1911 had toppled the emperors, but the Republic of China was soon torn by a civil war (1927–1949). The Civil War paused for a war with Japan (1937–45), but resumed after World War II. In 1949, Communist forces triumphed. Mao Zedong, Chairman of the Communist Party, led the new People's Republic of China; Zhou Enlai served as premier.

Mao's programs to reform China's ancient culture intensified class war. The Great Leap Forward (1958–61) aimed to reform agriculture; 36 million starved. China exported grain and pork to the world while its farmers ate elm bark, egret droppings, and clay.[4] A new plan was needed. Mao launched the Cultural Revolution (1966–1971) to purify the nation's ideology, rooting out capitalism, traditionalism, and Western ideas. From senior government officials down to ordinary citizens, anybody accused of harboring non-communist values could be fired from work and sent to prison, or moved to the country for re-education, or executed. China's youth joined the paramilitary Red Guard, which harassed and humiliated suspected "capitalist roaders." Widespread bullying drove people of all ages to suicide.[5]

Rubble left after a 7.8 earthquake demolished Tangshan. (NOAA)

Zhou died in January 1976. At 82, Mao was ailing. His speech slurred, his calligraphy wobbled, and he struggled to make his will known. What would happen when he died? Rival factions maneuvered

The Tangshan earthquake was the deadliest of the twentieth century. (Origiinal picture source unknown)

for advantage. One faction, led by Mao's wife Jiang Qing, was called the Gang of Four. They worked to discredit Vice-Premier Deng Xiaoping, who cared more about economic reconstruction than Maoist ideology. The political landscape of China was as treacherous as its earthquake-prone terrain.

Even earthquake prediction was a political minefield. Some scientists thought a quake was likely that summer. But when, exactly? The politically correct view was that "earthquakes can be prevented and can be detected."[6] This unrealistic idea burdened the seismologists. The economic costs of unnecessary precautions would be high, and the political costs higher still.

The cost of the quake, when it did come, was astronomical. Thousands of families were destroyed; 4,204 orphans were left with no families; an estimated 50,000 women and 70,000 men were widowed.[7]

The Gang of Four reportedly said, "The earthquake in Tangshan affected only one million people, of whom only a few thousand died. It's nothing compared to the criticism of Deng, which is a matter of eight hundred million people."[8] Mao died in September. The Gang of Four were arrested in October;

An Ancient Seismograph

In AD 132, court mathematician Zhang Heng made a device to help the Chinese emperor detect earthquakes. It was a bronze bowl with a dragon at each of the cardinal directions. If it detected a tremor, a ball would roll out of one dragon's mouth into the mouth of a toad below, triggering an alarm and pointing in the direction of the quake.[9]

This replica of Zhang Heng's invention was exhibited at the Chabot Space & Science Center in Oakland, California. (Kowloonese)

they were ideal scapegoats for the Cultural Revolution and other disasters. Deng led China from 1978 to 1992.

For years, Tangshanese lived in lean-to shacks, like refugees. Remarriage became more common; so did divorce. People had lost homes, workplaces, families, limbs, and confidence in the government's ability to protect them. The psychological damage struck deep. But new houses began to go up in 1979, and by 1986 a new Tangshan had risen from the ashes. It looked as if the city had won the war.

36

1981
MYSTERY DISEASE, AIDS, BECOMES A DREADED PANDEMIC

I n 1981 the U.S. Centers for Disease Control (CDC) reported a mystery: more than 100 gay men had been diagnosed with unexpected kinds of pneumonia and cancer. Diseases of the elderly were suddenly killing the young. A new illness, AIDS (acquired immunodeficiency syndrome), destroyed their immune systems. It also attacked Haitians and hemophiliacs. What was the connection?

Disease detectives investigated. In 1983, Luc Montagnier discovered the virus that causes AIDS. We now call it HIV (human immunodeficiency virus).

Marchers in Washington, D.C., July 22, 2012, protest a perceived lack of support for AIDS medical research. (Al Ungar/Thinkstock)

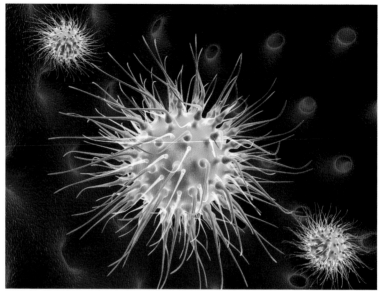

Like influenza, it mutates fast. By the time scientists develop a vaccine or treatment for one strain of HIV, a new strain will probably be spreading.

On the other hand, HIV progresses slowly through a human body. People can spread it for years before they know they have it. Some epidemics burn themselves out by killing their hosts before they can infect new hosts. HIV spreads first and kills later. In 1980, AIDS was rare. By 1985, 1 in 3 gay men in San Francisco had it.[1]

Scientists found that it had originated in Africa, where a monkey virus began infecting humans in the 1930s. It spread through blood and other body fluids. A patient could get AIDS from an infected blood transfusion; an emergency responder with an open cut could get it at a crime scene; a baby could get it from a mother. But the common ways to get HIV are intravenous (IV) drug use with shared needles, and unprotected sex with multiple partners.[2]

Finding effective treatments took time. In 1993, researchers learned to disable HIV with a combination of three drugs. The downside? Patients had to take 30 pills a day "at specific times, before and after specific meals, on either a full or empty stomach, with and without milk."[3] They had to tolerate side effects. And it cost over $20,000 a year—more than the average annual income in many countries with high infection rates. Pushed by ethical considerations and competition from Brazil and India, Western companies finally agreed to sell AIDS drugs for less in Africa.

Prevention was little easier than cure. Weapons that conquered other diseases worked poorly against AIDS. Mass vaccination? There was no safe vaccine. Quarantine? Victims would be prisoners for life. Surveillance? AIDS is harder to spot than smallpox, and victims often kept their condition secret. If identified, they might lose friends, jobs, or medical insurance. In Africa, at least one family was pelted with stones when neighbors learned they had AIDS. While public health officials need accurate records to do their work, victims had reasons for silence.

Education helped, but politics can limit education. In the U.S., for instance, some felt that educating teenagers about safer sex or drug use was like telling them it's all right to have sex and use drugs. Informing at-risk populations was undermining family values.

Rumors and conspiracy theories also get in the way of education. Some believe that AIDS originated as an American bioweapon to kill non-whites.[4] South Africa's president, Mbeki, denied that HIV caused AIDS and that drugs could slow its progress. His policy of refusing drugs may have hastened more than 330,000 deaths.[5]

In 2015, 1.1 million people in the U.S. are living with AIDS, and many of them—including many teenagers—don't know it. Each year there are about 50,000 new HIV infections. Most at risk are men who have sex with other men.[6] Since 1981, more than 636,000 people with AIDS diagnoses have died in the U.S.

But over 25 million have died worldwide.[7] In Africa, women are at high risk. Men who work far from their villages bring HIV home to their wives when they visit. Children die.[8] Grandparents raise orphans. The population of Africa is rising, but an imbalance is growing as members of one class—the educated middle-class workers—are the most likely to die of AIDS. Maybe HIV will change Africa as much as the Black Death changed medieval Europe.

The Venda Resist AIDS Education

It's 2005 in Venda, a region in South Africa where young women are at risk for AIDS. In the past, the Venda have fought Zulu warriors and European colonists. This evening, local men gather for a drinking session at the bottle store. A minivan arrives. Young women in red skirts crash the party. They are peer educators sponsored by a charity. They sing catchy songs about safe sex. "AIDS is killing us, like the *Boer* used to!" their leader shouts. "You fought apartheid, now fight with us against AIDS!"[9] Some of the men leave; others heckle the women. AIDS is not something to discuss in public. Anybody who knows too much about murder or witchcraft could be suspected of it. Venda see AIDS, too, as an unnatural death, better not mentioned. It is the "stubborn child of the white man who ignores other cultures," one traditional healer writes,[10] and many Venda have their own theories about what spreads it—starting with condoms and young women who break traditional rules. The peer educators are young and mostly unmarried. They are not authorities. How do they know so much about AIDS? Many suspect they are the ones spreading it. But in Venda, it is the funeral directors who are getting rich.

1984
LEAK FROM INSECTICIDE FACTORY POISONS CITY OF BHOPAL

I n the middle of the night, people woke up in pain. They couldn't breathe. They couldn't see. Their skin stung. They rushed from houses and shanties to escape the poisoned air, but outside it was worse.[1] Babies died; cattle died. Passengers in trains died as they sped through the city.

The Union Carbide India Limited (UCIL) plant in Bhopal was leaking methyl isocyanate (MIC), a highly toxic gas. In forty minutes, it covered 25 square miles (65 km²).[2] An estimated 2,000 died instantly and 20,000 more in the aftermath. Some 300,000 were injured. A generation later, many still suffer blindness, lung damage, post-traumatic stress, and other disabilities.[3]

This was an environmental disaster, but not a natural one. It was anthropogenic—brought about by human efforts to wring a better living from nature. In AD 1300, the world had 350 million people[4] and could barely feed them all. In 1984, more than twice that many lived in India alone.[5] But after 1968, the "Green Revolution" began to reach Asia and Latin America. New genetic strains of plants and farming techniques increased crop yields dramatically. Food became cheaper, and more people escaped poverty.[6]

Protestors in 2006 equate Warren Anderson (Union Carbide CEO) with Osama bin Laden (who headed Al-Qaeda at the time). (Credit unknown)

Modern agriculture uses chemical fertilizers and pesticides. In 1969, Union Carbide built a plant in Bhopal to manufacture carbaryl, an insecticide still used on grain crops in the U.S. One of the ingredients was MIC, and after 1979 the plant began making its MIC on site.

Manufacturing a toxic and unstable gas in a city of 800,000 was risky, as were many of UCIL's practices. Maintenance routines and equipment failed, and safety guidelines were ignored.[7] Management failed to communicate risks and emergency procedures to workers, neighbors, and local government.[8]

Communicating with neighbors might have been a challenge. Bhopal is the capital of Madhya Pradesh, whose people speak many dialects of Hindi and also Urdu, Gujarati, Marathi, and several tribal languages. In 1984, some of its poorest resi-

Ruins of the Bhopal chemical plant. (Julian Nitzsche)

dents squatted in a shanty town around the Union Carbide factory. Not all of them could read.

They might have understood a public warning siren—but after frequent minor leaks, management had stopped using it.[9] Critics said afterward that UCIL did not have a "culture of safety,"[10] but victims of the accident had been allowed to *feel* safe. If they had understood the risks, they might have *been* safer.[11] In the angry days and years after the accident, victims felt the company had stinted on safety to cut costs.

The Indian government sued Union Carbide for $3.3 billion. Union Carbide argued that their leak had been caused by sabotage. In 1989, they settled out of court, paying $470 million.[12] But the matter has never been truly settled. In 1991, toxic chemicals were reported in groundwater around the pesticide factory.[13] Union Carbide sold UCIL in 1994, and in 2012, a New York district court ruled that the parent company is not liable for ongoing clean-up and victim compensation.[14] Bhopal activists vowed to appeal, and protests continue. In 2015, the International Campaign for Justice in Bhopal urged India's Prime Minister Narendra Modi and visiting U.S. President Obama "to stop protecting corporate interests over the lives and health of ordinary people."[15]

38

1985
NEVADO DEL RUIZ ERUPTION
BURIES TOWN OF ARMERO
ON INTERNATIONAL TV

A lahar swept mud and debris from the volcano down the Rio Lagunillas and buried the town of Armero. (USGS)

The biggest volcanic explosions don't necessarily cause the most famous disasters. In 1912, a new volcano—Novarupta—emerged in Alaska. It was the twentieth century's largest eruption but went largely unnoticed. Until the 1950s, scientists thought it was Mt. Katmai that erupted.[1]

Colombia's 1985 Nevado del Ruiz eruption was much smaller. Yet it buried the town of Armero and killed over 22,000 people, more than any other volcano since 1902. It damaged or destroyed roads, bridges, power grids, aqueducts, schools, hospitals, industrial plants, livestock, crops, and businesses. It left about 7,700 homeless.[2]

The volcano had a history of small eruptions giving rise to lahars—deadly surges of mud, water, and debris. Armero was built on an 1845 mudflow. But at 28 miles (45 km) from the volcano, it seemed safe.[3]

In 1984, mountain climbers reported earthquakes and plumes of gas. Geologists monitored activity, especially after a minor eruption in September 1985. Long-term danger was obvious, but a visual inspection on November 12 gave no signs of immediate danger.[4] Without clear information, the government hesitated to order an unpopular evacuation. False alarms are expensive.

Omayra Sanchez, 13, was one of those who died before they could be extracted from the mud. (Frank Fournier, Contact Press Images)

On November 13, explosions began in the afternoon. Ash fell. Still no evacuation was ordered. By 7:30 P.M. the mountain quieted, and Armero's radio station told inhabitants to remain calm. At 9:08 a larger eruption melted snow on the peak and sent lahars roaring downstream. Two hours later, they hit Armero. Lights went out, the radio went off, and people rushed into the streets.[5]

Morning lit the ruins. Thousands reached high ground, but 21,000 had already died, and one or two thousand were still trapped alive in the mud. By noon, rescuers had managed to get only 65 of them out.[6] Reporters documented the effort on TV. People around the world watched the beautiful face of 13-year-old Omayra Sánchez as she died; divers could not free her lower body from the wreckage of her house.[7]

The Nevado del Ruiz volcano rears skyward, smoke rolling from its caldera and from fissures in its flanks. (USGS)

Some 80% of Armero's residents died. Another thousand were hospitalized, most with lacerations (69%), penetrating wounds (41%), fractures (37%), and complicating infections.[8] Months later, in camps for the homeless, many still suffered depression and post-traumatic stress.[9]

Colombia put a national disaster preparedness plan in place by 1987. Volcanologists worldwide increased their efforts to pool resources. The memory of Armero helped avert other tragedies as far away as the Philippines, where evacuation saved thousands from Mt. Pinatubo in 1991.

But it is still hard to know exactly when to evacuate, and evacuation does inflict costs. Worldwide, 490 volcanic events in the twentieth century resulted in evacuation, homelessness, and other trials for an estimated 4 to 6 million survivors.[10] In Ecuador, chronic ashfall from Mt. Tungurahua damages crops, and uprooted families may lack adequate food and water.[11] In the Philippines, Aeta culture is changing as indigenous hunter-gatherers relocate down Pinatubo's slopes.[12] And many people simply refuse to leave home, even for a volcano.

The Oso Mudslide

It does not take a volcano to bury a town. In March 2014, a mountain slope collapsed and buried homes in Oso, Washington. Rescuers could not cross the mud to find neighbors who were pinned in their houses. The area had experienced at least five major mudslides since 1949, and the Army Corps of Engineers had warned that a "large catastrophic failure" of the slope was likely. Yet seven of the damaged homes had been built since a 2006 slide. It was a beautiful neighborhood. Should people be allowed to settle where the risk is so great?[13]

(Washington National Guard)

39

1986
MELTDOWN AT CHERNOBYL NUCLEAR FACILITY LEAVES DEAD ZONE IN UKRAINE

In the twentieth century, humans discovered a new way to harness the forces of nature for heat and light: nuclear power. It seemed much cleaner than coal, oil, and other fossil fuels. By 1985, 374 nuclear power plants generated 15% of the world's electricity.[1] Then a nuclear accident turned a city of 45,000 into a ghost town.

It happened in Ukraine, which was then part of the Soviet Union—and it began with a safety test. Nuclear reactors produce energy, but they also use it. A constant flow of water cools the fuel, and nuclear-generated electricity powers the pumps to keep the water flowing. In case the electricity fails, plants have diesel generators. Engineers at Chernobyl were testing an alternative back-up

Lenin Square in Pripyat as seen from the ruins of the Hotel Polissya in 2009. A city of 50,000 founded in 1970, Pripyat was evacuated a few days after the Chernobyl meltdown. (Timm Suess)

113

The Chernobyl nuclear plant stands on the horizon 2.5 km from Pripyat. The Chernobyl Exclusion Zone–1,600 square miles (2,600 km²) of contaminated land around Chernobyl--is being reclaimed by forest and wildlife. Some scientists call it a biorefuge. Others call it a death zone. Possibly it's a little of both. (Timm Suess)

plan when fuel overheated and blew the top off a reactor.[2] By the morning of April 26, invisible radiation began to fall on the plant's neighbors and drift north over Europe.

That morning seemed normal. Children played outside. Stores opened. The next day, evacuation began.[3] It took days, but people who lived within 19 miles of the plant were moved, taking what they could carry.[4]

The Soviets lacked resources to fill people's needs quickly. They needed more trucks to carry safe food. They needed more health care professionals and supplies. They needed housing and work for the uprooted population.

As they struggled to meet the emergency, officials tried to maintain calm. They gave out reassuring information. Was it accurate? They said only 31 fire-

An abandoned classroom in Pripyat, 23 years after the disaster. (Timm Suess)

Radioactive contamination was most intense at the borders of Belarus, Russia, and Ukraine.

men and other heroic workers died from the accident, mostly of acute radiation disease (ARD).[5] But some observers angered Soviet authorities with higher estimates of deaths, radiation exposure, and predicted health consequences in the future. Evacuees had breathed contaminated air and eaten contaminated food. Would they get cancer soon? Would their children be all right?

Afterward, scientists saw an increase in thyroid cancers.[6] Children living on contaminated ground suffered higher levels of many diseases,[7] and children born after the disaster experienced genetic changes.[8] But it is not easy to prove a link between radiation exposure and one person's illness. Other factors could explain any given case. Stress, uncertainty, and "radiophobia"—fear of radiation—gave rise to psychosomatic illnesses as well as physical ones.

The Chernobyl accident endangered the physical, economic, and emotional health of countless people. It was an environmental disaster. In Norway, reindeer now graze on contaminated moss, and reindeer herders get as much radiation as people around Chernobyl.[9]

Politically, the disaster may have been healthy. In 1988, Soviet leader Mikhail Gorbachev introduced a policy of *glasnost*—transparency—giving people more freedom of speech. Public interest groups challenged energy officials, and "Chernobyl" became a key word in the ongoing debates.[10]

As of January 2015, 437 nuclear plants in 30 countries were generating 12.3% of the world's electricity. Another 71 nuclear plants were under construction.[11]

The Worst U.S. Nuclear Accident: Three Mile Island, Pennsylvania, 3/28/1979

In 1979, nuclear reactors provided 11.0% of U.S. electricity, and a movie—*The China Syndrome*—raised questions about how we would cope with a meltdown. Two weeks after its release came a partial meltdown at Three Mile Island. More than 3,500 pregnant women and children evacuated the area. Clean-up took until 1993. Long-term health effects are debated, but the most radiation a person might have received—100-mrem—was less than a CAT scan.[12] The NRC and the nuclear industry improved safety routines,[13] and reactors provided 19.4% of U.S. electricity in 2013.[14]

The Three-Mile Island nuclear plant on the Susquehanna River near Harrisburg, Pennsylvania. (Ted Van Pelt)

40

1993
ARSENIC IN BENGALI
DRINKING WATER

How much poison should you drink in a day? Take arsenic, for instance. A chemical element (abbreviated "As" in the periodic table), arsenic exists naturally. It wells up from hydrothermal vents in the deepest parts of the ocean. It bonds with other elements to make common rocks. All over the world, from Maine to China, there's arsenic in the bedrock—and arsenic in wells.[1]

It's natural, but it isn't good for you. The World Health Organization (WHO) considers water unhealthy if it has more than 10 parts per billion (ppb) of arsenic—two drops of arsenic in fifty drums of water.[2] Enough arsenic

A child in Bangladesh drinks water from a well with a red-painted spigot, indicating arsenic contamination. The village had no other source of drinking water in 2000, when this photo was taken. (Ian Berry/Magnum Photos)

can kill a person in hours. Smaller doses cause chronic illness. After about ten years of exposure, victims get black spots on their upper bodies. They may lose feeling in their hands and feet, and skin on their palms and soles may crack. Subsequent infections may lead to gangrene. Victims may suffer kidney failure.[3] Their risk of diabetes increases, and 10% of them are likely to die of cancer.[4] "Arsenic poisoning from drinking water has been called the worst natural disaster in the history of mankind," says an Indian newspaper, estimating that it affects 137 million people in 70 countries.[5]

Millions of those victims are in Bangladesh, where the Ganges and Brahmaputra flow into the Bay of Bengal. Water has always been a problem there. Cyclones drive storm surges up the rivers, and most of the country is no more than 10 meters (33 feet) above sea level. Bangladesh crowds the world's ninth largest population (about 166 million people) into an area smaller than Iowa[6] (which has about 3 million people). With so many people and so little high ground, there's no escaping the floods.

It's also hard to escape waterborne diseases, including cholera and diarrhea. We all need safe water, but to get it we have to find a clean supply, keep it clean, treat it to remove impurities, and distribute it.[7] Americans typically pipe water from reservoirs through protected pipes, filter and chlorinate it in treatment centers, and send it through local pipes to city residents' kitchens and bathrooms. Traditional Bangladeshis drank river water.

After Bangladesh won its independence from Pakistan in 1971, UNICEF and other agencies tried to help the government develop a better supply. They thought groundwater would be safer, and tube-wells with hand-pumps would be an affordable way to get it. By 1978, Bangladesh had one hand-pump for every 250 inhabitants.[8]

A decade passed. More and more cases of chronic arsenic poisoning appeared in Bangladesh, and in 1993, arsenic was found in many of the wells. UNICEF worked with the government again, and by 2008, they had tested 55% of the wells. Safe ones were painted green, unsafe ones red.[9] Most were safe, but in 3% of the villages, *all* the wells were contaminated.[10] Some had arsenic levels 100 times above the WHO limit.

Yet people kept using them. The alternatives were grim:

> ▷ Use river water and risk infectious diseases, which could kill quickly.
> ▷ Use red wells and risk arsenic poisoning, which could make them sick in ten years and kill them later.
> ▷ Use green wells and spend hours every day fetching and carrying water.[11]

It's been 20 years since the arsenic was found. Now nearly 20% of all adult deaths in Bangladesh are due to arsenic, and the skin of many ten year olds is spotted from life-long exposure to the poison.[12]

The search for an effective solution continues. In March 2014, the Lawrence Berkeley National Laboratory licensed new water-purification technology to a company that plans to use it in India and Bangladesh.[13] It takes advantage of arsenic's tendency to bond with rusty iron. Like the tube-wells, it's cheap and simple. Soon arsenic in well water may be a thing of the past.

The 2014 West Virginia Chemical Leak

Contaminated water is a problem everywhere in the world. In January 2014, a chemical leak in West Virginia's Elk River made tap water smell of licorice.[14] Suddenly, 300,000 people had to stop drinking, cooking, brushing their teeth, or even washing. Schools closed. So did restaurants and hotels. Stores ran out of bottled water, and the National Guard rationed supplies.

The licorice smell came from 4-methylcyclohexane methanol (MCHM) used to clean coal and reduce pollution. You can probably drink more MCHM than arsenic and still be safe. The Centers for Disease Control (CDC) recommends no more than one part per million (ppm) of MCHM, which would be like 200 drops in 50 drums of water. People can smell even smaller traces, so MCHM is also easier to detect than arsenic. The West Virginia spill was soon cleaned up, but the smell lingered, and residents felt uneasy.

The water problems in Bangladesh and West Virginia are both examples of the "law of unintended consequences." In both cases, people were trying to control other problems—waterborne diseases or air pollution. The new problems were accidents, and accidents, unfortunately, are natural.

1996-2014
NIGERIANS RESIST A POLIO ERADICATION CAMPAIGN

When does an epidemic become a disaster? Not everybody agrees. Take polio. The poliomyelitis virus enters the body through the mouth and multiplies in the intestine. In some cases it invades the spinal cord and the brain.

Where polio is common, children often get it before the age of five—and may never know they have it. Early symptoms are fever, fatigue, headache, vomiting, stiff neck, and aching limbs. One in 200 infections leaves a victim paralyzed for life, usually in the legs. One in about 2,000 infections leads to death.[1] When polio is contracted later in life, the suffering is likely to be greater. Franklin D. Roosevelt contracted polio in 1921 at the age of 39. He was paralyzed from the waist down for the last 24 years of his life, though that did not stop him from becoming governor of New York and ultimately president of the U.S.

The 1952 polio epidemic looked like a disaster in America, with 37 cases for every 100,000 people.[2] Thousands of middle-class children were stricken. Quarantine didn't stop the disease. Good sanitation even made it worse: children were not exposed to the virus until they were older and more likely to be paralyzed by it.[3] U.S. charities raised funds to fight polio. Celebrity scientists Albert Sabin and Jonas Salk led teams competing to develop the first vaccine, and both teams made critical contributions in the 1950s. The U.S. has been polio-free since 1979. But U.S. children are still vaccinated, because the disease survives in a few countries. It could be reintroduced.[4]

After a 1952 epidemic crippled thousands of children, the United States campaigned aggressively against polio, as in this billboard. (FDR Presidential Library & Museum)

A child in Nigeria receiving a polio vaccination. (Agnes Warner, Centers for Disease Control)

After the elimination of smallpox, health advocates launched an international Polio Eradication Initiative. Like smallpox, polio can only be spread from one human to another, and that makes it easier to control. It can't be spread by the bites of infected insects, for instance. Also like smallpox, polio can be prevented by a cheap, effective vaccine, protecting people against new infection. When most people in a community are immune to a virus, the virus runs out of new hosts. The chain of infection is broken, and the disease dies out.

One country where polio survives is Nigeria, which is beset with so many urgent problems that polio looks almost minor by comparison. Of every 1,000 children born in Nigeria, 124 die under the age of five. Malaria causes 20% of these early deaths, and pneumonia another 17%. Diarrhea (11%), HIV/AIDS (4%), and even measles (1%) kill far more Nigerian toddlers than polio.[5]

Especially in northern Nigeria in the early 2000s, many parents did not take their children to be vaccinated when medical teams visited their villages. Why? Some Nigerian leaders may have believed rumors that the vaccines were contaminated with HIV/AIDS virus or with infertility drugs.[6] A more real danger was that the oral vaccine contained live polio virus. The virus is weakened, but on rare occasions it can cause the disease it was designed to prevent.[7]

Apart from any danger, the aggressive eradication campaign stepped on family privacy and customs. Traditionally, Nigerians did not see polio as a dangerous childhood disease.[8] Then it became an international priority. Health workers went door to door with vaccines. They stained children's thumbs and marked doors to show who had taken the vaccine. Each child was supposed to get four doses of the oral vaccine. Some parents found all this unnecessary and intrusive.[9]

Workers made progress by addressing more basic Nigerian concerns. They added other public health activities to Immunization Plus Days. For instance, they gave out bednets treated with insecticides. Mosquitoes carry malaria, so everybody wanted the bednets.[10]

A rare photo of President Franklin Roosevelt on crutches. The president took great pains to hide his disability from the public. (FDR Presidential Library & Museum)

Polio debates in Nigeria raise questions about government's responsibility for public health. What sorts of programs matter most? How do religious, cultural, and political differences affect response to a public health program?[11] And if people must work constantly to give their children food, clothing, shelter, and treatment for common diseases, then how long should they have to stand in line for immunization against a disease that is less common and less deadly?

The World Health Organization (WHO) argues that eliminating polio would save billions of dollars over the next 20 years, mostly for low-income countries.[12] Vaccination is a cost-effective way to help poor children as well as rich ones. But some people think that "diseases of the affluent," like polio and HIV/AIDS, get more attention than scourges of the poor.

1997
SOUTHEAST ASIAN HAZE

n 1997, smoke hung over Malaysia, southern Thailand, Singapore, Brunei, and the Philippines.[1] Some days it was thick. Traffic slowed, schools and businesses closed, and health suffered around the South China Sea.[2] Eyes stung; breathing hurt. After the haziest days, death rates rose in Malaysian cities.[3]

But the smoke wasn't coming from Malaysia. It was blowing across the sea from Indonesia, where the worst forest fires on record raged in East Kalimantan and Sumatra. They started in April and didn't stop until the annual monsoon rains came in November. They broke out again when the rains ended. A volcano was erupting, but the fires produced more smoke.

How thick was the haze? The best evidence comes from satellite images. Scientists used data from NASA's Total Ozone Mapping Spectrometer (TOMS) to create an aerosol index—a measure of how many particles were floating in the air. The index goes from 0 (crystal clear) to 4 (so thick you can

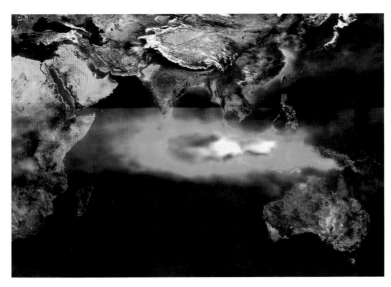

Enhanced satellite imagery shows how widely the smoke of 1997 fires spread. (NASA)

Smog over Southeast Asia remains a problem. This 2013 photograph shows Singapore haze.. (Brian Jeffery Beggerly)

hardly see the midday sun). On bad days in the haziest Indonesian cities that summer, the TOMS aerosol index topped 5 or 6.[4]

How did it happen? Climate was a factor, with the worst El Niño/Southern Oscillation (ENSO) drought in years. Terrain contributed, too. Much of Indonesia's peat-swamp forest grew over sandy, fast-draining soil; when drought caused the water level to drop, the dry forest burned easily. So did the peat itself.[5] And peat, given enough time, can turn into coal. Deep under the soil, fires smoldered in coal seams until the next dry season. This much was natural.

But humans set fires on purpose to clear land for cultivation. Small farmers had been doing this for centuries. Now Indonesia had huge commercial farms. Trees provided many of its major exports, including plywood,[6] tropical hardwood,[7] pulp and paper, and palm oil.[8] Loggers cleared more land, and their practices made it easier for fires to spread.[9] From 1982 on, wildfires increased. In 1995, Indonesia banned the use of fire for clearing land, but fires were set illegally. To put them out, the government needed more and better equipment, maps, personnel, access to water, and even roads.

Why was it a disaster? The haze reportedly killed 527 Indonesians between September and November. Another 16,000 were hospitalized, and 36,000 received outpatient care. Others died in collisions on land, sea, and in the air.[10] Malaysia and Singapore advised their citizens to avoid outdoor exercise and filter the air, but of course many had to work outside and could not afford air conditioning. Breathing the air in the worst-affected areas was as bad as smoking up to 80 cigarettes a day.[11]

The region's economy lost over $9 billion. Its ecology may have suffered more. Indonesia had some of the planet's most diverse wildlife and its third largest rain forest. The fires killed many plants and animals directly and destroyed the habitats of others. What survived was dry and brittle—more vulnerable to future fires. The government estimated that fire on Kalimantan consumed 520,000 hectares (over 2,000 square miles, about the area of Delaware) in 1997–98; satellite images showed ten times as much damage.[12]

The haze strained relationships between Indonesia and her neighbors. The Association of Southeast Asian Nations (ASEAN) adopted a Cooperative Plan on Transboundary Pollution in 1995, but it was hard to enforce.[13] Governments, NGOs (non-governmental organizations—i.e., non-profit citizens' groups), and private corporations struggled with the problem. In 2013, El Niño came back, and so did the haze.[14] Indonesia, with the world's fourth largest population, now has the third largest greenhouse gas emissions—and 75% of them come from deforestation and damage to forest and peatlands.[15] Environmentalists have boycotted some large companies until they agreed to zero-deforestation policies and more sustainable development.[16]

Restoring a Forest in Borneo

In 1989, Willie Smits met an orangutan. Smits was a forester, a microbiologist, and a Dutch-born citizen of Indonesia. The orangutan was caged in a marketplace when he first spotted her. Later, when he went back to rescue her, she had been thrown on a trash heap. He took her home, nursed her back to health, and in 1991 founded the Borneo Orangutan Survival Foundation (BOS) to rescue other orphans. But they needed habitat, and he could not prevent the burning of forests.[17]

In 2002, Smits bought approximately 5,000 acres of "biological desert." The land had already been stripped, and the local unemployment rate was 50%. He named the project "Samboja Lestari" (Everlasting Forest), and designed it with inner and outer zones. The villagers who sold land to the project live in the outer zone, where they plant acacia trees (for timber), sugar palms (for ethanol), and cash crops (including ginger, papayas, cocoa, and chilies). They circle (continued on page 126)

Tapping the sugar palm. (Dericks Tan)

Restoring a Forest in Borneo

(continued from page 125)
the new forest, where 1,600 species of trees, tall and short, fast-growing and slow-growing, shelter orangutans, sun bears, and 137 species of birds. "The greenery has lowered air temperatures by 3° to 5° C in the immediate vicinity and increased rainfall by 25%," reported *Science* in 2009.[18]

Critics point out that Smits has not submitted his findings for scientific review, and some fear that those who want to ravage more land will point to Smits's reforestation as proof that deforestation is not irreversible and not such a terrible thing.[19] The difficult truth is that the ecological and economic possibilities of destroyed habitat are different for every spot on earth, and a project like Samboja Lestari has to take into account national laws and local cultures. But Smits has shown that with patience and courage, one can begin to solve even the worst problems.

2003
WAS THE LETHAL EUROPEAN HEAT WAVE CAUSED BY CLIMATE CHANGE?

Europeans were dying of the heat. The summer of 2003 was probably Europe's hottest in 500 years—more than 1.9° C (3.42° F) hotter than the 1961–1990 average. In Switzerland the temperature was as much as 5° C (9.9° F) above average. And in August the European Heat Wave (EHW03) struck the continent.[1]

Forest fires raged out of control in Portugal. Pollution rose. Farm animals died and crops withered. EHW03 cost more than $10 billion. Demand for air conditioning shot up. So did hospital stays, visits to doctors, and ambulance rides. In France, nuclear plants overheated and power failed.[2]

Worse, the heat led to 40,000 or more "extra" deaths. In Italy, 20,000 more than usual died that summer.[3] In France, mortality rose by 60% in the

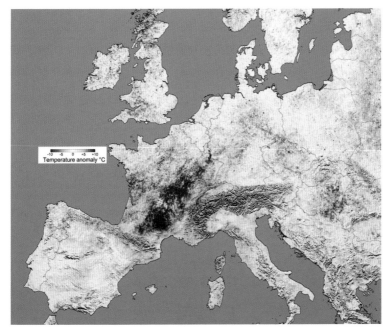

During the 2003 heat wave, daily high temperatures in parts of Europe rose over 10° C (18° F) above normal. (NASA)

The mighty Rhine, shrunk to a mere trickle in the heat. (Blue Breeze)

first three weeks of August, as 15,000 died of heat exposure. Most at risk were people over 75 years old, women, and city dwellers.

Would they have died soon anyhow? Did the heat wave just "harvest" the frailest people a few days or weeks before their time? France had fewer deaths than usual in 2004. But the "harvesting" hypothesis does not account for all the excess deaths.[4] People who live alone are more likely to die in heat waves, and those are people still healthy enough to take care of themselves. In Barcelona, adults who hadn't finished primary school were more likely to die.[5] They were also more likely to be poor and less likely to have air conditioners. In France, excess mortality was twice as high for residents of the poorest areas.[6]

Another factor was the "heat island" effect. Cities are hotter than surrounding countryside, especially at night.[7] With no relief from the day's heat, people's bodies do not recover. If elevators, air conditioners, and even cool running water fail during a heat wave, rooms on the upper floors of apartment buildings can turn into death traps.

Was this heat wave a symptom of global warming? It is hard to prove that any one weather event is caused by climate change. But several things helped make EHW03 possible. The North Atlantic Subtropical High (NASH), a high-pressure zone that usually centers near the Azores, shifted to the north. Soil in Europe was unusually dry.[8] These and other conditions interacted to cause the heat wave. High surface temperatures in the Mediterranean and North Seas may have helped prolong it.

Climatologists do predict more intense, long-lasting heat waves in the twenty-first century.[9] Over the past 30 years, the NASH has intensified and moved west—likely because of global warming caused by human activities.[10] Global temperatures have been rising steadily.[11] One way to help reduce the heat island effect: plant a garden on a building roof near you.[12]

Counting Excess Deaths in the 1995 Chicago Heat Wave

How do you know how many have died of heat? You can count the deaths one by one, assigning an exact cause of death for each. Or you can use statistics: calculate the difference between how many of a town's residents would be expected to die in a single week in July, and how many really did die.

Chicago's chief medical examiner, Edmund Donoghue, used the first method in 1995. He told investigators to classify a death as heat-related if body temperature was 105° at or immediately after death, or if there was good circumstantial evidence—for instance, if the body was closed up in a hot room or the person hadn't been seen alive since

before the heat wave. Counting one by one, Chicago had 485 deaths from heat between July 14 and July 20. Chicago Mayor Richard Daly pressured Donoghue to reduce the count. Could it really be proven that all these people died of heat? It reflected badly on the city.

But epidemiologists announced an even higher count: 739 extra Chicago residents died that week. The 1995 Chicago heat wave killed more than twice as many as the 1871 Chicago fire.[13] Ironically, fire-proof brick and stone buildings may have boosted the death toll. They help keep city blocks from cooling off at night.

Rooftop gardens, like this one atop the Chicago City Hall, relieve the urban "heat island" effect, reduce rainstorm run-off, and provide insulation in cold weather.

44

2004
INDONESIAN EARTHQUAKE
AND TSUNAMI
TRIGGER INTERNATIONAL
RELIEF EFFORT

O n December 26, 2004, the Indonesian island of Simeulue shook long and hard. Residents knew what would happen next. After shaking the earth, angry gods would send giant waves. Everybody raced for high ground. Thirty minutes later a 33-foot (10-meter) tsunami broke over the north coast.

A sudden wall The island was battered, but only 7 of its 75,000 residents died.[1]

of water pushes An hour or so later, waves still topped 10 feet (3 meters) when they

ashore in Thailand. reached Thailand.[2] Vacationing on the beach with her family, 10-year-old Tilly

(David Rydevik) Smith saw the tide rush out. The sea bubbled. Boats on the horizon tossed up

A street in downtown Banda Aceh no longer exists. (Michael L. Bak)

and down. Tilly's geography class had studied tsunamis two weeks earlier, and she knew the signs. She grabbed her parents and little sister; they warned other tourists and fled the beach.[3]

Local legend or geography lesson—knowledge saved lives that day. But many were lost. Even those who realized what was coming could not always find high ground fast enough.[4]

With a magnitude of 9.1, the earthquake was the third largest since 1900. It ruptured a fault longer than California, and raced north from Simeulue at 1.2 miles per second—for ten long minutes. (By comparison, the 1994 North-bridge earthquake ruptured about 12 miles and lasted 15 seconds.) As two tectonic plates broke free, the ocean floor sprang west as much as 20 feet and up as much as 6 feet.[5] Displaced water surged toward the coasts of the Indian Ocean and hammered 14 countries, leaving 227,898 people dead or missing and another 1.7 million homeless.[6] The victims were in 55 nations.[7] Many were tourists, far more were local.

The world grieved in many ways, ancient and modern. One Sri Lankan woman later went mad when a mass grave was opened near her village. Her family held an exorcism ritual and a sorcerer came, but she did not recover. Investigators had opened the grave to identify victims by DNA tests.[8] Finding the remains of loved ones brought comfort to some, pain to others.

News coverage was global and immediate. The tsunami registered on tide gauges on the other side of the world. Shocked tourists took videos as the sea poured over beaches and into towns, carrying automobiles, smashed furniture, broken houses, and struggling people. People everywhere could see the damage in real time, and aid flowed in: $7,100 per affected person, or more than the average Thai fisher makes in a year.[9] Still, victims struggled. Relief did not always reach the people who needed it most. Why? Aid workers tried to engi-

More of the tsunami aftermath in Banda Aceh, Indonesia.
(AusAID)

neer solutions for physical problems, but political and cultural problems could be even harder to solve.

Sri Lanka and Indonesia were both fighting rebellions in 2004. In 2005, after 30 years of warfare, the Free Aceh Movement (GAM) signed a peace accord with the Indonesian government. But in Sri Lanka, the Liberation Tigers of Tamil Eelam (LTTE) fought on until 2009. How could the tsunami lead to peace in one country and war in another? Many other factors influenced the outcomes.[10]

Even without open rebellion, local politics complicated the aid effort. In Thailand, the wave inundated 400 fishing communities, wrecked 5,300 fishing boats, and put more than 30,000 people out of work. The indigenous Moken, or "sea gypsies," often suffered worst. They had always lived by fishing, but jobs in tin mining and tourism had drawn outsiders to their villages since the 1970s. Newcomers included illegal Burmese and Cambodian immigrants, but many were ethnically dominant Thais. The Moken crowded into slums along the shore, and after the tsunami, land issues made it hard to relocate them safely after their homes were destroyed.[11]

One thing everybody could agree on: the need for a global tsunami warning system to reduce the loss of life from future events.[12] More secure housing and better evacuation routes could also save lives.[13] But to enrich lives and give them more solid long-term support, relief agencies must coordinate their efforts with governments, with each other, and—most important—with the people they are trying to help.

The Hyogo Framework for Action

Less than a month after the tsunami, the United Nations held a World Conference on Disaster Reduction at Kobe, Hyogo, Japan. The Hyogo Framework for Action (HFA), aimed at building national and community resilience and resources for coping with disaster, was endorsed by the U.N. General Assembly[14] and adopted by 168 member nations.[15] Indonesia, recovering from such a major disaster, was the first country to adopt the HFA.

2005
HURRICANE KATRINA
SWAMPS THE
U.S. GULF COAST

T he Mississippi River, like China's Yellow River, carries heavy loads of sediment between high levees. Its bed rises while wetlands around it subside.[1] Left to its own devices, the river would find a steeper channel and flow more directly to the sea. But the Mississippi is a great commercial waterway, surrounded by rich farmlands, cities, and industries. Allowing it to change course would dislocate things the American economy depends on—including the city of New Orleans. So the U.S. Army Corps of Engineers manages a vast system of levees, dams, locks, and spillways to tame the river and keep it in place. New Orleans, like the Netherlands, is largely below sea level. Between the Mississippi and the Gulf of Mexico, the city depends on engineering and

In the wake of Katrina, New Orleans houses were islands and a high-way led only to water. (Jocelyn Augustino/ FEMA)

Looking north over Interstate 10 toward Lake Ponchartrain. (Kyle Niemi/USCG)

careful water management. On August 29, 2005, Hurricane Katrina drove through the city's defenses with rain, winds, and a monster storm surge. The costliest storm in U.S. history smashed Alabama oil rigs, Mississippi casinos, and New Orleans schools. It damaged or destroyed roads, bridges, and ecosystems; erased whole coastal communities; knocked out power supplies; and killed over 1,800 people.[2] Years later, hundreds were still missing.[3]

New Orleans had 60 hours' warning.[4] Mayor Ray Nagin ordered an evacuation, and almost 80% of the city's 445,000 residents left. Another 10,000 sought shelter at the Superdome. But others could not or would not leave their homes.[5] Many lacked cars. Some didn't take the hype seriously. As one said, "Well, we always stayed through hurricanes or whatever."[6]

This hurricane was serious. Most of the city was flooded; draining it took weeks.[7] People were trapped on rooftops or crowded in rescue centers. Islamic countries, moved by the suffering, sent a billion dollars in relief to the U.S.[8]

Emergency evacuees didn't know their destinations until they landed, some as far away as Colorado.[9] A year later, New Orleans had only about

A Humvee next to the Superdome, the relatively high evacuation point where 10,000 New Orleans residents took shelter. (U.S. Army)

212,000 residents.[10] The city's African American residents were slow to return, probably because their low-lying neighborhoods had been worst damaged.[11] Families with school-age children also stayed away,[12] while schools struggled; more than 7,000 teachers were laid off.[13]

Many blamed the government. Black Americans believed the Federal Emergency Management Agency (FEMA) would have done more to help a richer city with a larger percentage of white residents.[14] Others theorized that a 1977 National Environmental Policy Act (NEPA) lawsuit caused the levee failures by forcing the Army Corps of Engineers to modify its hurricane protection project for New Orleans.[15]

New Orleans land continues to sink, and sea levels continue to rise. Is it possible to protect the city against a future Category 4 or 5 hurricane?[16]

FEMA Trailers and Formaldehyde Poisoning

To help homeless evacuees, the Federal Emergency Management Agency (FEMA) needed thousands of new housing units. They had 120,000 trailers built as fast as possible. Many people rushed home to Alabama, Louisiana, Mississippi, Texas—and a new set of problems. Wood in the trailers gave off a toxic chemical, formaldehyde. Soon occupants were suffering from asthma, pneumonia, nosebleeds, headaches, and ear infections. Journalists reported the illnesses, and dangerous levels of formaldehyde, in July 2006. But each symptom could have been caused by something else, and government was slow to condemn the trailers. In 2012, a class action suit was finally settled. FEMA and the trailer manufacturers paid $42.6 million. After lawyers were paid, an average of about $4,000 was left for each of the 55,000 plaintiffs.[17]

In 2013, the Environmental Protection Agency (EPA) proposed regulations to protect Americans against the risks of formaldehyde emission from wood products.[18]

2010
EARTHQUAKE MEETS POVERTY IN PORT-AU-PRINCE, HAITI

O n January 12, 2010, a magnitude 7.0 earthquake rocked southern Haiti. Officially 316,000 people were killed, 300,000 injured, and 1.3 million displaced in and around Port-au-Prince. A 2009 census counted fewer than 900,000 residents in Port-au-Prince, Haiti's capital, but there may be as many as 3 million living in its slums[1] without formal documentation, so total casualties are impossible to determine.[2] The suffering was huge. Survivors became first responders. They dug neighbors from the rubble, pooled food and water, and slept on the streets, huddled for warmth. They teamed up to bury the dead, care for the injured, and repair damages.[3]

Haiti sits west of the Dominican Republic on the island of Hispaniola, and it is very poor.[4] Most Haitians live on less than $2 a day.[5] In the country, peasants work tiny farms. In the city, many can only find work in the "informal" economy, with jobs like street vending.[6] Half the adult population is illiterate,[7] and children average less than five years of school.[8] Some never attend at all, because their parents cannot afford to send them.[9] They can't afford food, either. (In 2008, Haitians rioted against high food prices; U.N. soldiers quelled the riot.)[10] Many lack even clean water and decent sanitation.[11]

How did Haiti get so poor?

In 1492, when Columbus arrived at Hispaniola, the Taino people lived there, but after fifty years of forced labor and European diseases, only 500 Taino survived. To replace them, the Spanish brought slaves from Africa. Spain ceded the western part of Hispaniola to France in 1697, and Haiti became France's richest colony, exporting sugar, cotton, coffee, and indigo. In 1789, the year of the French Revolution, the colony had 450,000 slaves from almost 40 regions in Africa.[12] In 1791 the slaves began their own fight for liberty, and Haiti declared independence in 1804.

After the earthquake, homeless residents of Port-au-Prince camped out where they could. (Roosevelt Pinheiro/Abr)

136

An aerial view of a camp for earthquake victims in Port-au-Prince. (Spike Call/USN)

The fledgling nation got little support from abroad; other nations feared slave revolts of their own. The United States did not recognize Haiti until 1862, and then occupied it from 1915 to 1934.[13] Later generations of greedy dictators pillaged it, often with U.S. support. In 1978, the U.S. urged the slaughter of Creole pigs to prevent a spread of swine fever. The pigs were "like bank accounts" for many families, and losing them deepened Haitian poverty.[14]

A natural disaster is often taken as a sign of divine displeasure. Some interpret the Port-au-Prince quake that way.[15] Often, too, outsiders are blamed: witches in one century, political enemies in another. In Haiti, many resent the foreigners and charitable organizations involved in the relief effort. As of 2014, many new housing units stood empty, with rents too high for quake survivors.[16] Do outsiders know enough to be responsible for Haiti?

In 1791, Haitians took responsibility for their own future. Poverty still makes Haiti vulnerable to disaster more than two centuries later, but their own strong, compassionate communities offer the best hope for reconstruction.

The Haitian Cholera Epidemic and Donor Fatigue

In October 2010, cholera broke out near a U.N. peacekeepers' camp. It soon infected more than 6% of Haitians,[17] and more than 8,500 have died of it. The epidemic peaked in 2011, with more than 350,000 cases that year. In 2013 the number declined to 50,000, but the percentage of fatalities was rising. Supplies for treating the sick were harder to find. The U.N. struggled to raise funds, but could not manage even $5 million for vaccinations and $38 million for supplies like water purification tablets and oral rehydration salts—let alone $2 billion for water and sanitation infrastructure. One problem seemed to be "donor fatigue." Faced with too many humanitarian crises around the world, the rich were tired of giving.[18]

2010
DEEPWATER HORIZON OIL SPILL THREATENS GULF OF MEXICO AND ATLANTIC

The Gulf of Mexico is a vital resource. Its coastal wetlands support many fish and wildlife species. Its commercial fishermen landed $818 million in shrimp and other seafood in 2011.[1] It has a $20-billion-a-year tourism industry and seven of the busiest U.S. ports.[2] But the biggest money is in the fuel industry. Offshore drilling in the gulf produced 19% of the crude oil and 6% of the natural gas consumed in the U.S. in 2012.[3]

Over 25 million years ago, oil deposits formed deep under the gulf in the Lower Tertiary layer of the earth's crust. Explorers with new seismic equip-

Fire boats battle the blazing wreckage of the offshore oil rig Deepwater Horizon. (USGS)

An oiled pelican after the Deepwater Horizon *explosion.* (Photo courtesy of Governor Jindal's office)

ment can detect fuel beneath as much as 10,000 feet of water and five miles of earth.[4] To reach it, oil companies mount advanced drilling technology on oil platforms.

One of these was the *Deepwater Horizon,* a semi-submersible rig. Its tight-knit crew followed a detailed safety manual. They practiced emergency responses. But they were not ready for what happened on April 20, 2010.[5]

That day they worked hard and fast to meet a deadline. They had been drilling on the Macondo, a well with a mind of its own—given to "kicks" of surging gas and oil. Now they were trying to plug it so the *Horizon* could move on. At 8 P.M., company men and rig managers agreed that the well was under control. At 9:30, everything still looked good, but hundreds of barrels of oil and gas were speeding up through the well. By 9:38, the pressurized hydrocarbons burst through the blowout preventer, the failsafe device that should have helped crew members seal the well. Explosions followed, and flames engulfed the rig.[6]

The *Horizon* collapsed and sank. Most of the workers escaped, but 11 died and many were injured. The Macondo spewed up to 2.94 million gallons of gas and oil per day. The U.S. Coast Guard, commercial contractors, and volunteers used booms and chemical dispersants to contain the leak. The well was capped on July 12, but by then more than 5 million barrels of oil had washed onto beaches and wetlands around the gulf.[7]

Before 2010, the worst spill in U.S. history was in 1989, when the *Exxon Valdez* hit a reef in Prince William Sound, Alaska. Despite massive clean-up efforts, environmental damage is still felt there. But the 2010 leak came from the seabed, not the surface, and it presented new problems. There was no way to fight the damage without doing additional damage.[8] There were concerns for seafood safety,[9] wildlife habitats, economic impacts, and the health of people around the gulf.

The U.S. suspended offshore drilling for five months and stiffened safety rules; some rigs migrated to other countries. As of February 2015, BP could still be liable to pay $13.7 billion under the federal Clean Water Act.[10] But drilling in the gulf had increased by 2014,[11] and in spite of controversy, the Obama administration moved to open waters along the Atlantic seaboard to drilling.[12]

48

2011
TOHOKU EARTHQUAKE AND TSUNAMI BATTER FUKUSHIMA NUCLEAR REACTORS

On March 11, 2011, Japan suffered a magnitude 9.0 earthquake. It was caused by subduction of the Pacific plate along the Japan Trench, where scientists had thought such a massive event was unlikely.[1] Japan protects itself against earthquakes, designing quake-resistant structures. Even so, the event damaged 128,530 houses, 230,332 other buildings, and 78 bridges.[2] The major tsunami that followed swept whole towns into the sea.

Communities along Japan's Pacific coast are protected by seawalls—some

Post-earthquake tsunami in Japan, 2011. (© HO/ Reuters/Corbis)

at controversial expense. But this tsunami topped them.[3] It was up to 133 feet (40 meters) tall in places, and flooded points as far as 6 miles (10 km) inland.[4] It devastated a 1,200-mile (1,935 km) stretch of Japan's Pacific coast, pouring over 150 square miles (400 km^2) of land.

To the usual one-two earthquake-tsunami punch, the Tohoku earthquake added a third blow: nuclear disaster. Japan, in spite of its frequent earthquakes and the World War II atomic bombings of Hiroshima and Nagasaki, relied on 50 nuclear reactors for 30% of its energy needs.[5] Waves up to 49 feet (15 meters) high crashed over a 19-foot seawall onto the Fukushima Daichi power station, disabling 12 of its 13 backup generators.[6] Without power, the pumps failed. Temperatures rose toward meltdown.

In the chaotic minutes after the quake, coastal residents rushed for higher ground. Communication networks failed, and not all evacuation centers were high enough. As they raced uphill, people helped strangers and worried about loved ones. Ten months later, the official death count was 15,844, with another 3,394 missing.[7]

Disaster always brings uncertainty. People lose friends, family, homes, and work. Places they knew simply disappear. But March 11, 2011 brought even greater uncertainty. Neither the government nor the Tokyo Electric Power Company (TEPCO) wanted to announce how bad the situation was. Instead, top government spokesman Yukio Edano tried to reassure the nation. On March 16 he said that "radiation levels around the nuclear plant" did not pose "an immediate health risk."[8] People had heard of Chernobyl. Plant workers wondered if the hours and days they spent trying to contain the meltdown would give them cancer later on. Fish along the coast had high levels of radioactive cesium, and fishermen wondered if they would ever be allowed to fish again.

Three years later, people still wondered. Nobody had died of radiation exposure, but parents had toddlers checked for thyroid cancer, and Californians watched for radiation in the water. Over 1,600 evacuee deaths were blamed on the accident—including deaths from anxiety, depression, and suicide.[9]

Important questions are still debated. After the Tohoku quake, Japan idled reactors for safety inspections. This forced the nation to import fossil fuels, driving up its trade deficit. The price of uranium slumped.[10] Should Japan remain nuclear-free? That would limit economic growth. Should it put its nuclear reactors back in service? This was a major issue in 2014 elections, and voter response was inconclusive.[11] Government plans to restart a nuclear reactor were still controversial in 2015.[12]

Japanese Courage

The steady courage and civility of the Japanese in this crisis impressed foreign reporters. "There was no descent into lawlessness and savagery, or even rioting of the kind that worsened the aftermath of natural disasters elsewhere."[13] Could moral education after the 1923 earthquake be partly to thank? But some things never change. Tokyo governor Shintaro Ishihara called the disaster "divine punishment" for modern Japan's "selfish greed."[14]

2014
EBOLA VIRUS DISEASE (EVD) ERUPTS IN WEST AFRICA

It started with a sick child. He was only 18 months old, and he lived in a small village in Guinea. On December 26, 2013, he had a fever and vomiting; two days later he died. As the weeks passed, his family sickened and died, and so did midwives and healers who treated them. Was it malaria, or cholera? These and other illnesses cause high fevers and dehydration, and are common in Guinea. But the child had Ebola, an infectious virus that was new in Guinea.[1] Bats and other wild animals can be infected with the Ebola virus, however, and that may be how the disease reached the child's village.

In the Democratic Republic of the Congo, where Ebola first erupted in 1976, it would have been identified quickly and the sick would have been isolated. Ebola causes internal bleeding, septic shock, organ failure, and—in at least half of all cases—death.[2] It is passed on through contact with body fluids, including vomit, feces, and even sweat.[3] The incubation period can last for 21 days. Once symptoms appear, the victims become highly contagious. Simply by absent-mindedly dabbing at her own eye after changing a dirty sheet or patting a sweaty forehead, a caregiver could infect herself. But early symptoms of Ebola look like early symptoms of other diseases, and it can spread easily if it is not recognized. In places with a history of Ebola outbreaks, hospital staff wear protective gear; they are trained to prevent and control infection. But Guinea had only one or two doctors per 100,000 inhabitants.[4] The illness went unidentified for nearly three months.

By then it had spread across borders and become the largest Ebola epidemic ever. As of February 2015, there had been more than 14,000 confirmed cases in the three most affected countries and another 9,000 suspected cases; more than 9,000 victims had died.[5] The World Health Organization said the outbreak "behaved like a fire in a peat bog," spreading underground and flaring up unexpectedly.[6]

Researchers in Biosafety Level 4 hazmat suits work with Ebola virus. Samples are handled in a negative-pressure biological safety cabinet to provide an additional layer of protection. Compare seventeenth-century plague doctor's protective gear, page 31. (Randal Schoepp, USAMRIID)

The sister of an Ebola patient speaks with him through a protective fence at an Ebola treatment center in Nzérékoré, Guinea. (UN Photo/ Martine Perret)

Guinea and its neighbors, Liberia and Sierra Leone, are desperately poor, and their recent civil wars blocked education as well as economic growth. Poverty contributed to Ebola's spread, as people traveled throughout the region in search of work. Traditional culture also played a role, as they traveled home to their villages to care for loved ones, attend funerals, or die. Affected communities refused to cooperate with medical workers. They hid Ebola victims and held secret burial services after dark.

Like other disasters, this one brought fear, suspicion, and rumor. Like the British in 1832—who suspected that doctors gave poor folks cholera in order to steal their bodies for dissection (Chapter 19)—many West Africans believed that Ebola was a conspiracy. Medical staff risked not only contagion, but also attack by angry mobs.[7]

Still, the need for international aid was obvious, and NGOs joined with governments to fight the epidemic. In December 2014, the Sierra Leone government launched its Operation Western Area Surge initiative with help from the Bill and Melinda Gates Foundation, the UK government, MSF (Médecins Sans Frontières, or Doctors without Borders), and WHO. To build trust, they began by distributing antimalarial medicines. Fear of Ebola kept people from getting treatment for other illnesses, too, and malaria—spread by mosquitoes—kills far more victims than Ebola.

As of September 2014, vaccines and drug therapies for Ebola were still under development.[8] Early treatment with rehydration did help prevent organ breakdown; scary as they looked in their protective gear, the hard-working medics saved lives.[9] But the WHO concluded that the most needed weapon against in this fight is community engagement. The Ebola virus alone did not cause the epidemic; it was abetted by "the fear and misunderstanding that fuelled high-risk behaviours."[10] Going forward, the disease fighters must persuade communities that doctors are allies, not enemies, and that Ebola survivors are to be supported, not shunned. Working respectfully with local culture, disease fighters will become educators.

Ebola Concerns in the United States

In 2014, at least 26 deaths in the U.S. were caused by lightning;[11] only 2 were caused by Ebola.[12] Clearly Ebola is not a major health concern in the U.S., yet it dominated the media for weeks. People feared a disease that forbids the comfort of touching loved ones, and even though victims do not become contagious until they show symptoms, there was public demand for quarantines of anybody who had been exposed to the disease. Nurse Kaci Hickox made headlines when she refused the Maine governor's order to quarantine herself for the three-week incubation period. Judge Charles LaVerdiere ruled in her favor, but said that even if people's fear was "not entirely rational," it had to be respected: "Respondent's actions, at this point, as a health care professional, need to demonstrate her full understanding of human nature and the real fear that exists."[13] While Hickox defended her individual civil liberties, others argued about the ethics of airlifting Ebola-infected doctors to the United States. Did the heroic altruism of medical volunteers entitle them to better treatment than they could get in the desperately poor countries they were trying to help? Was the focus on experimental drugs and vaccines a distraction from public health measures that could have saved more West Africans? One ethicist stated flatly, "The global response to the Ebola epidemic has so far been a catastrophe."[14] Irrational fear of Ebola in the U.S. could actually turn out to be helpful—if it mobilizes lasting support for improvements to the global health infrastructure.

DISASTER IN
THE MAKING
ANTHROPOGENIC
CLIMATE CHANGE IN THE
TWENTY-FIRST CENTURY

E arth's climate changes naturally. The planet orbits a little closer to the sun or a little farther away. The sun gives off a little more energy or a little less. Volcanoes spread ash and sulfur compounds through the stratosphere, reducing the amount of sunlight that reaches the ground. All this has happened more than once without human intervention.

Technically, we are living in an ice age that began about 2.5 million years ago.[1] Anatomically Modern Humans (AMHs) emerged just 200,000 years ago,[2] so we are children of the ice age. Even during an ice age, however, there are interglacial periods. One of them—the Holocene Epoch—began about 11,700 years ago. Civilization developed in the comfortable Holocene climate, in fertile river valleys around the world. The average temperature has been higher by half a degree Celsius in one century and lower in another, but civilized humans have adapted. This is the climate we know.

1999–2008 mean temperature anomalies, compared to 1940–1980 averages (NASA)

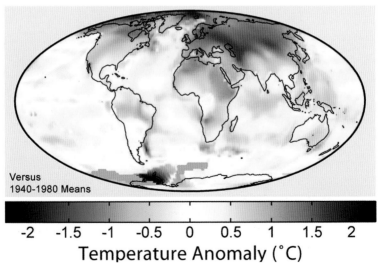

Versus
1940-1980 Means

-2   -1.5   -1   -0.5   0   0.5   1   1.5   2
Temperature Anomaly (°C)

Ships stranded by the disappearance of Kazakhstan's Aral Sea. (P. Christopher Staecker)

Now our climate is changing fast, and human activity seems to be driving the change. Since 1750, when humans began burning more fossil fuels, levels of greenhouse gases in the atmosphere have risen by as much as 40%. Increased carbon dioxide acidifies seawater and eats away the shells and exoskeletons of many ocean species. As tiny creatures become rare or go extinct, larger fish suffer, and so do human fisheries. Sulfur dioxide and nitrogen oxide cause acid rain that damages forests, rivers, lakes, and the animals who live in them.

But the single most obvious effect of greenhouse gases is global warming. In the middle of a cold winter, it can be hard to believe this, but in 2014 the Intergovernmental Panel on Climate Change (IPCC) reported that:

> ▷ Climate change is real.
> ▷ There is strong evidence that human activity has been the dominant influence on warming since 1950.
> ▷ By the end of the 21st century, the average global sea-level temperature will probably be more than 1.5°C above its 1850–1900 level. Some years and regions will be warmer than others, but the trends will continue.
> ▷ Even if we stop all CO_2 emissions now, most aspects of climate change will persist and worsen for centuries.[3] But by acting now, we could prevent the problem from getting even worse than it otherwise will.

Since 1980, each decade has been warmer than the one before. The year 2014 was the warmest year on record, and the ten warmest years (with the lone exception of 1998) have all occurred since 2000. Animals (such as penguins, butterflies, and Atlantic cod) are moving away from the equator to escape the heat. Alder trees are taking root in bare northern grasslands. Even tropical storms are peaking farther away from the equator, menacing coasts where they used to be rare.[4]

Rapid global warming may be a disaster for civilization in several ways. Melting ice sheets raise sea levels; great coastal cities will be more vulnerable to flooding. One island nation—the Marshall Islands, consisting largely of coral atolls—is already in danger of being evacuated.[5] As the ocean rises and acidic water eats away the coral, their land shrinks. Elsewhere in the world, heat and drought have damaged water supplies and crop yields, making food more expensive.[6]

To bring global warming under control, humans need to cut greenhouse gas emissions in half by mid-century and to near-zero by 2100. We will have to change how we produce and use energy, transport people and goods, design buildings, and organize towns. Luckily, renewable wind and solar energy are becoming more efficient and affordable, and inventors are finding sustainable new solutions. For instance, Indonesian Willie Smits makes sure local people are the ones who benefit when he restores a burned rain forest.[7] He integrates trees, energy-efficient machinery, and cultural values in a new system that really works.[8] Meanwhile, as New York and New Jersey communities grapple with damage done by Hurricane Sandy, Dutch expert Henk Ovink suggests designs that work with the water instead of fighting it.[9]

Humans have invented ways out of trouble before. Climate change is a major hazard, but the solutions of thinkers like Smits and Ovink show ways of handling the risk. With empathy and respect, including vulnerable people in new plans, they demonstrate ways to make our society more resilient in the future.

Working for International Cooperation

The IPCC aims to limit future climate change by reducing CO_2 emissions, removing pollutants from the environment, and other mitigation activities. The nations of the world struggle to work out rules for this. The 1997 Kyoto Protocol, an international agreement adopted in Japan, committed industrialized nations to reduce greenhouse gas emissions by up to 8%.[10] But the United States did not ratify it, and Canada withdrew from the agreement.[11] Meanwhile, populations and economies keep growing, using more energy and emitting more carbon.[12] More than 190 nations are scheduled to meet in Paris in December 2015 to grapple with the problems again.[13]

Could a Microbe Trigger Rapid Global Warming and Mass Extinctions?

Whether it's caused by large or seemingly small events, sudden climate change can lead to mass extinctions. When the Cretaceous period ended with global cooling about 65 million years ago, an estimated 75% of Earth's plants and animals (including the dinosaurs) became extinct. When the Paleozoic Era ended about 252 million years ago, global warming ended as many as 96% of all marine species and 70% of terrestrial vertebrates. One theory is that the Siberian Traps eruptions, one of the largest known volcanic events, fueled a runaway greenhouse effect.[14] But a recent MIT study suggests that the real culprit was the *Methanosarcina* microbe, which had just acquired a new power. Gene transfer with another microbe equipped it to produce methane very efficiently. *Methanosarcina* needed nickel to grow, and the volcanoes released nickel into the environment. Empowered by volcanic nutrients and a handy mutation, *Methanosarcina* may have been the major contributor to a heat wave that ended Paleozoic life.[15]

CONCLUSION

There have always been natural hazards. Earth's tectonic plates have pushed against each other, jammed, and shaken apart in huge earthquakes. Magma has welled up under volcanoes and erupted, propelling broken rocks and sulfur compounds into the stratosphere. Tsunamis and storm surges have battered the coasts; rivers have flooded their valleys; wild winds have torn across the land. These are all natural hazards.

Humans have often found the greatest opportunities right where the greatest hazards occur. We have worked the rich soil around volcanoes and great rivers, fished along the coasts, and established great cities near the edges of tectonic plates. Over time we've learned to understand the hazards, but the opportunities entice us. We keep risking disaster.

When disaster strikes, people respond in a number of ways.

- ▷ Some are heroes. Even though he had asthma, Pliny rushed toward Mount Vesuvius in AD 79 to rescue his friends and other people in danger. Even though they knew what had happened at Chernobyl, Japanese workers put themselves at risk to stop the meltdown at the Fukushima nuclear plant in 2011.
- ▷ Some are looters, and some punish looters harshly. This happened in Lisbon after the 1755 earthquake, and it happened in New Orleans after the 2005 hurricane.
- ▷ Some organize relief efforts. Nero requisitioned supplies for victims of the Great Fire of Rome in AD 64, and FEMA contracted for trailers as emergency dwellings after Hurricane Katrina in 2005.
- ▷ Some try to fix blame. King Charles II was suspected of torching London in 1666; Mrs. O'Leary's cow was blamed for burning Chicago in 1871.
- ▷ Some try to shift blame. Nero tried to shift it onto Christians (or the even more unpopular worshippers of Isis) in AD 64, and the United States Industrial Alcohol company tried to shift it onto an imaginary bomb-throwing Italian anarchist in 1919.

And in the end, there are always some who try to prevent similar disasters in the future. After fires, they rebuild cities with wider streets and fire-resistant roofs. After epidemics, they search for vaccinations against new and emerging diseases. After famines, they develop ways to increase crop yields.

Sometimes our activities have unintended results. We find that everything is connected to everything else, often in ways that are hard to see. Great levees on the Yellow River and the Mississippi, intended to control flooding, have contributed to major floods. Fossil fuels have made industry more profitable and homes more comfortable, but they have also added greenhouse gases to the air and helped raise Earth's temperature.

The more civilization advances, the more humans contribute to environmental disasters. We have always lived near hazards like volcanoes and rivers; now we create new hazards, like molasses holding tanks and chemical fertilizers. We are vulnerable both to natural hazards and to our own mistakes.

Yet we are a resilient species, and we grow more resilient—better able to anticipate hazards, resist them, cope with them, and recover from their impact. Children and teens participate in risk reduction. For instance, they map and analyze local hazards; help plan effective responses; join community activities to prevent or recover from disasters; and spread useful information. Tilly Smith (see Chapter 45) is just one example of a girl who saved lives.

GLOSSARY

aerosol particles: Tiny solid or liquid particles (such as fine ash from a volcano) suspended in a gas (such as earth's atmosphere).

AMH: Anatomically Modern Human; *Homo sapiens sapiens*. See also *Neanderthal*.

anemometer: A device for measuring wind speed.

anthropogenic: Caused by humans.

aqueduct: A structure, often bridgelike, built as a conduit for water.

arsenic: A poisonous chemical element, naturally occurring in many minerals.

arsonist: A criminal who deliberately sets a fire.

asphyxiation: Severe oxygen deficiency caused by impairment of normal breathing, as by choking or by lack of oxygen in the air.

asteroid: A small rocky body that orbits the sun.

bacillus: A genus of bacteria that includes *Vibrio cholerae* and *Yersinia pestis*.

bacteriology: The scientific study of bacteria.

bioweapon: A poison, virus, fungus, or other agent used to cause disease in enemies. Early bioweapons included the bodies of dead plague victims, and blankets deliberately infected with smallpox.

Black Death: The bubonic plague pandemic that hit Europe in the Middle Ages.

caldera: A geographic formation; a broad, cauldron-shaped depression formed by volcanic eruption.

carbon dioxide (CO_2): A naturally occurring chemical compound, found in the atmosphere and necessary for plants; an important greenhouse gas.

coral atoll: A ring-shaped coral reef encircling a lagoon.

cyclone: A large-scale tropical storm, wheeling around an area of low pressure. A cyclone with winds exceeding 74 mph is called a hurricane in the North Atlantic, or a typhoon in some regions of the Pacific.

Deism: Belief in a single Creator, coupled with disbelief in religious authority or revelation. Deists believed the existence of God was supported by reason and by direct observation of nature.

delta: The land formed at a river's mouth, where sediment is deposited as the river flows out to sea.

dialect: A variant way of speaking a language; often regional, a dialect uses words, pronunciations, and grammatical constructions that differ from the standard language.

dike: A levee or embankment built to protect land against flooding.

EHW03: European Heat Wave of 2003.

El Niño/Southern Oscillation (ENSO): In El Niño years, the Pacific is warmer than usual; this affects weather patterns around the world.

endemic: (Of a disease or condition) regularly found among a certain population or in a certain area.

epidemic: A breakout of disease in a region or country.

epidemiology: The scientific study of how diseases spread and can be controlled.

fault: In geology, a fracture or discontinuity.

feudalism: A medieval social and economic system requiring serfs to work land for lords, who held it from greater lords, who held it from kings. At each level those in the lower rank owed work, obedience, and possibly military service to their overlords, who owed them protection in return.

flagellants: Persons who flog either themselves or others; in the Middle Ages, this was sometimes done for religious discipline or penance.

gangrene: The death or decomposition of body tissue, usually at the victim's extremities (fingers and toes), resulting from lack of blood flow or bacterial infection.

geyser: A hot spring that throws an intermittent column of water and steam into the air.

glacier: A slowly moving mass of ice, which builds up and is compacted.

Great Plague: The 1665 bubonic plague epidemic in London.

Green Revolution: Increased crop yields per acre, made possible by the adoption of new plant varieties, fertilizers, technologies, and techniques, especially from about 1968 to 1982.

greenhouse gas: A gas in the atmosphere that absorbs and gives off infrared radiation. Greenhouse gases include water vapor, carbon dioxide, methane, nitrous oxide, and ozone. As levels of greenhouse gas in the atmosphere rise, more heat is retained near Earth's surface and less is released into space; the atmosphere grows warmer.

guild: A medieval association of craftsmen or merchants. Like today's unions and professional organizations, the guilds influenced recruitment, training, and advancement in their occupations.

hallucinate: See or otherwise sense things that are not actually present; high fevers can cause *hallucinations,* or delusions.

Heinrich Event: within a glacial period, a climate fluctuation associated with the break-up of northern ice shelves and release of melting icebergs into the sea.

hemophiliac: A person who suffers from hemophilia, a bleeding disorder that prevents blood from clotting. Before 1985, some hemophiliacs contracted HIV/AIDS after being treated with contaminated blood supplies.

hydrochloric acid: A highly corrosive acid; one ingredient in London's 1952 killer smog.

ice age: An extended period when cold temperatures result in ice sheets at the North and South Pole. Within a long-term ice age, there may be glacial periods (when ice sheets spread over continents) and interglacial periods (when mountain glaciers and polar ice caps shrink). An ice age began 2.6 million years ago, and since there are still ice sheets at the poles, it has not yet ended.

ice core: A tube-shaped sample of ice, taken from a sheet of ice that has built up over many centuries. Each year's snow carries particles of dust, pollen, and other substances in the atmosphere. Because they fall layer by layer, with the newest layers on top, scientists can use the cores to reconstruct climate history.

ignimbrite: A volcanic rock in which shards of erupted minerals are welded by pressure and heat. Even on the slopes of a single volcano, the deposits of an individual eruption will have unique characteristics, depending on the chemistry of source magma.

immunity: The ability of an organism to resist a disease by mobilizing white blood cells or antibodies specific to that disease. Immunity may result when an individual's immune system is primed by surviving the disease or being vaccinated against it. Herd immunity may result when most members of a population are already immune.

incubation period: The time after one is infected with a disease and before symptoms show themselves.

indigo: Plant from which a deep blue dye is made.

Industrial Revolution: Beginning around 1760, a transition to new manufacturing methods, including steam power and mechanized processes.

Inquisition: In the past, an organization within the Roman Catholic Church that was responsible for finding and punishing those who did not believe its approved doctrine.

Isis, cult of: In the Roman Empire, a religion devoted to the Egyptian goddess Isis.

jaundice: Yellowing of the skin and/or whites of the eyes; a symptom of certain medical conditions.

Justinian's Plague: The first bubonic plague pandemic, which swept the Mediterranean area in 541.

lahar: A semiliquid surge of volcanic debris, typically flowing down a stream or river during an eruption.

lava: Magma that flows down the sides of volcanoes.

Little Ice Age: A period of cooling after the Medieval Warm Period. Scientists date its onset anywhere from 1300 to 1570, and its ending between 1850 and 1950.

magma: Molten (melted) rock.

malnutrition: An unhealthy condition resulting from not eating enough healthy food.

Medieval Warm Period: A period of slightly warmer temperatures, dated from approximately 800 to 1300; its warmest years, between 950 and 1100, were probably almost as warm as the 1961–1990 average.

methane: One of the greenhouse gases; produced naturally by the decomposition of plants and animals, and by the carbonization of coal. It is colorless, odorless, and easy to burn; it can be used as a fuel.

Neanderthal: An extinct species or subspecies of human, variously classified as *Homo neanderthalis* (a separate species from Anatomically Modern Humans, *Homo sapiens)* or *Homo sapiens neanderthalis,* a separate subspecies. Neanderthals lived in Europe until approximately 35,000 years ago.

negligence: Failure to use the same level of care that a reasonably sensible person would have used in the same circumstances.

NGO: A non-governmental organization; usually a voluntary group organized to provide services or advocate public policy.

nitrous oxide: One of the greenhouse gases; emitted during agricultural and industrial activities. Sometimes called "laughing gas," it is used as an anesthetic.

nor'easter: A storm with strong northeast winds, typically bringing heavy rain or snow and coastal flooding to the eastern U.S. and Canada.

pandemic: A worldwide breakout of disease. The 1918 influenza pandemic infected half a billion people around the world and killed over 50 million.

Penal Laws: In Ireland, a series of laws intended to force Catholics to accept the established Protestant religion (the Church of Ireland) by depriving them of civil rights.

pious: Devoutly religious.

polder: A low-lying tract of land enclosed by dikes.

post-traumatic stress: The stress experienced after danger is past, by survivors or witnesses of an ordeal.

psychosomatic: Having mental or emotional rather than physical causes.

pumice: Light-weight, porous volcanic rock, formed by the sudden cooling of gas-rich lava.

pyroclastic flow: A rapid flow of hot gas and rock from a volcano.

radiocarbon dating: A dating technique that uses the decay of carbon-14 (^{14}C; an unstable isotope of carbon) to estimate the age of organic material.

reservoir: A natural or artificial lake used as a water supply.

resistance (to disease): An organism's natural capacity to withstand disease.

rinderpest: An infectious disease that killed sheep and cattle; declared extinct in 2010.

sanitation: In public health, the provision of clean drinking water and adequate sewage disposal.

savanna: A grassland with widely spaced trees.

scapegoat: A person or group unfairly blamed. (Sometimes the true guilty party does the blaming.)

seismology: The scientific study of earthquakes.

serf: Under feudalism, a person bound to the land and required to work for its owner.

siege: Isolating a city or fort by surrounding it with a hostile army, so that defenders inside the walls are cut off from help and supplies.

socialist: One who advocates that the community or state, rather than individuals, should own and control major industries, land, and other sources of wealth.

storm surge: Water pushed toward the shore by the force of storm winds. Like a tsunami, a storm surge may look like a wall of water rushing onto the land.

subduction zone: The boundary where the edge of one tectonic plate is forced below another.

sulfur dioxide: A foul-smelling toxic gas, emitted by volcanoes and coal fires.

sulfuric acid: A strong, corrosive chemical that can burn skin.

sustainable: Able to continue without exhausting resources or destroying balance needed for optimum use and enjoyment. In environmental science, sustainability has to do with conserving and replenishing natural resources and living in balance with nature.

tax amnesty: Government forgiveness of tax liability, usually to a specific group of taxpayers for a limited time.

tectonic plates: According to the theory of plate tectonics, about a dozen sections of the earth's crust, whose motion relative to each other causes earthquakes, volcanoes, continental drift, and related phenomena.

tephra: Magma forced up into the air by volcanic explosion; ash, rocks, and other volcanic debris.

tsunami: A set of ocean waves caused by a large, sudden disturbance of the sea surface—for instance, an earthquake on the ocean floor, or the sudden collapse of an erupting volcano, or a landslide.

tube-well: A type of well made by boring a stainless steel pipe into an underground water source.

Vibrio cholerae (V. cholerae): A waterborne bacterium, some strains of which cause the disease cholera.

virus: A small infectious agent that replicates only within the cells of other living organisms.

Yersinia pestis (Y. pestis): The bacterium that caused the Plague of Justinian and the Black Death.

SOURCES AND ADDITIONAL RESOURCES
A WORD ABOUT THE RESEARCH PROCESS

Original research—"primary" research—is based on direct investigation. Research scientists may devise experiments to test their hypotheses; historians may gather and analyze data from archives.

This book is not a work of original research. Instead, it is based on secondary research—looking things up and making sense of them. To write the book, I had to gather sources on each topic, compare and synthesize them, and summarize each story. You may often have to do secondary research for school reports, and you probably go about it much the way I did. We rely on our "information literacy."

Basic information literacy skills include defining the task; deciding on an information-seeking strategy; locating and accessing sources; reading (or viewing or listening to) the sources and taking from them what you need; synthesizing what you've taken from multiple sources and presenting it; and, finally, evaluating and possibly revising your product[1]—whether it's a book or a class presentation. Each time you go through this process you get a little more efficient, which helps you the next time.

I don't always do the steps in order. Often I go back and forth between them. For instance, I define my task, start searching—and redefine my task. I locate a source, jump forward to read it, and decide not to use it—or find it mentions three other sources I need to locate. Here are my first three steps:

Defining the task: For this book, the task was clear. I had to introduce 50 different disasters, in chapters between 500 and 700 words long. Each chapter had to tell what the disaster was, and how it affected civilization—or how civilization affected the disaster.

Plotting a search strategy: First I looked for lists of disasters in general—and found hundreds of them. To limit the search, I used these rules of thumb:

▷ The disaster had to involve the environment, pitting humans against natural forces—whether volcanoes or viruses or chemicals. I eliminated war.

▷ The disaster had to be well documented. Did 230,000 people really die in an 1138 Aleppo earthquake? I wanted to include it, since it happened during the Crusades, but I just couldn't find enough.

For a few of the disasters I found entire books, by writers who had already located and collated many sources. For others, I sometimes started with Wikipedia. (Wikipedia should be handled carefully, as should any source; but it's constantly being reviewed and corrected, and most of its articles have sources you can follow up. Think of it as a jumping-off point, and keep going.) For many of my disaster stories, I pieced together information from scholarly articles that I accessed through my university library, using databases such as Academic Search Complete and JSTOR.

Locating and accessing sources: Physical access was not a problem. School, public, and university libraries have online catalogs of their holdings, and online databases of articles. Before going to the library, I make a list of things I want to look at when I get there.

But not every source is useful. Before leaving the library, I check the index of each book and look at the pages that should be most relevant to my question. Before reading a whole article online, I use "find" the same way. Is the book or article really about my topic? Can I understand it? Do I trust it? If not, I will not borrow it from the library or download it.

How do I know what to trust? I look for documentation—bibliographies, endnotes and other evidence that the authors have done their homework. I look for balance— if there's a controversy, I want both sides to be explained fairly. On the internet, I tend to trust academic or non-profit sources more than commercial sources, but that's not a

foolproof guide to reliability. The best strategy is to compare multiple sources and see where they agree.

Reading, synthesizing, writing, and rewriting: In the later stages of my secondary research, I go back and forth between steps more and more. Writing makes me notice questions that still need answering. My writing is not a fast or predictable process. But it absorbs me; it is a process of discovery. I hope you can use this book—with its source lists and additional resources—as a jumping off point for your own voyage of discovery.

Introduction

Ambraseys, Nicholas N. "The 12th Century Seismic Paroxysm in the Middle East: A Historical Perspective." *Annals of Geophysics* 47 (April/June 2004): 733–58.

Republic of the Philippines National Disaster Risk Reduction and Management Council. "SitRep No. 104 Effects of Typhoon 'Yolanda' (Haiyan)." www.ndrrmc.gov.ph/attachments/article/1329/Effects_of_Typhoon_YOLANDA_(HAIYAN)_SitRep_No_104_29JAN2014_0600H.pdf (accessed 28 May 2014).

1. 37,000 BC: Neanderthals and the Campanian Ignimbrite Eruption

Davies, Siwan, and Peter Abbott. "Volcanic Secrets in the Ice." *Planet Earth Online* (March 19, 2010): http://planetearth.nerc.ac.uk/features/story.aspx?id=674 (accessed 12 January 2014).

Fitzsimmons, Kathryn E., Ulrich Hambach, Daniel Veres, and Radu Iovita. "The Campanian Ignimbrite Eruption: New Data on Volcanic Ash Dispersal and Its Potential Impact on Human Evolution." *PLoS ONE* 8, 6 (June 17, 2013): http://journals.plos.org/plosone/article?id=10.1371/journal.pone.0065839 (accessed 17 February 2015).

Golovanova, Liubov Vitaliena, *et al.* "Significance of Ecological Factors in the Middle to Upper Paleolithic Transition." *Current Anthropology* 51, 5 (October 2010): 655–91.

Hansell, A. L., C. J. Horwell, and C. Oppenheimer. "Education: The Health Hazards of Volcanoes and Geothermal Areas." *Occupational and Environmental Medicine* 63, 2 (February 2006): 149–56.

"Kissing Cousins." *The Economist* (February 1, 2014): www.economist.com/news/science-and-technology/21595403-genetic-contribution-neanderthal-man-made-modern-humanity.

Rampino, Michael R., and Stanley H. Ambrose. "Volcanic Winter in the Garden of Eden: The Toba Supereruption and the Late Pleistocene Human Population Crash." In *Volcanic Hazards and Disasters in Human Antiquity*, ed. Floyd W. McCoy and Grant Heiken, 71–82 (Boulder, CA: Geological Society of America, 2000).

Sriram Sankararaman *et al.* "The Genomic Landscape of Neanderthal Ancestry in Present-day Humans." *Nature* (January 29, 2014): http://sriramsankararaman.com/publications/sankararaman.nature.2014.pdf (accessed 6 July 2015).

Scarth, Alwyn. *Vesuvius: A Biography*. Princeton, NJ: Princeton University Press, 2009.

Self, S. "The Effects and Consequences of Very Large Explosive Volcanic Eruptions." *Philosophical Transactions: Mathematical, Physical and Engineering Sciences*, 364, No. 1845, Extreme Natural Hazards (August 15, 2006): 2073–97.

Sepulchre, Pierre, *et al.* "H4 Abrupt Event and Late Neanderthal Presence in Iberia." *Earth and Planetary Science Letters* 258 (2007): 283–92.

Sigurdsson, Haraldur. *Melting the Earth: The History of Ideas on Volcanic Eruptions*. New York: Oxford University Press, 1999.

Vernot, Benjamin, and Joshua M. Akey, "Resurrecting Surviving Neandertal Lineages from Modern Human Genomes," *Science* 343, no. 6174 (28 February 2014): 1017-21.

Wikipedia. "Human Evolution." http://en.wikipedia.org/wiki/Human_evolution.

Wikipedia. "Anatomically Modern Humans." http://en.wikipedia.org/wiki/Anatomically_modern_humans.

Additional Resources

Amos, Jonathan. "Toba Super-Volcano Catastrophe Idea 'Dismissed.'" *BBC News*, 30 April 2013. www.bbc.co.uk/news/science-environment-22355515 (Accessed 12 January 2014).

Choi, Charles Q. "Ancient Super-Eruption Larger Than Thought," *LiveScience*, June 21, 2012 www.livescience.com/31560-ancient-super-eruption-larger.html (accessed 11 January 2014).

"Volcanoes Wiped Out Neanderthal, New Study Suggests." *Science Daily*, October 7, 2010. www.sciencedaily.com/releases/2010/10/101006094057.htm (accessed 11 January 2014).

2. 1600 BC: Eruption at Santorini Undermines Minoan Civilization

Bruins, Hendrik J., *et al.* "Geoarchaeological Tsunami Deposits at Palaikastro (Crete) and the Late Minoan IA Eruption of Santorini." *Journal of Archaeological Science* 35, 1 (January 2008): 191-212.

Höflmayer, Felix. "The Date of the Minoan Santorini Eruption: Quantifying the 'Offset.'" *Radiocarbon* 54 (2012): 435–48.

Knappett, Carl, Ray Rivers, and Tim Evans. "The Theran Eruption and Minoan Palatial Collapse: New Interpretations Gained from Modelling the Maritime Network." *Antiquity* 85 (2011): 1008–23.

Sigurdsson, Haraldur. *Melting the Earth: The History of Ideas on Volcanic Eruptions.* New York: Oxford University Press, 1999.

Wiener, Malcolm H. "Cold Fusion: The Uneasy Alliance of History and Science." In *Tree-Rings, Kings, and Old World Archaeology and Environment: Papers Presented in Honor of Peter Ian Kuniholm.* Edited by Sturt W. Manning and Mary Jaye Bruce, 277–92. Oxford: Oxbow Books, 2009.

Additional Resources

Archaeology, Mythology and History of Crete: Minoan Civilization. www.explorecrete.com/archaeology/minoan-civilization-destruction.html (accessed 13 January 2014).

Baird, W. Sheppard. "The 'Sinking Atlantis' Tsunami Myth Debunked." www.minoanatlantis.com/Sinking_Atlantis_Myth.php (accessed 29 May 2014).

"Sinking Atlantis: The Fall of the Minoans." *Secrets of the Dead* (May 9, 2011). www.pbs.org/wnet/secrets/the-fall-of-the-minoans/61/ (accessed 13 January 2014).

Whipps, Heather. "How the Eruption of Thera Changed the World." *LiveScience* (Feb 24, 2008). www.livescience.com/4846-eruption-thera-changed-world.html (accessed 13 January 2014).

3. AD 64: Emperor Nero Blames Great Fire on Unpopular Cult

Champlin, Edward. "Nero reconsidered." *New England Review* 19, Issue 2 (Spring 1998): 97–108.

Dando-Collins, Stephen. *The Great Fire of Rome: The Fall of the Emperor Nero and His City.* Cambridge, MA: Da Capo Press, 2010.

Additional Resources

"Secrets of the Dead Case File: The Great Fire of Rome." PBS. www.pbs.org/wnet/secrets/previous_seasons/case_rome/index.html?utm_source=Tumblr&utm_medium=ThisDayHistory&utm_campaign=July%2B18%2BRome%2BFire.

"The Burning of Rome, 64 AD." EyeWitness to History (1999). www.eyewitnesstohistory.com/rome.htm.

"July 19, 64 A.D.: Nero's Rome Burns." History.com. www.history.com/this-day-in-history/neros-rome-burns.

4. AD 79: Vesuvius Buries Pompeii and Herculaneum

Clarke, John. *Physical Science in the Time of Nero: Being a Translation of the* Quaestiones Naturales *by Seneca.* London: Macmillan and Company, 1910.

Pliny the Younger. *Letters of Pliny.* Ed. F. C. T. Bosanquet; Trans. William Melmoth. Project Gutenberg release date September, 2001 (Etext #2811). www.gutenberg.org/files/2811/2811-h/2811-h.htm (accessed 15 January 2014).

Scarth, Alwyn. *Vesuvius: A Biography.* Princeton, NJ: Princeton University Press, 2009.

Sigurdsson, Haraldur. *Melting the Earth: The History of Ideas on Volcanic Eruptions.*

New York: Oxford University Press, 1999.

USGS. "Invisible CO2 Gas Killing Trees at Mammoth Mountain, California." U.S. Geological Survey Fact Sheet 172–96, Online Version 2.0, http://pubs.usgs.gov/dds/dds-81/Intro/facts-sheet/GasKillingTrees.html (accessed 30 June 2014).

Additional Resources

BBC. Pompeii Live. www.britishmuseum.org/whats_on/past_exhibitions/2013/pompeii_and_herculaneum/pompeii_live/eruption_timeline.aspx.

"Deadly Shadow of Vesuvius." NOVA, PBS. www.pbs.org/wgbh/nova/vesuvius/.

"Secrets of the Dead: Herculaneum Uncovered." PBS. www.pbs.org/wnet/secrets/previous_seasons/case_herculaneum/index.html.

University of Rhode Island Graduate School of Oceanography. "Vesuvius Volcano." www.gso.uri.edu/vesuvius/Vesuvius/Vesu.html.

5. 536: The Case of the Mysterious Ash

Arjava, Antti. "The Mystery Cloud of 536 CE in the Mediterranean Sources." *Dumbarton Oaks Papers* 59 (2005): 73–94.

Keys, David. Catastrophe: An Investigation into the Origins of the Modern World (New York: Ballantine Books, 1999).

Franck Lavigne *et al.* "Source of the Great A.D. 1257 Mystery Eruption Unveiled, Samalas Volcano, Rinjani Volcanic Complex, Indonesia." *PNAS* 110, 42 (15 October 2013): 16742–47.

Southon, John, Mahyar Mohtadi, and Ricardo De Pol-Holz. "Planktonic

Foram Dates from the Indonesian Arc: Marine ^{14}C Reservoir Ages and a Mythical AD 535 Eruption of Krakatau," *Radiocarbon* 55, 2 (2013): 1164–72.

Whitby, Michael. "Catastrophe. An Investigation into the Origins of the Modern World, by D. Keys." [Review.] The Classical Review, New Series 50, 1 (2000): 350.

Wohletz, KH. "Were the Dark Ages Triggered by Volcano-related Climate Changes in the 6th Century? *EOS, Transactions American Geophysical Union* 48, 81 (2000): F1305. www.ees.lanl.gov/geodynamics/Wohletz/Krakatau.htm (accessed 1/18/2014).

Additional Resources

"Detective story: King Arthur." Discover myths. Discovery series. TES Connect (11 May 2008): www.tes.co.uk/teaching-resource/Detective-story-King-Arthur-Discover-myths-Discovery-series-308846/.

Hirst, K. Kris. "Ragnarok, the Vikings, and the Dust Veil of 536: Scholarly Articles on the Environmental Catastrophe." http://archaeology.about.com/od/medieval/qt/Dust-Veil-of-AD-536_2.htm.

Stewart, Rhea Talley. "A Dam at Marib." Aramco, www.saudiaramcoworld.com/issue/197802/a.dam.at.marib.htm.

6. 541: Justinian's Plague Weakens the Byzantine Empire

Arjava, Antti. "The Mystery Cloud of 536 CE in the Mediterranean Sources." *Dumbarton Oaks Papers* 59 (2005): 73–94.

Drancourt, M., et al. "*Yersinia pestis* Orientalis in Remains of Ancient Plague Patients." *Emerging Infectious Diseases*

13, 2 (February 2007). wwwnc.cdc. gov/eid/article/13/2/06-0197.htm (accessed 2 November 2013).

Keys, David. Catastrophe: An Investigation into the Origins of the Modern World (New York: Ballantine Books, 1999).

Tyson, Peter. "A Short History of Quarantine." *NOVA* (12 October 2004). www.pbs.org/wgbh/nova/body/short-history-of-quarantine.html (accessed 25 January 2014).

Kinder, Hermann, and Werner Kilgemann. *The Anchor Atlas of World History*, trans. Ernest A. Menze. New York: Anchor Press/Doubleday, 1974.

Wagner, David M., *et al.* "*Yersinia pestis* and the Plague of Justinian 541-543 AD: A Genomic Analysis." *The Lancet* (January 28, 2014): http://eeid.cornell.edu/files/2012/12/Wagner-1te9if4.pdf (accessed 18 February 2015).

Additional Resources

GreenfieldBoyce, Nell. "Ancient Plague's DNA Revived from a 1,500-Year-Old Tooth." *Morning Edition*, NPR (January 29, 2014): www.npr.org/blogs/health/2014/01/29/267598868/ancient-plagues-dna-revived-from-a-1-500-year-old-tooth.

North, Joshua. "The Death Toll of Justinian's Plague and Its Effects on the Byzantine Empire." *Armstrong Undergraduate Journal of History* 3, 1 (January 2013): www.armstrong.edu/Initiatives/history_journal/history_journal_the_death_toll_of_justinians_plague_and_its_effects_on.

Rosen, William. Justinian's Flea: The First Great Plague and the Fall of the Roman Empire. New York: Penguin Books, 2008.

Than, Ker. "Two of History's Deadliest Plagues Were Linked, With Implica-tions for Another Outbreak: Scientists Discover a Link between the Justinian Plague and the Black Death." *National Geographic News* (January 29, 2014): http://news.nationalgeographic.com/news/2014/01/140129-justinian-plague-black-death-bacteria-bubonic-pandemic/ (Accessed 18 February 2015).

7. 1287: St. Lucia's Flood Creates a New Sea

Fagan, Brian. *The Little Ice Age: How Climate Made History, 1300–1850*. New York: Basic Books, 2000.

Harrabin, Roger. "Careless Farming Adding to Floods." *BBC News* (6 March 2014): www.bbc.com/news/science-environment-26466653.

Information Britain. "Deadly Storm Changes UK Coastline." www.information-britain.co.uk/famdates.php?id=1205.

Kentucky Geological Survey. "How Is Coal Formed?" www.uky.edu/KGS/coal/coalform.htm (accessed 7 May 2014).

Medieval Sourcebook: Tables on Population in Medieval Europe. www.fordham.edu/halsall/source/pop-in-eur.asp (accessed 17 October 2013).

Shorto, Russell. "How to Think Like the Dutch in a Post-Sandy World." *NYT Magazine* (April 9, 2014): www.nytimes.com/2014/04/13/magazine/how-to-think-like-the-dutch-in-a-post-sandy-world.html.

TeBrake, William H. "Taming the Waterwolf: Hydraulic Engineering and Water Management in the Netherlands during the Middle Ages." *Technology and Culture* 43, 3 (July 2002): 475–499.

Van Dam, Petra J. E. M. "Sinking Peat Bogs: Enviornmental [*sic*] Change Holland, 1350–1550." *Environmental History* 6, 1 (Jan., 2001): 32–45.

Wikipedia. St. Lucia's Flood. http://en.wikipedia.org/wiki/St._Lucia%27s_flood.

Zwart, Hub. "Aquaphobia, Tulipmania, Biophilia: A Moral Geography of the Dutch Landscape." *Environmental Values* 12, 1 (February 2003): 107–128.

Additional Resources

The Consequences of a Flood Disaster. Zuiderzee Museum. www.zuiderzeemuseum.nl/en/132/news/the-consequences-of-a-flood-disaster/ ?id=3195.

USGS. "Peat." http://minerals.usgs.gov/minerals/pubs/commodity/peat/ (accessed 6/7/2014).

USGS Energy Resources Program. "Peat." http://energy.usgs.gov/Coal/Peat.aspx#378846-overview (accessed 6/7/2014).

8. 1315–17: Great Famine Starves Northwestern Europe

Wallace S. Broecker, "Was the Medieval Warm Period Global?" *Science*, New Series, 291, No. 5508 (Feb. 23, 2001): 1497–1499.

Crowley, Thomas J. and Thomas S. Lowery. "How Warm Was the Medieval Warm Period?" *Ambio* 29, 1 (Feb., 2000): 51–54.

de Blij, H.J. "*The Little Ice Age: How Climate Made History, 1300–1850* by Brian Fagan" [Review], *Annals of the Association of American Geographers* 92, No. 2 (June 2002): 377–379.

Fagan, Brian. *The Little Ice Age: How Climate Made History, 1300–1850.* New York: Basic Books, 2000.

Maasch, Kirk A. "What Triggers Ice Ages?" *PBS Nova* (1 January 1997). www.pbs.org/wgbh/nova/earth/cause-ice-age.html.

Matthews, John A., and Keith R. Briffa. "The 'Little Ice Age': Re-Evaluation of an Evolving Concept." *Geografiska Annaler* Series A, Physical Geography, 87, 1 (2005): 17–36.

Medieval Sourcebook: Tables on Population in Medieval Europe. www.fordham.edu/halsall/source/pop-in-eur.asp (accessed 17 October 2013).

Rosen, William. The Third Horseman: Climate Change and the Great Famine of the 14th Century (New York: Viking, 2014).

Jeff Tollefson, "The 8,000-year-old Climate Puzzle," *Nature* (25 March 2011): www.nature.com/news/2011/110325/full/news.2011.184.html.

Wikipedia. "Holocene." http://en.wikipedia.org/wiki/Holocene.

Additional Resources

El Niño: Making Sense of the Weather. http://kids.earth.nasa.gov/archive/nino/intro.html.

United States National Oceanic and Atmospheric Administration. NOAA Ocean Service Education. "The Global Conveyor Belt." http://oceanservice.noaa.gov/education/tutorial_currents/05conveyor2.html.

United States National Oceanic and Atmospheric Administration. "Climate.gov: Science and Information for a Climate-Smart Nation." www.climate.gov/.

9. 1348–1353: The Black Death Depopulates Europe

Byrne, Joseph P. *Daily Life during the Black Death.* Westport, CT: Greenwood Press, 2006.

Herlihy, David. *The Black Death and the Transformation of the West*. Cambridge: Harvard University Press, 1997.

Medieval Sourcebook: Tables on Population in Medieval Europe. www.fordham.edu/halsall/source/pop-in-eur.asp (accessed 2 November 2013).

Morelli, G., *et al*. "Phylogenetic Diversity and Historical Patterns of Pandemic Spread of *Yersinia Pestis*." *Nature Genetics* 42, 12 (December 2010): 1140–43. www.ncbi.nlm.nih.gov/pmc/articles/PMC2999892/ (accessed 18 September 2013).

Porter, Stephen. *The Great Plague* (Stroud, Gloucestershire: Sutton Publishing, 1999).

Thirsk, Joan. Alternative Agriculture: A History from the Black Death to the Present Day (New York: Oxford University Press, 1997).

Wagner, David M., *et al*. "*Yersinia pestis* and the Plague of Justinian 541-543 AD: A Genomic Analysis." *The Lancet* (January 28, 2014): http://eeid.cornell.edu/files/2012/12/Wagner-1te9if4.pdf (accessed 18 February 2015).

Wheelis, M. "Biological Warfare at the 1346 Siege of Caffa." *Emerging Infectious Diseases* 8, 9 (September 2002). wwwnc.cdc.gov/eid/article/8/9/01-0536.htm (accessed 2 November 2013).

Wheeler, Kip. "The Black Death: Did It Save English?" web.cn.edu/Kwheeler/ppt/Black_Death_Language.ppt (accessed 2 November 2013).

Wikipedia. Black Death. http://en.wikipedia.org/wiki/Black_Death.

10. 1450: Little Ice Age Empties a Viking Colony

Di Bacco, Mario, *et al*. "The Effect of an Unbalanced Demographic Structure on Marriage and Fertility Patterns in Isolated Populations: The Case of Norse Settlements in Greenland." *Genus* 62, 1 (2006): 97–119.

Diamond, Jared. Collapse: How Societies Choose to Fail or Succeed (New York: Penguin, 2011).

Fagan, Brian. *The Little Ice Age: How Climate Made History, 1300–1850* (New York: Basic Books, 2000).

Hebsgaard, Martin B., *et al*. "'The Farm Beneath the Sand'—an Archaeological Case Study on Ancient 'Dirt' DNA." *Antiquity* 83 (2009): 430–444.

Kolbert, Elizabeth. *The Sixth Extinction: An Unnatural History* (New York: Henry Holt, 2014).

McGovern, Thomas H. "Climate, Correlation, and Causation in Norse Greenland." *Arctic Anthropology* 28, No. 2 (1991): 77–100.

Panagiotakopulu, Eva, Peter Skidmore, and Paul Buckland. "Fossil Insect Evidence for the End of the Western Settlement in Norse Greenland." *Naturwissenschaften* 94 (2007): 300–306

Stockinger, Günther. "Abandoned Colony in Greenland: Archaeologists Find Clues to Viking Mystery," translated by Christopher Sultan, *Der Spiegel*, 10 January 2013, www.spiegel.de/international/zeitgeist/archaeologists-uncover-clues-to-why-vikings-abandoned-greenland-a-876626.html (accessed 24 January 2014).

Additional Resources

North Atlantic Biocultural Organization: www.nabohome.org/.

Vikings: The North Atlantic Saga. Smithsonian National Museum of Natural History. www.mnh.si.edu/vikings/.

11. 1507–1537: Smallpox Conquers the Western Hemisphere

Giblin, James Cross. *When Plague Strikes: The Black Death, Smallpox, AIDS*. New York: HarperCollins, 1995.

Henderson, D. A. *Smallpox: The Death of a Disease*. Amherst, NY: Prometheus Books, 2009.

Mann, Charles C. *1491: New Revelations of the Americas before Columbus*, 2d ed. New York: Vintage Books, 2011.

Oldstone, Michael B. A. *Viruses, Plagues, and History*. New York: Oxford University Press, 1998.

Wikipedia. "Bartolomé de las Casas." http://en.wikipedia.org/wiki/Bartolom%C3%A9_de_las_Casas (accessed 4 June 2014).

Additional Resources

"Defeat of the Inca Empire Conquistador" [film clip], Splash ABC, http://splash.abc.net.au/home#!/media/533424/conquistador-conquest-defeat-of-the-inca-empire.

Russo, Ralph. "Multiple Perspectives on the Spanish Invasion of Mexico." Yale National Institute to Strengthen Teaching in Public Schools. http://teachers.yale.edu/curriculum/viewer/initiative_05.02.07_u.

"The Story of . . . Smallpox—and Other Deadly Eurasian Germs." Variables, WGBH. www.pbs.org/gunsgermssteel/variables/smallpox.html.

12. 1556: Deadliest Earthquake Ever Levels Shaanxi

Britannica. "Shaanxi Province Earthquake of 1556." britannica.com/EBchecked/topic/1483629/Shaanxi-province-earthquake-of-1556.

Smith, Roff. "The Biggest One." *Nature* 465, 6 (May 6 2010): 24–25.

Stone, Richard "China Grapples with Seismic Risk in Its Northern Heartland." *Science*, New Series 313, 5787 (August 4, 2006): 599.

United States Geological Survey. "Earthquakes with 50,000 or More Deaths." https://web.archive.org/web/20140820090633/http://earthquake.usgs.gov/earthquakes/world/most_destructive.php (accessed 7 July 2015).

USGS Earthquake Hazards Program, "Measuring the Size of an Earthquake," http://earthquake.usgs.gov/learn/topics/measure.php (accessed 7 July 2015).

USGS Earthquake Hazards Program, "The Modified Mercalli Intensity Scale," http://earthquake.usgs.gov/learn/topics/mercalli.php (accessed 7 July 2015).

USGS Earthquake Hazards Program, Seismic Glossary, "seismic moment," http://earthquake.usgs.gov/learn/glossary/?term=seismic%20moment (accessed 7 July 2015).

Wang, Jian "Historical Earthquake Investigation and Research in China," *Annals of Geophysics* 47 (April/June 2004): 831–38.

Wikipedia. Shaanxi Earthquake. http://en.wikipedia.org/wiki/1556_Shaanxi_earthquake.

Yeats, Robert. *Active Faults of the World*. New York: Cambridge University Press, 2012.

Yoon, Hong-key. "Loess Cave-Dwellings in Shaanxi Province, China." *GeoJournal* 21, 1/2 (May/June 1990): 95–102.

Zhang Zhenzhong and Wang Lanmin. "Geological Disasters in Loess Areas during the 1920 Haiyuan Earthquake, China." *GeoJournal* 36, 2/3 (June/July 1995): 269–74.

Additional Resources

"Deadliest Earthquake in History Rocks China." This Day in History. www.history.com/this-day-in-history/deadli-est-earthquake-in-history-rocks-china.

Disaster Pages of Dr. George Pararis-Carayannis: www.drgeorgepc.com/EarthquakesChina.html.

Science Museum of China, Museum of Earthquakes: www.kepu.net.cn/english/quake/ruins/rns03.html.

"Yaodong, a Little Treatise on Construction." http://vimeo.com/69690514.

13. 1600: Huaynaputina Erupts in Peru

de Silva, Shanaka, Jorge Alzueta, and Guido Salas. "The Socioeconomic Consequences of the A.D. 1600 Eruption of Huaynaputina, Southern Peru." In *Volcanic Hazards and Disasters in Human Antiquity*, ed. Floyd W. McCoy and Grant Heiken, 15–24. Boulder, CA: Geological Society of America, 2000.

Duncan, M., D. K. Chester and J. E. Guest. "Mount Etna Volcano: Environmental Impact and Problems of Volcanic Prediction." *The Geographical Journal* 147, 2 (July 1981): 164–178.

Mann, Charles. *1491: New Revelations of the Americas before Columbus*, 2d ed. New York: Vintage, 2011.

Thouret, Jean-Claude and Jasmine Davila. "Large-Scale Explosive Eruption at Huaynaputina Volcano, 1600 AD, Southern Peru." *Fourth ISAG, Goettingen (Germany), 04-06/10/1999*, 758–760.

Witze, Alexandra. "The Volcano That Changed the World: Eruption in 1600 May Have Plunged the Globe into Cold Climate Chaos." *Nature* (11 April 2008). www.nature.com/news/2008/080411/full/news.2008.747.html.

Additional Resources

Bagley, Mary. "Mt. Etna: Facts about Volcano's Eruptions." *LiveScience* (25 February 2013). www.livescience.com/27421-mount-etna.html (accessed 25 January 2014).

"Etna." Italy's Volcanoes. www.italysvolcanoes.com/ETNA_1669.html (accessed 25 January 2014).

"This Dynamic Planet." Smithsonian Institution, dynamic online map: http://nmnh-arcgis01.si.edu/thisdynamicplanet/ (accessed 7 July 2015).

14. 1616–1619: Epidemic Readies Massachusetts for English Settlement

d'Errico, Peter. "Jeffrey Amherst and Smallpox Blankets" (2010). http://people.umass.edu/derrico/amherst/lord_jeff.html (accessed 4 November 2013).

Giblin, James Cross. *When Plague Strikes: The Black Death, Smallpox, AIDS*. New York: HarperCollins, 1995.

Gill, Harold B., Jr. "Colonial Germ Warfare." *Colonial Williamsburg Journal* (Spring 2004). www.history.org/foundation/journal/spring04/warfare.cfm (accessed 4 November 2013).

Henderson, D. A. *Smallpox: The Death of a Disease*. Amherst, NY: Prometheus Books, 2009.

Mann, Charles C. *1491: New Revelations of the Americas before Columbus*, 2d ed. New York: Vintage Books, 2011.

Marr, J. S. and J. T. Cathey. "New Hypothesis for Cause of an Epidemic among Native Americans, New England, 1616–1619." *Emerging Infectious Diseases* 16, 2 (2010 Feb): wwwnc.cdc.gov/eid/article/16/2/09-0276.htm.

15. 1666: The Great Fire of London— Papist Plot Burns Out the Plague?

Cooper, Michael. 'A More Beautiful City': Robert Hooke and the Rebuilding of London after the Great Fire (London: Sutton Publishing, 2003).

Hanson, Neil. The Great Fire of London in That Apocalyptic Year, 1666 (New York: John Wiley & Sons, 2002).

Additional Resources

Fire of London Game. www.fireoflondon. org.uk/.

Fly through 17th Century London. http:// londonist.com/2013/10/fly-through-17th-century-london.php.

Museum of London. "What Happened in the Great Fire of London?" www. museumoflondon.org.uk/explore-online/pocket-histories/what-happened-great-fire-london/.

Museum of London. "A History of London in 10 Archaeological Objects." http:// blog.museumoflondon.org.uk/a-histo-ry-of-london-in-10-archaeological-ob-jects-object-8/.

Schofield, John. "London after the Great Fire." BBC. www.bbc.co.uk/history/british/civil_war_revolution/after_fire_01.shtml.

16. 1755: Earthquake in Lisbon Shakes Europe's Philosophers

Aguirre, Benigno E. "Better Disaster Statistics: The Lisbon Earthquake." Journal of Interdisciplinary History 43, 1 (Summer, 2012): 27–42.

Chester, David K., and Olivia K. Chester. "The Impact of Eighteenth Century Earthquakes on the Algarve Region, Southern Portugal." The Geographical Journal 176, 4 (December 2010): 350–370.

Neiman, Susan. Evil in Modern Thought: An Alternative History of Philosophy. Princeton, NJ: Princeton University Press, 2002.

Shrady, Nicholas. The Last Day: Wrath, Ruin & Reason in the Great Lisbon Earth-quake of 1755. New York: Penguin, 2008.

Additional Resources

"The Lisbon Earthquake." Lisbon Guide. www.lisbon-guide.info/about/lisbon_earthquake.

U.S. Geological Survey. "Historic Earthquakes." http://earthquake. usgs.gov/earthquakes/world/events/1755_11_01.php.

U.S. NWS Pacific Tsunami Warning Center. "Tsunami Animation for the Great Lisbon Earthquake of 1755." https:// www.youtube.com/watch?v=_TrTZ-YfMYhI.

17. 1815: Mt. Tambora Takes More Lives Than the Battle of Waterloo

Cao, Shuji, Yushang Li, and Bin Yang. "Mt. Tambora, Climatic Changes, and China's Decline in the Nineteenth Century." Journal of World History 23, 3 (2012): 587–607.

Klingaman, William K. and Nicholas P. Klingaman. The Year Without Sum-mer: 1816 and the Volcano That Dark-ened the World and Changed History. New York: St. Martin's Press, 2013.

Oppenheimer, Clive. "Climatic, Environ-mental and Human Consequences of the Largest Known Historic Eruption: Tambora Volcano (Indonesia) 1815." Progress in Physical Geography 27, 2 (2003): 230–259.

Sigurdsson, Haraldur. Melting the Earth: The History of Ideas on Volcanic Eruptions.

New York: Oxford University Press, 1999.

Von Storch, Hans, and Nico Stehr. "Anthropogenic Climate Change: A Reason for Concern since the 18th Century and Earlier." *Geografiska Annaler* 88, 2 (2006): 107–13.

Additional Resources

Evans, Robert. "Blast from the Past: The Eruption of Mount Tambora Killed Thousands," *Smithsonian Magazine* (July 2002): www.smithsonianmag.com/history/blast-from-the-past-65102374/?no-ist.

McNamara, Robert, "Mount Tambora Was the Largest Volcanic Eruption of 19th Century." About Education. http://history1800s.about.com/od/crimes-anddisasters/a/Eruption-Of-Mount-Tambora.htm.

"Tambora Volcano." Volcano Discovery. www.volcanodiscovery.com/tambora.html.

18. 1817: Colonialism Helps Cholera Go Global

Arnold, David. "Cholera and Colonialism in British India." *Past & Present* 113 (Nov., 1986): 118–151.

Borroto, René J. "Global Warming, Rising Sea Level, and Growing Risk of Cholera Incidence: A Review of the Literature and Evidence." *GeoJournal* 44, 2 (1998): 111–120.

Centers for Disease Control. "Cholera—*Vibrio cholerae* Infection." www.cdc.gov/cholera/illness.html.

Centers for Disease Control and Prevention. Travelers' Health. wwwnc.cdc.gov/travel/yellowbook/2014/chapter-3-infectious-diseases-related-to-travel/cholera.

Clark, Gregory. "Farm Wages and Living Standards in the Industrial Revolution: England, 1670–1850." www.econ.ucdavis.edu/faculty/gclark/papers/farm_wages_&_living_standards.pdf.

Colwell, Rita R. "Global Climate and Infectious Disease: The Cholera Paradigm." *Science, New Series* 274, 5295 (December 20, 1996): 2025–2031.

Colwell, Rita R. "Cholera Outbreaks and Ocean Climate." *Social Research* 73, 3 (2006): 753–760.

DiRita, Victor J. "Genomics Happens." *Science, New Series* 289, 5484 (September 1, 2000): 1488–1489.

Evans, Richard J. "Epidemics and Revolutions: Cholera in Nineteenth-Century Europe." *Past & Present* 120 (August 1988): 123–146.

Greenberg, D. "Two Historic World-Pestilences Robbed of Their Terrors by Modern Sanitation." *The Scientific Monthly* 4, 6 (Jun., 1917): 554–566.

Lacey, Stephen W. "Cholera: Calamitous Past, Ominous Future." *Clinical Infectious Diseases* 20, 5 (May, 1995): 1409–1419.

Roos, Robert. "Cholera Has Struck More Than 6% of Haitians." Center for Infectious Disease Research and Policy (January 9, 2013). www.cidrap.umn.edu/news-perspective/2013/01/cholera-has-struck-more-6-haitians.

Sahadeo, Jeff. "Epidemic and Empire: Ethnicity, Class, and "Civilization" in the 1892 Tashkent Cholera Riot." *Slavic Review* 64, 1 (Spring, 2005): 117–139.

Wade, Nicholas. "Gene Sleuths Find How Some Naturally Resist Cholera." *New York Times* (3 July 2013): www.nytimes.com/2013/07/04/health/gene-sleuths-find-how-some-naturally-resist-cholera.html.

Wikipedia. "Burke and Hare Murders." http://en.wikipedia.org/wiki/Burke_and_Hare_murders (accessed 1 June 2014).

Additional Resources

Ball, Laura. "Cholera and the Pump on Broad Street: The Life and Legacy of John Snow." *The History Teacher* 43, 1 (November, 2009), 105–119.

Centers for Disease Control and Prevention. "Cholera." www.cdc.gov/cholera/general/index.html.

The John Snow Site. "Who First Discovered *Vibrio cholerae*?" www.ph.ucla.edu/epi/snow/firstdiscoveredcholera.html.

World Health Organization. "Cholera." www.who.int/topics/cholera/en/.

19. 1845–52: The Irish Potato Famine Sows Bitterness and Distrust

Gray, Peter. "The Irish Poor Law and the Great Famine." IEHC 2006 Helsinki Session 123. www.academia.edu/419878/The_Irish_poor_law_and_the_Great_Famine.

Kelly, John. *The Graves Are Walking: The Great Famine and the Saga of the Irish People* (New York: Picador, 2012).

McNeill, William H. "How the Potato Changed the World's History." *Social Research* 66, 1 (1999): 67–83.

Metress, Seamus P. "The History of Irish-American Care of the Aged." *Social Service Review* 59, 1 (March, 1985): 18–31.

Additional Resources

Bigelow, Bill. "Hunger on Trial: An Activity on the Irish Potato Famine and Its Meaning for Today." http://zinnedproject.org/materials/hunger-on-trial/.

"Forced to Flee: Famine and Plague." Lesson Plan Library, Discovery Education. www.discoveryeducation.com/teachers/free-lesson-plans/forced-to-flee-famine-and-plague.cfm.

"Irish Potato Famine." Teaching Resources, TES Connect. https://www.tes.co.uk/teaching-resource/irish-potato-famine-6129532.

"A Very Sad Period in Irish History." *Faces of America with Henry Louis Gates, Jr.* PBS. www.pbs.org/wnet/facesofamerica/lessons/they%E2%80%99re-coming-to-america-immigrants-past-and-present/video-segments/25/.

20. 1871: Irish Poor Blamed for Burning of Dry, Windy Chicago

Hemphill, Stephanie. "Peshtigo: A Tornado of Fire Revisited." Minnesota Public Radio (27 November 2002): http://news.minnesota.publicradio.org/features/200211/27_hemphills_peshtigofire/.

Horton, Madelyn. *Mother Jones.* San Diego: Lucent, 1996.

Murphy, Jim. *The Great Fire.* New York: Scholastic, 1995.

Additional Resources

Boda, John. "Great Chicago Fire 1871." Weather Channel [video]: https://www.youtube.com/watch?v=a3Q3w-wRAGiw.

The Great Chicago Fire and the Web of Memory. www.greatchicagofire.org/.

"People & Events: The Great Fire of 1871." American Experience. WGBH. www.pbs.org/wgbh/amex/chicago/peopleevents/e_fire.html

21. 1878: Yellow Fever in the American South

Centers for Disease Control and Prevention. "Yellow Fever." www.cdc.gov/yellow-fever/symptoms/index.html (accessed 22 October 2013).

Ellis, John H. *Yellow Fever & Public Health in the New South.* Lexington: University of Kentucky, 1992.

"Timelines: Yellow Fever." The History of Vaccines. www.historyofvaccines.org/content/timelines/yellow-fever (accessed 4 June 2014).

Oldstone, Michael B. A. *Viruses, Plagues, and History.* New York: Oxford University Press, 1998.

Schladweiler, John. *Tracking Down the Roots of Our Sanitary Sewers.* Timelines (2011). www.sewerhistory.org/chronos/design_choices.htm (accessed 2 November2013).

World Health Organization. "Yellow Fever." www.who.int/csr/disease/yellowfev/en/ (accessed 22 October 1913).

World Health Organization. "Yellow Fever Factsheet." www.who.int/mediacentre/factsheets/fs100/en/ (accessed 4 June 2014).

Additional Resources

Louisiana State University, Hill Memorial Library. "Topic Guide to Yellow Fever (1853–1905)." www.lib.lsu.edu/collections/digital/dlnp/topic_guides/yellow_fever.html.

National Library of Medicine, National Institutes of Health. "The Silent War: Colombia's Fight against Yellow Fever." (1943 documentary about vaccination campaign during WWII, 10 minutes, b/w), www.youtube.com/watch?v=EohPRleYbvA&feature=youtube_gdata.

Piggott, Felice. "Yellow Fever: Resources for Teaching about the Yellow Fever Epidemic of 1793." http://newvisions.libguides.com/yellowfevers.

"The Great Fever." PBS. www.pbs.org/wgbh/amex/fever/peopleevents/e_1878.html.

Shapiro, Joel. "Lessons from America's Tropical Epidemic." *NPR* (26 February 2008): www.npr.org/templates/story/story.php?storyId=19241319.

22. 1883: Eruption of Krakatoa Drives Scientific Advance and Colonial Discord

"How Volcanoes Work: Krakatau, Indonesia (1883)." www.geology.sdsu.edu/how_volcanoes_work/Krakatau.html (accessed 26 September 2013).

Keys, David. *Catastrophe: An Investigation into the Origins of the Modern World.* New York: Ballentine, 1999.

van Sandick, R. A. "The Eruption of Krakatoa," in *The Indonesia Reader: History, Culture, Politics,* ed. Tineke Hellwig and Eric Tagliacozzo, 252–55. Durham, NC: Duke University Press, 2009.

Wikipedia. "Ethnic Groups in Indonesia." http://en.wikipedia.org/wiki/Ethnic_groups_in_Indonesia.

Winchester, Simon. *A Crack in the Edge of the World: America and the Great California Earthquake of 1906.* New York: Harper Perennial, 2006.

Winchester, Simon. *Krakatoa: The Day the World Exploded, August 27, 1883.* New York: Harper Perennial, 2003.

Additional Resources

BBC interview with Simon Winchester; audio account from survivor: www.bbc.co.uk/programmes/p0098gdy.

Clary, Renee, and James Wandersee. "Krakatoa Erupts!" *Science Teacher* 78, 9 (December 2011): 42–47.

Gregory, Jonathan. "Is Sea Level Lower Because of Krakatoa?" National Centre for Environmental Research, 2012. www.ncas.ac.uk/index.php/en/climate-blog/400-is-sea-level-lower-because-of-krakatoa.

23. 1887: The Yellow River Floods

Chen, Yunzhen, *et al.* "Socio-economic Impacts on Flooding: A 4000-Year History of the Yellow River, China." *AMBIO* 41 (2012): 682–698.

Fan, Hui, Haijun Huang and Thomas Zeng. "Impacts of Anthropogenic Activity on the Recent Evolution of the Huanghe (Yellow) River Delta." *Journal of Coastal Research* 22, 4 (July, 2006): 888+919–929.

Ma Junya and Tim Wright, "Sacrificing Local Interests: Water Control Policies of the Ming and Qing Governments and the Local Economy of Huaibei, 1495–1949." *Modern Asian Studies*, 47, 4 (July 2013): 1348–1376.

Walling, Desmond E. "Water: Provision and Control." *Geography* 74, 4 (October 1989): 356–358.

Wikipedia. "1887 Yellow River Flood." http://en.wikipedia.org/wiki/1887_Yellow_River_flood.

Additional Resources

Asia for Educators. http://afe.easia.columbia.edu/tps/1750.htm.

Kendall, Anthony. "China's Sorrow." *Damned Interesting.* www.damninteresting.com/chinas-sorrow/.

Hudec, Kate. "Dealing with the Deluge." PBS, Nova (March 26, 1996). www.pbs.org/wgbh/nova/earth/dealing-deluge.html.

24. 1889: The Honolulu Board of Health Burns Out Bubonic Plague

Carmichael, D. A. "Hawaiian Islands: Further Concerning Plague." *Public Health Reports* 15, 7 (16 February 1900): 360–61.

Echenberg, Myron. *Plague Ports: The Global Urban Impact of Bubonic Plague, 1894–1901.* New York University Press, 2007.

Jew Ho vs. Williamson, 103 F. 10, 1990. In Lawrence Gostin, *Public Health Law and Ethics: A Reader* (2002), www.publichealthlaw.net/Reader/docs/JewHo.pdf (accessed 3 November 2013).

Morelli, G., *et al.* "Phylogenetic Diversity and Historical Patterns of Pandemic Spread of *Yersinia Pestis.*" *Nature Genetics* 42, 12 (December 2010): 1140–43; www.ncbi.nlm.nih.gov/pmc/articles/PMC2999892/ (accessed 18 September 2013).

World Health Organization (WHO). "Plague." www.who.int/topics/plague/en/ (accessed 16 September 2013).

Additional Resources

Honolulu Advertiser, "The Black Plague of 1900," www.hawaiinewsnow.com/story/5080433/the-black-plague-of-1900.

Hōʻike o Haleakalā Curriculum, "Plagues Past and Present," www.hoikecurriculum.org/activity/plagues-past-and-present/.

25. 1902: Mt. Pelée Buries a City

Zebrowski, Eugene, Jr. The Last Days of St. Pierre: The Volcanic Disaster That Claimed Thirty Thousand Lives. New Brunswick, NJ: Rutgers University Press, 2002.

Simkin, Tom, Lee Siebert and Russell Blong. "Volcano Fatalities: Lessons from the Historical Record." *Science, New Series* 291, 5502 (January 12, 2001: 255.

Additional Resources

Nature, Place and Peoples of the Antilles' Bioregion: http://myweb.rollins.edu/jsiry/AntillesMaps.html (accessed 19 January 2014).

Montagne Pelée 1902 (Slide lecture): www.geo.mtu.edu/~gbluth/Teaching/GE4150/lecture_pdfs/L8_pelee.pdf.

26. 1906: San Francisco Shakes and Burns

U. S. Census. No. HS-7. "Population of the 75 Largest Cities: 1900–2000." www.census.gov/statab/hist/HS-07.pdf.

Winchester, Simon. *A Crack in the Edge of the World: America and the Great California Earthquake of 1906.* New York: Harper Perennial, 2006.

Additional Resources

"The Great 1906 Earthquake and Fires of San Francisco." http://mceer.buffalo.edu/1906_earthquake/san-francisco-earthquake.asp.

Library of Congress. "San Francisco Earthquake and Fire, April 18, 1906" [silent film footage, b/w]. www.loc.gov/item/00694425.

USGS, Earthquake Hazards Program. "The Great 1906 San Francisco Earthquake." http://earthquake.usgs.gov/regional/nca/1906/18april/index.php.

Virtual Museum of the City of San Francisco. "Great 1906 Earthquake and Fire." www.sfmuseum.net/1906/06.html.

27. 1908: Tunguska Asteroid Levels Forest in Siberia

Beatty, Kelly. "New Chelyabinsk Results Yield Surprises." *Sky and Telescope* (7 November 2013): www.skyandtelescope.com/community/skyblog/newsblog/New-Chelyabinsk-Results-Surprising-Sobering-231008971.html.

Brannen, Peter. "The Death of the Dinosaurs." *The New York Times* (January 31, 2015). www.nytimes.com/2015/02/01/opinion/sunday/the-death-of-the-dinosaurs.html.

Collins, G. S., *et al.* "Evidence that Lake Cheko Is Not an Impact Crater." *Terra Nova* 20 (2008): 165–68.

Kluger, Jeffrey. "The Man Who Guards the Planet" [profile of astronomer Don Yeomans]. *Time* (9 June 2014): 34–37.

Kolbert, Elizabeth. *The Sixth Extinction: An Unnatural History.* New York: Henry Holt, 2014.

Lerbekmo, J. F. "The Chicxulub-Shiva Extraterrestrial One-two Kller Punches to Earth 65 Million Years Ago." *Marine and Petroleum Geology* 49 (January 2014): 203–207.

Napier, Bill, and David Asher. "The Tunguska Impact Event and Beyond." *Astronomy and Geophysics* 50 (Feb 2009): 1.18–1.26.

NASA, Near Earth Object Program, NEO Basics. "Near-Earth Objects and Life on Earth." http://neo.jpl.nasa.gov/neo/life.html (accessed 4 June 2014).

NASA, Near Earth Object Program, NEO Basics. "Target Earth," http://neo.jpl.nasa.gov/neo/target.html.

NASA. "The Tunguska Explosion—100 Years Later." *Science News* (June 30 2008). http://science.nasa.gov/science-news/science-at-nasa/2008/30jun_tunguska/.

"Tunguska Explosion Conspiracy." Georgia Tech Conspiracy Wiki. https://web.archive.org/web/20131011013916/http://conspiracytheories.lmc.gatech.edu/index.php/Tunguska_Explosion_Conspiracy.

Watson, Nigel. "The Tunguska Event." *History Today* (July 2008), 7.

Wikipedia. "2014 AA." http://en.wikipedia.org/wiki/2014_AA (accessed 22 February 2015).

Additional Resources

Earth Impact Database. www.passc.net/EarthImpactDatabase/.

NASA ScienceCasts. "What Exploded Over Russia?" www.youtube.com/watch?v=-qZ6oiaSm00.

"Near Earth Objects Animation." Armagh Observatory. http://star.arm.ac.uk/neos/anim.html.

"Sentry Risk Table." NASA Near Earth Object Program. http://neo.jpl.nasa.gov/risk/.

28. 1918: Influenza Kills More Than World War I

Barry, John M. *The Great Influenza: The Story of the Deadliest Pandemic in History*. New York: Penguin, 2005.

Erkora, Anton. "Origins of the Spanish Influenza Pandemic (1918–1920) and Its Relation to the First World War." *Journal of Molecular and Genetic Medicine* 3, 2 (2009 December): 190–194. www.ncbi.nlm.nih.gov/pmc/articles/PMC2805838/ (accessed 20 January 2014)

Fanning, Patricia J. *Influenza and Inequality: One Town's Tragic Response to the Great Epidemic of 1918*. Amherst: University of Massachusetts Press, 2010.

The Great War: WWI Casualty and Death Tables. PBS. www.pbs.org/great-war/resources/casdeath_pop.html (accessed 20 January 2014).

Olson, Donald R., *et al.* "Epidemiological Evidence of an Early Wave of the 1918 Influenza Pandemic in New York City." *Proceedings of the National Academy of Sciences of the United States of America* 102, 31 (Aug. 2, 2005): 11059–63.

Taubenberger, Jeffery, and David M. Morens. "1918 Influenza: The Mother of All Pandemics." *Emerging Infectious Diseases* 12, 1 (January 2006). http://dx.doi.org/10.3201/eid1209.050979.

Additional Resources

The Great Pandemic: The United States in 1918–1919. www.flu.gov/pandemic/history/1918/ (accessed 20 January 2014).

The Deadly Virus: The Influenza Epidemic of 1918. www.archives.gov/exhibits/influenza-epidemic/ (accessed 20 January 2014)

29. 1919: The Great Molasses Flood Blamed on Anarchists

"233,000 Gallons of Molasses Spills into Honolulu Harbor Kausing Fish Kill." *Hawaii News Now* (September 10, 2013). www.hawaiinewsnow.com/story/23396971/faulty-pipe-caused-honolulu-harbor-molasses-spill

Daysog, Rick. "Molasses Spill Caused Massive Coral Die-off." *Hawaii News Now* (December 14, 2013): www.hawaiinewsnow.com/story/24189342/exclusive-molasses-spill-disastrous-for-coral.

Garcia, Oskar. "Hawaii Lawmakers Call for Changes after Molasses Spill." *Huffington Post* (January 27, 2014). www.

huffingtonpost.com/2014/01/27/ hawaii-law-molasses-spill_n_4677113. html.

Potter, Sean. "Retrospect: January 15, 1919: Boston Molasses Flood." *Weatherwise* 64, 1 (2011): 10–11.

Puleo, Steve. *Dark Tide: The Great Boston Molasses Flood of 1919.* Boston: New Beacon Press, 2004.

Puleo, Steve. "Death by Molasses." *American History* 35, 6 (2001): 60–66.

Additional Resources

Jabr, Ferris. "The Science of the Great Molasses Flood." *Scientific American* (July 17, 2013): www.scientificameri-can.com/article/molasses-flood-phys-ics-science/.

National Fire Protection Association. "The Great Boston Molasses Flood." www.nfpa.org/newsandpublications/ nfpa-journal/2011/may-june-2011/ features/the-great-boston-molasses-flood.

Travel Channel. "Boston's Great Molasses Flood." www.travelchannel.com/ video/bostons-great-molasses-flood.

30. 1923: Kanto Earthquake Flattens Tokyo and Yokohama; Koreans Massacred

Borland, Janet. "Capitalising on Catastro-phe: Reinvigorating the Japanese State with Moral Values through Education Following the 1923 Great Kantô Earthquake." *Modern Asian Studies* 40, 4 (October, 2006): 875–907.

Hammer, Joshua. "Aftershocks." *Smithsonian* 42, 2 (May 2011): 50–53.

Ishiguro, Yoshiaki. "A Japanese National Crime: The Korean Massacre after the Great Kanto Earthquake of 1923." *Korea Journal* 38, 4 (Winter 1998):

331–354. www.ekoreajournal.net/ issue/index2.htm?Idx=383#.

Ryang, Sonia. "The Great Kanto Earthquake and the Massacre of Koreans in 1923: Notes on Japan's Modern National Sovereignty." *Anthropological Quarterly* 76, 4 (Fall 2003): 731–748.

Schencking, J. Charles. "The Great Kanto Earthquake and the Culture of Catastrophe and Reconstruction in 1920s Japan." *Journal of Japanese Studies* 34, 2 (Summer, 2008): 295–331.

U. S. Geological Survey. "Historic Earth-quakes: Kanto (Kwanto), Japan." http:// earthquake.usgs.gov/earthquakes/ world/events/1923_09_01.php.

Additional Resources

Brown University Center for Digital Schol-arship. "The Great Kanto Earthquake of 1923." http://library.brown.edu/ cds/kanto/about.html.

Schencking, J. Charles. "The Great Kanto Earthquake of 1923." www.greatkan-toearthquake.com/.

31. 1938: Unpredicted Hurricane Batters New England

Allen, Everett S. *A Wind to Shake the World: The Story of the 1938 Hurricane.* Bev-erly, MA: Commonwealth Editions, 1976.

Gibson, Christine. "How the Hurricane Got Its Name." *American Heritage* 57, 4 (2006). www.americanheritage.com/ content/how-hurricane-got-its-name.

Gibson, Christine. "Our 10 Greatest Natural Disasters," *American Heritage* 57, 4 (2006). www.americanheritage.com/content/ our-10-greatest-natural-disasters.

"The Long Island Express: The Great Hurri-cane of 1938." www2.sunysuffolk. edu/mandias/38hurricane/.

National Weather Service. "The Great Hurricane of 1938." www.weather.gov/box/1938hurricane.

Scott, R. A. *Sudden Sea: The Great Hurricane of 1938*. Boston: Back Bay Books, 2003.

Smil, Vaclav. "The Next 50 Years: Fatal Discontinuities." *Population and Development Review* 31, 2 (June 2005): 201-36.

University of Rhode Island Graduate School of Oceanography. "Hurricanes: Science and Society." www.hurricanescience.org/history/timeline/#/?decade=pre1900.

WGBH, American Experience. "The Hurricane of '38, Interview: Norman Caswell." PBS. www.pbs.org/wgbh/americanexperience/features/interview/hurricane-norman-caswell/.

Additional Resources

NOAA Education Resources. www.education.noaa.gov/.

National Weather Service. "The Great New England Hurricane of 1938." www.weather.gov/okx/1938Hurricane-Home.

New York Times, The Learning Network. "Teaching Hurricane Sandy: Ideas and Resources." http://learning.blogs.nytimes.com/2012/10/30/teaching-hurricane-sandy-ideas-and-resources/?_php=true&_type=blogs&_r=0

WGBH, American Experience. "The Hurricane of '38." PBS. www.pbs.org/wgbh/americanexperience/features/trailer/hurricane-trailer/.

Works Progress Administration (WPA). "1938 Hurricane" [11-minute documentary newsreel]. www.youtube.com/watch?v=RA-3zULhCvM.

32. 1952: Killer Smog Shrouds London

Davenport, Coral. "Obama to Take Action to Slash Coal Pollution." *New York Times* (1 June 2014). www.nytimes.com/2014/06/02/us/politics/epa-to-seek-30-percent-cut-in-carbon-emissions.html.

International Energy Agency. "Coal." www.iea.org/topics/coal/ (accessed 5 June 2014).

Moretto, Mario. "Environmentalists Decry Proposal to Loosen Maine Smog Rules." *Bangor Daily News* (September 10, 2013). https://bangordailynews.com/2013/09/10/politics/environmentalists-decry-proposal-to-loosen-maine-smog-rules-paper-mill-officials-say-change-will-spur-job-creation/.

NASA, Earth Observatory. "How Is Today's Warming Different from the Past?" http://earthobservatory.nasa.gov/Features/GlobalWarming/page3.php.

Parris, Thomas M. "Smog Season." *Environment* (May 2006), 3.

United Nations Economic Commission for Europe (UNECE). *Convention on Long-Range Transboundary Air Pollution*. www.unece.org/env/lrtap/lrtap_h1.html (accessed 7 July 2015).

United Nations Treaty Collection. "Convention on Long-range Transboundary Air Pollution, Geneva, 13 November 1979." https://treaties.un.org/Pages/ViewDetails.aspx?src=TREATY&mtdsg_no=XXVII-1&chapter=27&lang=en (accessed 7 July 2015).

U.S. Energy Information Administration. "What Is U.S. Electricity Generation by Energy Source?" www.eia.gov/tools/faqs/faq.cfm?id=427&t=3 (accessed 5 June 2014).

U.S. Environmental Protection Agency, Clean Air Research. "Science to Protect the Air We Breathe" [video]. www.epa. gov/research/video/ca/index.html.

U.S. Environmental Protection Agency, Clean Energy. "Coal." www.epa.gov/ cleanenergy/energy-and-you/affect/ coal.html (accessed 5 June 2014).

United States Environmental Protection Agency. "History of Air Pollution." www.epa.gov/airscience/air-historyofairpollution.htm.

United States Environmental Protection Agency. "U.S. Canada Air Quality Agreement." www.epa.gov/airmarkets/ progsregs/usca/index.htm.

Wikipedia. "Coal." http://en.wikipedia.org/ wiki/Coal (accessed 5 June 2014).

Wikipedia. "1930 Meuse Valley Fog." http://en.wikipedia.org/wiki/1930_ Meuse_Valley_fog.

Wise, William. *Killer Smog: The World's Worst Air Pollution Disaster*. Chicago: Rand McNally, 1968.

World Health Organization, Regional Office for Europe. "Health Aspects of Long-Range Transboundary Air Pollution." www.euro.who.int/en/health-topics/ environment-and-health/air-quality/ activities/health-aspects-of-long-rangetransboundary-air-pollution.

Additional Resources

Damocles. "Animation about the Greenhouse Effect." www.damocles-eu.org/ education/Animation_about_the_ greenhouse_effect_182.shtml.

Met Office. "The Great Smog of 1952." www.metoffice.gov.uk/education/ teens/case-studies/great-smog.

"Mystery Fog Engulfs Nigerian City." BBC News (October 12, 2005) news.bbc. co.uk/2/hi/africa/4335550.stm.

"Nigeria: The Lagos Mystery Fog." AllAfrica.com (October 27, 2005): allafrica. com/stories/200510280254.html.

Pennsylvania Historical and Museum Commission. "The Donora Smog Disaster, October 30–31, 1948." www.portal.state.pa.us/portal/ server.pt/community/documents_ from_1946_-_present/20426/ donora_smog_disaster/999079.

"Smog Deaths in 1948 Led to Clean Air Laws." NPR. www.npr.org/templates/ story/story.php?storyId=103359330.

U.S. Environmental Protection Agency, Clean Air Research. "Science to Protect the Air We Breathe." www.epa.gov/ research/video/ca/index.html.

World Health Organization. "Chapter 11, Polluted Cities: The Air Children Breathe." In *Inheriting the World: The Atlas of Children's Health and the Environment*, 28–29. www.who.int/ceh/ publications/11airpollution.pdf?ua=1.

33. 1968–1985: Drought in the Sahel Starves Sub-Saharan Africa

Batterbury, Simon. "The Sahel Region: Assessing Progress 25 Years after the Great Drought." www.simonbatterbury. net/pubs/geogmag.html.

Bonnifield, Paul. *The Dust Bowl: Men, Dirt, and Depression*. Albuquerque: University of New Mexico Press, 1979.

Butzer, K.W. "Paleo-Environmental Perspectives on the Sahel Drought of 1968–73," *GeoJournal* 7, 4 (1983): 369–374.

"The Dust Bowl Returns." *New York Times* (February 10, 2014): www.nytimes. com/2014/02/10/opinion/the-dust-bowl-returns.html?_r=0.

Environment and Society Portal. "Sahel Drought and Famine, 1968–1985." www.environmentandsociety.org/ tools/keywords#/id/1865.

Held, I. M., *et al.* "Simulation of Sahel Drought in the 20th and 21st Centuries." *Proceedings of the National Acad-*

emy of Sciences of the United States of America 102, 50 (December 13, 2005): 17891–96.

IRIN News and Analysis. "Sahel: Backgrounder on the Sahel, West Africa's Poorest Region" (2 June 2008). www.irinnews.org/report/78514/sahel-backgrounder-on-the-sahel-west-africa-s-poorest-region.

National Drought Mitigation Center. "Drought in the Dust Bowl Years." http://drought.unl.edu/DroughtBasics/DustBowl/DroughtintheDustBowlYears.aspx.

NOAA. "North American Drought: A Paleo Perspective." www.ncdc.noaa.gov/paleo/drought/drght_home.html.

Sollod, Albert E. "Rainfall Variability and Twareg Perceptions of Climate Impacts in Niger." Human Ecology 18, 3 (September 1990): 267–281.

United Nations Environmental Programme, Africa Environment Outlook. "West Africa." www.unep.org/dewa/Africa/publications/AEO-1/056.htm.

"UN Seeks $2 Billion in International Aid for Africa's Sahel Region." U.N. News Centre (3 February 2014): un.org/apps/news/story.asp/html/realfile/story.asp?NewsID=47065&Cr=sahel&Cr1=#.UwDyvJWPI5s.

U.S. House of Representatives, Natural Resources Committee. "The Man-Made California Drought." http://natural-resources.house.gov/issues/issue/?IssueID=5921 (accessed 7 July 2015).

U.S., NOAA. "January Precipitation Deficits Keep California Drought Outlook Grim." Climate.gov (February 7, 2014), www.climate.gov/news-features/event-tracker/january-precipitation-deficits-keep-california-drought-outlook-grim.

U.S., NOAA, Earth System Research Laboratory. "El Niño/Southern Oscillation (ENSO)." www.esrl.noaa.gov/psd/enso/.

Zeng, Ning. "Drought in the Sahel." Science, New Series 302, 5647 (November 7, 2003): 999–1000.

Additional Resources

Al Jazeera. "Analysis: Understanding the Sahel Drought." www.aljazeera.com/indepth/spotlight/saheldrought/2012/06/2012616174721352901.html.

Jeffries, Michael. "The Great Depression, Displaced Mountaineers, and the C.C.C." YouTube. www.youtube.com/watch?v=2jvbTwxdbvE.

Library of Congress, American Memory. "Voices from the Dust Bowl." http://memory.loc.gov/ammem/afctshtml/tshome.html.

"NASA Explains the Dust Bowl Drought." nasa.gov/centers/goddard/news/topstory/2004/0319dustbowl.html.

Oklahoma Historical Society. "Dust Bowl." okhistory.org/publications/enc/entry.php?entry=DU011

PBS. "American Experience: Surviving the Dust Bowl." www.pbs.org/wgbh/americanexperience/features/introduction/dustbowl-introduction/.

PBS. "The Dust Bowl: A Film by Ken Burns." www.pbs.org/kenburns/dustbowl/.

USAID Famine Early Warning Systems Net. http://earlywarning.usgs.gov/adds/index.php.

United Nations Environmental Programme, UNEP Regional Office for Africa. www.unep.org/roa/.

Vital Climate Graphics Africa. www.grida.no/publications/vg/africa/page/3109.aspx.

Wessels Living History Farm. "Farming in the 1930s." www.livinghistoryfarm.org/farminginthe30s/water_02.html.

34. 1970–75: Smallpox Eradicated in Bangladesh

Fenner, F., *et al*. *Smallpox and Its Eradication*. History of International Public Health, No. 6. Geneva: World Health Organization, 1988. http://whqlibdoc.who.int/smallpox/9241561106.pdf.

Giblin, James Cross. *When Plague Strikes: The Black Death, Smallpox, AIDS*. New York: HarperCollins, 1995.

Gill, Jr., Harold B. "Colonial Germ Warfare." *Colonial Williamsburg Journal* (Spring 2004). www.history.org/foundation/journal/spring04/warfare.cfm (accessed 4 November 2013).

Henderson, D. A. *Smallpox: The Death of a Disease*. Amherst, NY: Prometheus Books, 2009.

Additional Resources

Center for Global Development. "Case 1: Eradicating Smallpox." cgdev.org/page/case-1-eradicating-smallpox.

College of Physicians of Philadelphia. "Disease Eradication." *The History of Vaccines*. www.historyofvaccines.org/content/articles/disease-eradication.

World Health Organization. "Global Alert and Response, Smallpox." www.who.int/csr/disease/smallpox/en/.

35. 1976: Earthquake Wipes Out Chinese City of Tangshan as Mao Lies Dying

Chen, Xiangming, Dai Kejing, and Allan Parnell. "Disaster Tradition and Change: Remarriage and Family Reconstruction in a Post-Earthquake Community in the People's Republic of China." *Journal of Comparative Family Studies* 23, 1 (Spring 1992): 115–132.

"Museum Built for Tangshan Quake." *China Today* (January 2011): 8.

Palmer, James. *Heaven Cracks, Earth Shakes: The Tangshan Earthquake and the Death of Mao's China*. New York: Basic Books, 2012.

Waldron, Arthur. "Starving in China." *The New Criterion* (May 2013): 4–8.

Zhang, Hon-Can, and Yi-Jong Zhang. "Psychological Consequences of Earthquake Disaster Survivors." *International Journal of Psychology* 26, 5 (November 1991): 613–621.

Zhao, Shaorong and Shuzo Takemoto. "Aseismic Fault Movement before the 1976 Tangshan Earthquake Detected by Levelling: Implications for Pre-seismic Stress Localization?" *Geophysical Journal International* 136 (1999): 68–82.

Additional Resources

Earnshaw, Grahame. "Tangshan Earthquake Survivors in Terror of New Quake" (November 2, 1983): *Danwei*, www.danwei.org/the_earnshaw_vault/remembering_the_tangshan_earth.php.

"Tangshan: The Deadliest Earthquake." AboutEducation. http://history1900s.about.com/od/horribledisasters/a/tangshan.htm

Wang Fang. "Historic Earthquakes: The 1976 Tangshan Earthquake." USGS Earthquake Hazards Program, http://earthquake.usgs.gov/earthquakes/world/events/1976_07_27_eib.php.

36. 1981: Mystery Disease, AIDS, Becomes a Dreaded Pandemic

Engel, Jonathan. *The Epidemic: A Global History of Aids*. New York: HarperCollins, 2006.

McNeill, Fraser G. *AIDS, Politics, and Music in South Africa*. New York: Cambridge University Press, 2011.

Nattrass, Nicoli. *The AIDS Conspiracy: Science Fights Back*. New York: Columbia University Press, 2012.

United States, Aids.gov. "U.S. Statistics." http://aids.gov/hiv-aids-basics/hiv-aids-101/statistics/.

World Health Organization. "HIV/AIDS: Data and Statistics." www.who.int/hiv/data/en/.

World Health Organization. "South Africa: Health Profile." www.who.int/gho/countries/zaf.pdf?ua=1.

Additional Resources

Centers for Disease Control and Prevention. "HIV/AIDS." www.cdc.gov/hiv/

"Singing Songs of AIDS in South Africa." London School of Economics. www.lse.ac.uk/researchAndExpertise/researchHighlights/WorldRegionsAndDevelopment/singing_songs_of_AIDS.aspx.

Unicef. "Child Survival: HIV/AIDS." www.unicefusa.org/work/hivaids/?gclid=COmYza72gb0CFYc7Ogodln0AZA.

World Health Organization. "HIV/AIDS." www.who.int/hiv/en/

37. 1984: Leak from Insecticide Factory Poisons City of Bhopal

Bhattacharyar, Prasenjit. "Court Rules Union Carbide Not Liable in Bhopal Case." *Wall Street Journal* (June 28, 2012): http://online.wsj.com/news/articles/SB10001424052702303561504577493642502980690.

Bogard, William. *The Bhopal Tragedy: Language, Logic, and Politics in the Production of a Hazard*. Boulder, CO: Westview Press, 1989.

Dhara, V. Ramana, *et al.* "Personal Exposure and Long-Term Health Effects in Survivors of the Union Carbide Disaster at Bhopal." *Environmental Health Perspectives* 110, 5 (May, 2002): 487–500.

India Blooms News Service. "Bhopal Victims Protest for Clean Water" (February 17, 2014). www.indiablooms.com/NewsDetailsPage/2014/newsDetails170214d1.php.

International Food Policy Research Institute. *Green Revolution: Curse or Blessing?* www.ifpri.org/sites/default/files/pubs/pubs/ib/ib11.pdf.

Iyengar, Radhika, and Monisha Bajaj. "After the Smoke Clears: Toward Education for Sustainable Development in Bhopal, India." *Comparative Education Review* 55, 3 (August 2011): 424–56.

Morehouse, Ward and M. Arun Subramaniam. *The Bhopal Tragedy: What Really Happened and What It Means for American Workers and Communities at Risk*. New York: Council on International and Public Affairs, 1986.

"NGOs want Modi to take up issues of Bhopal gas tragedy victims with Obama." *Hindustan Times* (25 January 2015): www.hindustantimes.com/bhopal/ngos-want-modi-to-take-up-issues-of-bhopal-gas-tragedy-victims-with-obama/article1-1310623.aspx.

Rosencranz, Armin. "Bhopal, Transnational Corporations, and Hazardous Technologies." *Ambio* 17, 5 (1988): 336–41.

Trotter, R. Clayton, Susan G. Day and Amy E. Love. "Bhopal, India and Union Carbide: The Second Tragedy." *Journal of Business Ethics*, 8, 6 (Jun., 1989): 439–54.

U.S. Census Bureau, International Programs, Historical Estimates of World Population, https://www.census.gov/population/international/data/worldpop/table_history.php.

Wikipedia. "Bhopal Disaster." http://
en.wikipedia.org/wiki/Bhopal_disas-
ter#Legal_action_against_Union_
Carbide (accessed 17 February 2014).

Additional Resources

Bhopal and Chernobyl Disasters, Teaching Resources, TES, www.tes.co.uk/
teaching-resource/bhopal-and-cher-
nobyl-disasters-6136646.
"The Bhopal Memory Project." http://
bhopal.bard.edu/classroom/teaching.
shtml.
Bhopal Medical Appeal. www.bhopal.org/.
Union Carbide Corporation. www.union-
carbide.com/.

38. 1985: Nevado del Ruiz Eruption Buries Town of Armero on International TV

BBC. "Picture Power: Tragedy of Omayra
Sanchez." http://news.bbc.co.uk/2/
hi/4231020.stm.
Gaillard, Jean-Christophe. "Was it a *Cultural
Disaster? AETA Resilience Following
the 1991 Mt. Pinatubo Eruption." *Phil-
ippine Quarterly of Culture and Society*
34, 4 (December 2006): 376–99.
Hansell, A. L., C. J. Horwell and C.
Oppenheimer. "Education: The Health
Hazards of Volcanoes and Geothermal
Areas." *Occupational and Environmental Medicine* 63, 2 (February 2006):
149–56.
Johnson, Kirk. "After Mountain's Collapse,
Uncertainty and Loss." *New York Times*
(March 26, 2014): www.nytimes.
com/2014/03/27/us/washing-
ton-mudslide-search.html?hp&_r=0.
King, Hobart. "Novarupta: The Most Powerful Volcanic Eruption of the Twentieth Century." http://geology.com/
novarupta/.

Lima, Bruno R., *et al.* "Disasters and Mental
Health: Experience in Colombia and
Ecuador and Its Relevance for Primary
Care in Mental Health in Latin Amer-
ica." *International Journal of Mental
Health* 19, 2 (Summer 1990): 3–20.
Murray, M. "Scientists Predict Second Ruiz
Blast." *Science News* 129, 25 (June 21,
1986): 390–91.
Naranjo, J. L., *et al.* "Eruption of the Nevado
Del Ruiz Volcano, Colombia, on 13
November 1985: Tephra Fall and
Lahars." *Science*, New Series 233, 4767
(August 29, 1986): 961–63.
Thouret, Jean-Claude, and Christophe
Laforge. "Hazard Appraisal and Haz-
ard-Zone Mapping of Flooding and
Debris Flowage in the Rio Combeima
Valley and Ibague City, Tolima Depart-
ment, Colombia." *GeoJournal* 34, 4
(December 1994): 407–413.
Tobin, Graham A., and Linda M. White-
ford. "Provisioning Capacity: A Critical
Component of Vulnerability and Resil-
ience under Chronic Volcanic Erup-
tions." Chapter 8 in *Forces of Nature and
Cultural Responses*, ed. Katrin Pfeifer
and Niki Pfeifer, 139–166. New York:
Springer, 2013.
USGS, Hawaiian Volcano Observatory.
"Lessons Learned from the Armero,
Colombia Tragedy" (2009): http://
hvo.wr.usgs.gov/volcanowatch/
archive/2009/09_10_29.html.
Voight, Barry. "The 1985 Nevado del Ruiz
Volcano Catastrophe: Anatomy and
Retrospection." *Journal of Volcanology
and Geothermal Research* 44 (1990):
349–386.

Additional Resources

*The Eruption of the Nevado del Ruiz Vol-
cano—Colombia, 1985* [15-minute
documentary]. www.youtube.com/
watch?v=5KkylPM1oYU.

"How Volcanoes Work: Nevado Del Ruiz." www.geology.sdsu.edu/how_volcanoes_work/Nevado.html.

National Geophysical Data Center. *Teacher's Guide to Stratovolcanoes of the World.* www.ngdc.noaa.gov/hazard/stratoguide/nevadofact.html.

39. 1986: Meltdown at Chernobyl Nuclear Facility Leaves Dead Zone in Ukraine

Baverstock, Keith and Dillwyn Williams. "The Chernobyl Accident 20 Years on: An Assessment of the Health Consequences and the International Response." *Environmental Health Perspectives* 114, 9 (September, 2006): 1312–17.

Bennett, L. L. and R. Skjoeldebrand. "Pages from the Past: Nuclear Power Redux." *IAEA Bulletin* 50, 2 (May 2009), 58–60: www.iaea.org/Publications/Magazines/Bulletin/Bull502/50201215860.html.

Ginzburg, Harold M., and Eric Reis. "Consequences of the Nuclear Power Plant Accident at Chernobyl." *Public Health Reports* 106, 1 (January, 1991): 32–40.

Lomat, Leonid, *et al.* "Incidence of Childhood Disease in Belarus Associated with the Chernobyl Accident." *Environmental Health Perspectives* 105, Supplement 6: Radiation and Human Health (December, 1997): 1529–32.

Marples, David R. *The Social Impact of the Chernobyl Disaster.* New York: St. Martin's Press, 1988.

NEI Knowledge Center. "World Statistics: Nuclear Energy Around the World." www.nei.org/Knowledge-Center/Nuclear-Statistics/World-Statistics.

Osif, Bonnie A., Anthony J. Baratta, and Thomas W. Conkling. *TMI 25 Years Later: The Three Mile Island Nuclear Power Plant Accident and Its Impact.* University Park: The Pennsylvania State University Press, 2004.

Schmid, Sonja D. "Transformation Discourse: Nuclear Risk as a Strategic Tool in Late Soviet Politics of Expertise." *Science, Technology, & Human Values* 29, 3 (Summer, 2004): 353–76.

Snell, Victor. "The Cause of the Chernobyl Accident," Introduction, in David R. Marples, *The Social Impact of the Chernobyl Disaster*, 1–24. New York: St. Martin's Press, 1988.

U.S. Energy Information Administration, *Monthly Energy Review* (February 2014), 115: www.eia.gov/totalenergy/data/monthly/pdf/sec8.pdf.

U.S. NRC Backgrounder on Three Mile Island, nrc.gov/reading-rm/doc-collections/fact-sheets/3mile-isle.html.

Weinberg, Hava-Shifra, *et al.* "Molecular Changes in the Offspring of Liquidators Who Emigrated to Israel from the Chernobyl Disaster Area." *Environmental Health Perspectives* 105, Supplement 6: Radiation and Human Health (Dec., 1997), 1479–81.

Additional Resources

ABC. *Chernobyl: Revisiting the Nuclear Accident Site.* www.youtube.com/watch?v=ldYeFLZqh3Q.

Higginbotham, Adam. "Is Chernobyl a Wild Kingdom or a Radioactive Den of Decay?" *WIRED* (14 April 2011): www.wired.com/magazine/2011/04/ff_chernobyl/all/.

Live Science. "Chernobyl: Facts about the Nuclear Disaster." www.livescience.com/39961-chernobyl.html.

Morris, Holly. "After Chernobyl, They Refused to Leave" [special to CNN]. (November 7, 2013). www.cnn.com/2013/11/07/opinion/morris-ted-chernobyl/. See also www.ted.com/talks/holly_morris_why_stay_in_chernobyl_because_it_s_home.html.

New York Times, The Learning Network. "A Blast from the Past." http://learning.blogs.nytimes.com/2005/09/07/a-blast-from-the-past/.

PennState University Libraries. "Three Mile Island 2 Recovery and Decontamination Collection." www.libraries.psu.edu/psul/eng/tmi.html.

Physicians for Social Responsibility. *The Lessons of Fukushima and Chernobyl Briefing Book.* www.psr.org/resources/the-lessons-of-fukushima-and-chernobyl.html.

Science Net Links. "The Chernobyl Disaster." http://sciencenetlinks.com/lessons/the-chernobyl-disaster/.

Taylor, Alan. "The Chernobyl Disaster: 25 Years Ago." *The Atlantic* (March 23, 2011): www.theatlantic.com/photo/2011/03/the-chernobyl-disaster-25-years-ago/100033/.

Three Mile Island Emergency, Virtual Museum and Resource Center. www.threemileisland.org/index.html.

40. 1993: Arsenic in Bengali Drinking Water

Ayotte, Joseph D., Denise L. Montgomery, and Sarah M. Flanagan. "Arsenic in Groundwater in Eastern New England: Occurrence, Controls, and Human Health Implications." *Environmental Science & Technology* 37, 10 (2003): 2075–83.

Brown, Steven E. F. "Berkeley Lab Licenses Arsenic-Cleaning Technology to Indian Company." *San Francisco Business Times* (March 5, 2014). www.bizjournals.com/sanfrancisco/news/2014/03/05/berkeley-lab-licenses-arsenic-cleaning.html.

Central Intelligence Agency. "Bangladesh." *The World Fact Book.* https://www.cia.gov/library/publications/the-world-factbook/geos/bg.html.

Gadgil Lab for Energy and Water Research. "Arsenic Removal." http://gadgillab.berkeley.edu/research/water/arsenic_removal/.

"Luminous Water Technologies Licenses Berkeley Lab Invention for Arsenic Free Water in India, Bangladesh." *Business Standard* (March 28, 2014). www.business-standard.com/article/news-ani/luminous-water-technologies-licenses-berkeley-lab-invention-for-arsenic-free-water-in-india-bangladesh-114032100361_1.html.

Osnos, Evan. "Chemical Valley: The Coal Industry, the Politicians, and the Big Spill." *New Yorker* (April 7, 2014): www.newyorker.com/magazine/2014/04/07/chemical-valley (accessed 22 February 2015).

Salzman, James. *Drinking Water: A History.* New York: Overlook Duckworth, 2013.

Smith, Allan H., Elena O. Lingas, and Mahfuzar Rahman. "Contamination of Drinking-Water by Arsenic in Bangladesh: A Public Health Emergency." *Bulletin of the World Health Organization* 78, 9 (Jan. 2000), 1093–1103: www.who.int/bulletin/archives/78(9)1093.pdf.

UNICEF, Arsenic Mitigation in Bangladesh, www.unicef.org/bangladesh/Arsenic.pdf.

UNICEF, Bangladesh Overview, History, www.unicef.org/bangladesh/overview_4842.htm.

World Health Organization, Water Sanitation Health, Arsenic in Drinking Water, www.who.int/water_sanitation_health/dwq/arsenic/en/.

Additional Resources

Deborah Blum, "The Arsenic in Our Drinking Water," *New York Times* (September 20, 2013), http://well.blogs.nytimes.com/2013/09/20/the-arsenic-in-our-drinking-water/?_php=true&_type=blogs&_r=0.

Jefferson Lab, "The Element Arsenic," *It's Elemental: The Periodic Table of Elements*, http://education.jlab.org/itselemental/ele033.html.

41. 1996: Nigerians Resist a Polio Eradication Campaign

Oshinsky, David M. *Polio: An American Story*. New York: Oxford University Press, 2005.

Polio Global Eradication Initiative. "Circulating Vaccine-Derived Poliovirus 2000–2013." www.polioeradication.org/Dataandmonitoring/Poliothisweek/Circulatingvaccinederivedpoliovirus.aspx.

Renne, Elisha P. *The Politics of Polio in Northern Nigeria*. Bloomington: Indiana University Press, 2010.

United States Centers for Disease Control and Prevention. "Global Health: Nigeria." www.cdc.gov/globalhealth/countries/nigeria/why/default.htm.

United States Centers for Disease Control and Prevention. "A Polio-Free U.S. Thanks to Vaccine Efforts." www.cdc.gov/features/poliofacts/.

World Health Organization. "Nigeria: Health Profile." www.who.int/gho/countries/nga.pdf?ua=1.

World Health Organization. Poliomyelitis Fact Sheet. www.who.int/mediacentre/factsheets/fs114/en/.

World Health Organization. "What Is Vaccine-derived Polio?" www.who.int/features/qa/64/en/.

Additional Resources

Global Polio Eradication Initiative, Independent Monitoring Board. *Polio's Last Stand?* (November 2012): polioeradication.org/Portals/0/Document/Aboutus/Governance/IMB/7IMB-Meeting/7IMB_Report_EN.pdf

Global Polio Eradication Initiative. www.polioeradication.org/.

"Room for Debate: Making Vaccination Mandatory for All Children." *New York Times* (23 March 2014). www.nytimes.com/roomfordebate/2014/03/23/making-vaccination-mandatory-for-all-children?hp&rref=opinion.

42. 1997: Southeast Asian Haze

Aiken, S. Robert. "Runaway Fires, Smoke-Haze Pollution, and Unnatural Disasters in Indonesia." *Geographical Review* 94, 1 (2004): 55–79.

Frankenberg, Elizabeth, Douglas McKee and Duncan Thomas. "Health Consequences of Forest Fires in Indonesia." *Demography* 42, 1 (2005): 109–29.

Gellert, Paul K. "A Brief History and Analysis of Indonesia's Forest Fire Crisis." *Indonesia* 65 (April, 1998): 63–85.

Little, Jane Braxton. "Regrowing Borneo, Tree by Tree." *Scientific American* 18, 5 (December 2008).

Normile, Dennis. "Restoring a 'Biological Desert' on Borneo." *Science*, New Series 325, 5940 (31 June 2009): 557.

Rosenberg, David. "Environmental Pollution around the South China Sea: Developing a Regional Response." *Contemporary Southeast Asia* 21, 1 (1999): 119–145.

Sastry, Narayan. "Forest Fires, Air Pollution, and Mortality in Southeast Asia." *Demography* 39, 1 (2002): 1–23.

United States Central Intelligence Agency. "Indonesia." *World Fact Book*. www.cia. gov/library/publications/the-world-factbook/geos/id.html.

Wardani, Ekoningtyas Margu. "A Nation of Fire: What Should We Learn from the 1997/1998 Haze?" *Jakarta Post* (June 25 2013). www.thejakartapost.com/ news/2013/06/25/a-nation-fire-what-should-we-learn-19971998-haze.html.

Additional Resources

Kwok, Yenni. "The Southeast Asian Haze Is Back and Worse May Follow." *Time Magazine* (July 30, 2013). http:// world.time.com/2013/07/30/the-southeast-asian-haze-is-back-and-worse-may-follow/.

Pyne, Stephen J. "Passing the Torch." *American Scholar* (Spring 2008). http:// theamericanscholar.org/passing-the-torch/#.UzGdp5VOV2t.

"Sumatra's Orangutans Under Threat." http://content.time.com/time/audioslide/0,32187,1926657,00.html.

43. 2003: Was the Lethal European Heat Wave Caused by Climate Change?

Borrell, Carme, *et al*. "Socioeconomic Position and Excess Mortality during the Heat Wave of 2003 in Barcelona." *European Journal of Epidemiology* 21, 9 (2006): 633–40.

Dahlman, LuAnn. "Climate Change: Global Temperature." NOAA, Climate.gov (August 30, 2009). www.climate.gov/ news-features/understanding-climate/ climate-change-global-temperature (accessed 6 March 2014).

García-Herrera, R., *et al*. "A Review of the European Summer Heat Wave of 2003." *Critical Reviews in Environmental Science and Technology* 40, 4 (2010): 267–306.

Klinenberg, E. *Heat Wave: A Social Autopsy of Disaster in Chicago*. Chicago: The University Chicago Press, 2002.

Li, Wenhong, *et al*. "Changes to the North Atlantic Subtropical High and Its Role in the Intensification of Summer Rainfall Variability in the Southeastern United States. *Journal of Climate* 24, 5 (March 2011): 1499–1506.

Meehl, Gerald A. and Claudia Tebaldi. "More Intense, More Frequent, and Longer Lasting Heat Waves in the 21st Century." *Science*, New Series 305, 5686 (August 13, 2004): 994–97.

Rey, Grégoire, *et al*. "Heat Exposure and Socio-Economic Vulnerability as Synergistic Factors in Heat-Wave-Related Mortality." *European Journal of Epidemiology* 24, 9 (2009): 495–502.

Scott, Michon. "Heat Hammers Europe in July & August." NOAA (August 22, 2013). www.climate.gov/news-features/event-tracker/heat-hammers-europe-july-and-august.

Toulemon, Laurent, and Magali Barbieri. "The Mortality Impact of the August 2003 Heat Wave in France: Investigating the 'Harvesting' Effect and Other Long-Term Consequences." *Population Studies* 62, 1 (March 2008): 39–53.

Additional Resources

U.S. Environmental Protection Agency. "Heat Island Effect." www.epa.gov/ heatisland/ (accessed 6 March 2014).

NASA, Goddard Institute for Space Studies. "GISS Surface Temperature Analysis" [generate a global map, comparing a selected time period to a 30-year base average]. data.giss.nasa.gov/gistemp/ maps/.

44. 2004: Indonesian Earthquake and Tsunami Trigger International Relief Effort

Baird, Abigail A. "Sifting Myths for Truths about Our World: *When They Severed Earth from Sky: How the Human Mind Shapes Myth* by Elizabeth Wayland Barber; Paul T. Barber" [review], *Science*, New Series, 308, 5726 (May 27, 2005): 1261–62.

Beardsley, Kyle and Brian McQuinn. "Rebel Groups as Predatory Organizations: The Political Effects of the 2004 Tsunami in Indonesia and Sri Lanka." *The Journal of Conflict Resolution* 53, 4 (August 2009): 624–45.

Bernard, E. N., *et al.* "Tsunami: Scientific Frontiers, Mitigation, Forecasting and Policy Implications." *Philosophical Transactions: Mathematical, Physical and Engineering Sciences* 364, 1845 (Aug. 15, 2006): 1989–2007.

California Institute of Technology Tectonics Observatory. "What Happened During the 2004 Sumatra Earthquake." www.tectonics.caltech.edu/outreach/highlights/sumatra/what.html.

Deraniyagala, Sonali. *Wave.* New York: Knopf, 2013.

"Girl, 10, Used Geography Lesson to Save Lives." *The Telegraph* (January 1, 2005). www.telegraph.co.uk/news/1480192/Girl-10-used-geography-lesson-to-save-lives.html.

Hutanuwatr, Khanin, Bob Bolin, and David Pijawka. "Vulnerability and Disaster in Thailand: Scale, Power, and Collaboration in Post-tsunami Recovery." Chapter 5 in *Forces of Nature and Cultural Responses*, edited by Katrin Pfeifer and Niki Pfeifer, 69–92. Dordrecht: Springer, 2005.

Jaffe, Bruce, Eric Geist, and Helen Gibbons. "Indian Ocean Earthquake Triggers Deadly Tsunami." *Sound Waves* (USGS Newsletter), http://soundwaves.usgs.gov/2005/01/ (accessed 9 June 2014).

Kelman, Ilan, *et al.* "Tourists and Disasters: Lessons from the 26 December 2004 Tsunamis." *Journal of Coastal Conservation* 12, 3 (September, 2008): 105–13.

Martin, Mary-Laure. "Child Participation in Disaster Risk Reduction: The Case of Flood-Affected Children in Bangladesh." *Third World Quarterly* 31, 8 (2011): 1357–75.

Sato, Jin. "Matching Goods and People: Aid and Human Security after the 2004 Tsunami." *Development in Practice* 20, 1 (February, 2010): 70–84.

United Nations Office for Disaster Risk Reduction. Hyogo Framework for Action. www.unisdr.org/we/coordinate/hfa.

United States Geological Survey. "Earthquakes with 50,000 or More Deaths," https://web.archive.org/web/20140820090633/http://earthquake.usgs.gov/earthquakes/world/most_destructive.php.

Additional Resources

McDaris, John, and Monica Bruckner. "Tsunami Visualizations." Science Education Resource Center, Carleton College. serc.carleton.edu/NAGTWorkshops/hazards/visualizations/tsunami.html.

NOAA Education Resources. "Tsunamis." www.education.noaa.gov/Ocean_and_Coasts/Tsunami.html.

Richards, Glenn A. "The Boxing Day Tsunami: Teaching with Google Earth." Pedagogy in Action, SERC. https://serc.carleton.edu/sp/library/google_earth/examples/boxing_day_tsunami.html.

45. 2005: Hurricane Katrina Swamps the U.S. Gulf Coast

Brunker, Mike. "Class-Action Suit Against FEMA Trailer Manufacturers Settled for $42.6 Million." NBC News (September 28, 2012). http://investigations.nbcnews.com/_news/2012/09/28/14140222-class-action-suit-against-fema-trailer-manufacturers-settled-for-426-million.

Dreilinger, Danielle. "7,000 New Orleans Teachers, Laid Off after Katrina, Win Court Ruling." *The Times-Picayune* (January 17, 2014). www.nola.com/crime/index.ssf/2014/01/7000_new_orleans_teachers_laid.html.

Elliott, Diana B. "Understanding Changes in Familes and Households Pre- and Post-Katrina." U.S. Census Bureau. San Francisco: American Sociological Association Meeting, August 10, 2009.

Fussell, Elizabeth, Narayan Sastry and Mark Van Landingham. "Race, Socioeconomic Status, and Return Migration to New Orleans after Hurricane Katrina." *Population and Environment* 31, 1/3 (January 2010): 20–42.

Knabb, Richard D., Jamie R. Rhome, and Daniel P. Brown. "Tropical Cyclone Report: Hurricane Katrina, 23–30 August 2005." National Hurricane Center (20 December 2005; updated 14 September 2011). www.nhc.noaa.gov/pdf/TCR-AL122005_Katrina.pdf.

Kysar, Douglas A., and Thomas O. McGarity. "Did NEPA Drown New Orleans? The Levees, the Blame Game, and the Hazards of Hindsight." *Duke Law Journal* 56, 1 (October, 2006): 179–235.

Locke, Dr. William W. "Understanding Katrina," in Laurie Cantwell, *Teaching with Hurricane Katrina: The Physiography, Climate, Storm, and Impact,* Science Education Resource Center, Carleton College, http://serc.carleton.edu/research_education/katrina/understanding.html.

McCallum, Ewen, and Julian Heming. "Hurricane Katrina: An Environmental Perspective." *Philosophical Transactions: Mathematical, Physical and Engineering Sciences* 364, 1845 (Aug. 15, 2006): 2099–2115.

Olsen, Lise. "5 Years after Katrina, Storm's Death Toll Remains a Mystery." *Houston Chronicle* (Aug. 30, 2010), www.chron.com/news/nation-world/article/5-years-after-Katrina-storm-s-death-toll-remains-1589464.php.

Petterson, John S., *et al.* "A Preliminary Assessment of Social and Economic Impacts Associated with Hurricane Katrina." *American Anthropologist,* New Series 108, 4 (December, 2006): 643–670.

Reich, Jennifer A., and Martha Wadsworth. "Out of the Floodwaters, but Not Yet on Dry Ground: Experiences of Displacement and Adjustment in Adolescents and Their Parents Following Hurricane Katrina." *Children, Youth and Environments* 18, 1 (2008): 354–70.

Smil, Vaclav. "The Next 50 Years: Fatal Discontinuities." *Population and Development Review* 31, 2 (June 2005): 201–36.

United States Environmental Protection Agency. "Formaldehyde Emissions from Composite Wood Products." www.epa.gov/opptintr/chemtest/formaldehyde/ (accessed 24 March 2014).

White, Ismail K., *et al.* "Feeling the Pain of My People: Hurricane Katrina, Racial Inequality, and the Psyche of Black America." *Journal of Black Studies* 37, 4 (March, 2007) 523–38.

Additional Resources

Cantwell, Laurie. *Teaching with Hurricane Katrina: The Physiography, Climate, Storm, and Impact.* Science Education Resource Center, Carleton College, serc.carleton.edu/research_education/katrina/index.html.

Swenson, Dan. "Flash Flood: Hurricane Katrina's Inundation of New Orleans, August 29, 2005." *Times Picayune*, www.nola.com/katrina/graphics/flash-flood.swf.

"Hurricane Katrina." History.com. www.history.com/topics/hurricane-katrina.

U.S. Census Bureau. "Census Bureau Releases First Detailed Data on Katrina Damage to New Orleans Area Housing." (February 14, 2011). www.census.gov/newsroom/releases/archives/housing/cb11-28.html.

Zimmerman, Kim Ann. "Hurricane Katrina: Facts, Damage, & Aftermath." LiveScience (August 20, 2012). www.livescience.com/22522-hurricane-katrina-facts.html.

46. 2010: Earthquake Meets Poverty in Port-au-Prince, Haiti

Archimbold, Randal C., and Samini Sangupta. "U.N. Struggles to Stem Haiti Cholera Epidemic." *New York Times* (19 April 2014): www.nytimes.com/2014/04/20/world/americas/un-struggles-to-stem-haiti-cholera-epidemic.html?hp.

Beasley, Myron M. "Women, *Sabotaj*, and Underground Food Economies in Haiti." *Gastronomica: The Journal of Food and Culture* 12, 2 (Summer 2012): 33–44.

Global Research, Haiti Grassroots Watch. "Haiti: Reconstruction's Housing Proj-ects Still Plagued with Problems Four Years after the Earthquake." (January 8, 2014): www.globalresearch.ca/haiti-reconstructions-housing-projects-still-plagued-with-problems-four-years-after-the-earthquake/5364749.

Haiti Partners, Haiti Statistics. http://haiti-partners.org/who-we-are/haiti-statistics/.

Lundahl, Mats. *Poverty in Haiti: Essays on Underdevelopment and Post Disaster Projects.* New York: Palgrave Macmillan, 2011.

McAlister, Elizabeth. "Humanitarian Adhocracy, Transnational New Apostolic Missions, and Evangelical Anti-Dependency in a Haitian Refugee Camp." *Nova Religio: The Journal of Alternative and Emergent Religions* 16, 4 (May 2013): 11–34.

Presutti, Carol. "Haiti Struggles to Begin Free Public Education." *Voice of America* (October 31, 2011): www.voanews.com/content/haiti-struggles-to-begin-free-public-education-133018688/164638.html.

Roos, Robert. "Cholera Has Struck More Than 6% of Haitians." Center for Infectious Disease Research and Policy (January 9, 2013). www.cidrap.umn.edu/news-perspective/2013/01/cholera-has-struck-more-6-haitians.

Schuller, Mark, and Pablo Morales, ed. *Tectonic Shifts: Haiti Since the Earthquake.* Sterling, VA: Kumarian Press, 2012.

UN Data. "World Statistics Pocketbook: Haiti." http://data.un.org/CountryProfile.aspx?crName=Haiti.

UN Development Programme, 2013 Human Development Report. "Haiti." http://hdr.undp.org/sites/default/files/Country-Profiles/HTI.pdf.

United States Central Intelligence Agency. World Fact Book: Haiti. https://www.

cia.gov/library/publications/the-world-factbook/geos/ha.html.

USGS, Earthquake Hazards Program. "Haiti Region Magnitude 7.0." http://earthquake.usgs.gov/earthquakes/eqinthenews/2010/us2010rja6/#summary.

World Bank, Data. "Haiti." http://data.worldbank.org/country/haiti.

Additional Resources

EERI Haiti Earthquake Clearinghouse. http://eqclearinghouse.org/co/20100112-haiti/.

Google Earth. Satellite View and Map of the City of Port-au-Prince (Pòtoprens), Haiti. www.nationsonline.org/oneworld/map/google_map_Port-au-Prince.htm.

Incorporated Research Institutions for Seismology (IRIS). Recent Earthquakes Teachable Moments. www.iris.edu/hq/retm and www.iris.edu/hq/retm/event/918.

United States Central Intelligence Agency. World Fact Book: Haiti. https://www.cia.gov/library/publications/the-world-factbook/geos/ha.html.

USGS, Woods Hole Coastal and Marine Science Center. "Caribbean Tsunami and Earthquake Hazard Studies." http://woodshole.er.usgs.gov/project-pages/caribbean/atlantic+trench_large.html.

47. 2010: *Deepwater Horizon* **Oil Spill Threatens Gulf of Mexico and Atlantic**

Barstow, David, David Rohde, and Stephanie Saul. "Deepwater Horizon's Final Hours." *New York Times* (December 12, 2010). www.nytimes.com/2010/12/26/us/26spill.html?pagewanted=all.

Davenport, Coral. "Obama's Plan: Allow Drilling in Atlantic, but Limit It in Arctic." *New York Times* (January 27, 2015). www.nytimes.com/2015/01/28/us/obama-plan-calls-for-oil-and-gas-drilling-in-the-atlantic.html (accessed 22 February 2015).

Gohlke, Julia M., *et al.* "A Review of Seafood Safety after the "Deepwater Horizon" Blowout." *Environmental Health Perspectives* 119, 8 (August 2011): 1062–69.

Klump, Edward. "Wildcatter Hunch Unlocks $1.5 Trillion Oil Offshore U.S." *Bloomberg* (September 13, 2013). www.bloomberg.com/news/2013-09-12/wildcatter-hunch-unlocks-1-5-trillion-oil-offshore-u-s-.html.

Mendelssohn, Irving A., *et al.* "Oil Impacts on Coastal Wetlands: Implications for the Mississippi River Delta Ecosystem after the *Deepwater Horizon* Oil Spill," *BioScience* 62, 6 (June 2012): 562–574.

NOAA Fisheries, Office of Science & Technology. *Fisheries Economics of the U.S., 2009.* www.st.nmfs.noaa.gov/st5/publication/econ/2009/gulf_ALL_econ.pdf.

NOAA Fisheries, Office of Science & Technology. *Fisheries Economics of the U.S., 2011.* www.st.nmfs.noaa.gov/Assets/economics/documents/feus/2011/FEUS2011%20-%20Gulf%20of%20Mexico.pdf.

Peterson, Charles H., *et al.* "A Tale of Two Spills: Novel Science and Policy Implications of an Emerging New Oil Spill Model," *BioScience* 62, 5 (May 2012): 461–69.

Reuters. "BP Loses Bid to Cut Maximum $13.7 Billion Gulf Spill Fine." *New York Times* (February 19, 2015): www.nytimes.com/reuters/2015/02/19/business/19reuters-bp-spill.html?_r=0 (accessed February 22, 2015).

U.S. Energy Information Administration. Gulf of Mexico Fact Sheet. www.eia. gov/special/gulf_of_mexico/data. cfm.

U.S. Environmental Protection Agency. "BP Oil Spill (Deepwater Horizon), Description of the Event and EPA's Response/Role." www.epa.gov/aed/html/research/bpspill.html.

U.S. Environmental Protection Agency. "Gulf of Mexico Program, General Facts about the Gulf of Mexico." www.epa.gov/gmpo/about/facts.html#resources.

Wethe, David. "U. S. Oil Profits Lure $16 Billion More Rigs by 2015." *Bloomberg* (July 17, 2013). www.bloomberg.com/news/2013-07-16/u-s-gulf-oil-profits-lure-16-billion-more-rigs-by-2015.html.

Wines, Michael. "U.S. Moves Toward Atlantic Oil Exploration, Stirring Debate over Sea Life." *New York Times* (February 27, 2014). http://www.nytimes.com/2014/02/28/us/us-moves-toward-atlantic-oil-exploration-stirring-debate-over-sea-life.html.

Additional Resources

Children of the Spills [oral histories and drawings from youth impacted by Exxon Valdez and Deepwater Horizon spills]. http://childrenofthespills.org/

de Melker, Saskia. "'Louisiana Water Stories' Documents the Culture and Curses of SOLA" [video interview]. PBS (April 21, 2011). www.pbs.org/newshour/rundown/-in-southern-louisiana-life/.

Energy Information Administration. Energy KIDS. www.eia.gov/KIDS/index.cfm.

NOAA Deepwater Horizon Archive. www.noaa.gov/deepwaterhorizon/.

NOAA Gulf Restoration videos. www.gulfspillrestoration.noaa.gov/media-center/videos/.

NOAA. Deepwater Horizon Trajectory Map Archive. http://archive.orr.noaa.gov/topic_subtopic_entry.php?RECORD_KEY%28entry_subtopic_topic%29=entry_id,subtopic_id,topic_id&entry_id(entry_subtopic_topic)=830&subtopic_id(entry_subtopic_topic)=2&topic_id(entry_subtopic_topic)=1.

Times Topics. "Gulf of Mexico Oil Spill (2010)." *New York Times*, topics.nytimes.com/top/reference/timestopics/subjects/o/oil_spills/gulf_of_mexico_2010/index.html.

"Tracking the Oil Spill in the Gulf" [interactive map]. *New York Times* (May 1, 2010). www.nytimes.com/interactive/2010/05/01/us/20100501-oil-spill-tracker.html.

USGS. Oil Spill Response. www.usgs.gov/oilspill/.

48. 2011: Tohoku Earthquake and Tsunami Batter Fukushima Nuclear Reactors

Birmingham, Lucy, and David McNeill. *Strong in the Rain: Surviving Japan's Earthquake, Tsunami, and Fukushima Nuclear Disaster.* New York: Palgrave MacMillan, 2012.

Fackler, Martin. "Nuclear Issue in Limbo as Indecision Grips Japan." *New York Times* (February 11, 2014): www.nytimes.com/2014/02/12/world/asia/nuclear-issue-in-limbo-as-indecision-grips-japan.html.

Mori, Nobohito, Tomoyuki Takahashi, and the 2011 Tohoku Earthquake Tsunami Joint Survey Group. "Nationwide Post Event Survey and Analysis of the 2011 Tohoku Earthquake Tsunami." *Coastal*

Engineering Journal 54, 1 (2012): 1250001-1—1250001-27.

NOAA. "Japan's 'Harbor Wave': The Tsunami One Year Later." www.noaa. gov/features/03_protecting/japantsunami_oneyearlater.html.

Reuters. "Japan Aims to Restart Nuclear Reactor in June." *New York Times* (February 6, 2015): www.nytimes. com/reuters/2015/02/06/world/ asia/06reuters-japan-nuclear-restart. html (accessed 22 February 2015).

Sharples, Ben, and Tsuyoshi Inujima. "Uranium Poised for Bull Market as Japan Reviews Reactors: Energy." *Bloomberg* (January 22, 2014). www.bloomberg. com/news/2014-01-21/uranium-poised-for-bull-market-as-japan-reviews-reactors-energy.html.

Stimson, Ian. "Japan's Tohoku Earthquake and Tsunami." *Geology Today* 27, 3 (May–June 2011): 96–98.

Tabuchi, Hiroko. "Reversing Course, Japan Makes Push to Restart Dormant Nuclear Plants." *New York Times* (February 25, 2014): www.nytimes. com/2014/02/26/world/asia/ japan-pushes-to-revive-moribund-nuclear-energy-sector.html.

Wingfield-Hayes, Rupert. "Fukushima: Is Fear of Radiation the Real Killer?" *BBC Asia* (11 March 2014). www.bbc.com/ news/world-asia-26483945.

World Nuclear Association. "Nuclear Energy in Japan" (updated February 2014). www.world-nuclear.org/info/ Country-Profiles/Countries-G-N/ Japan/ (accessed 14 February 2014).

Additional Resources

NOAA Center for Tsunami Research: nctr. pmel.noaa.gov/. See especially nctr.pmel.noaa.gov/honshu20110311/.

49. 2014: Ebola Virus Disease (EVD) Erupts in West Africa

Bah, Elhadj Ibrahima, *et al.* "Clinical Presentation of Patients with Ebola Virus Disease in Conakry, Guinea." *New England Journal of Medicine* 2015; 372:40-47 (January 1, 2015): www.nejm.org/ doi/full/10.1056/NEJMoa1411249.

Centers for Disease Control and Prevention. "Ebola: Ebola Virus Disease." www.cdc. gov/vhf/ebola/.

Centers for Disease Control and Prevention. "How to Talk with Your Children about Ebola." www.cdc.gov/vhf/ebola/ pdf/how-talk-children-about-ebola-factsheet.pdf.

World Health Organization. "Ebola Virus Disease Fact Sheet." www.who.int/ mediacentre/factsheets/fs103/en/.

World Health Organization. "Liberia: Channelling hope – how psychosocial support breaks boundaries between families and Ebola patients" (January 2015). www.who.int/features/2015/ ebola-patients-mental-health/en/.

World Health Organization. *One Year into the Ebola Epidemic: A Deadly, Tenacious, and Unforgiving Virus* (January 2015): www. who.int/csr/disease/ebola/one-year-report/ebola-report-1-year.pdf?ua=1.

Additional Resources

Centers for Disease Control and Prevention. "Ebola: Resources for Parents, Schools, and Pediatric Healthcare Workers." www.cdc.gov/vhf/ebola/children/ index.html (accessed 23 February 2015).

"The Latest: Ebola in the United States." *The Atlantic* (November 20, 2014): www.theatlantic.com/ health/archive/2014/11/ebola-in-the-us/381575/.

50. Disaster in the Making: Anthropogenic Climate Change in the Twenty-First Century

Chandler, David L. "Ancient Whodunit May Be Solved: The Microbes Did It!" *MIT News* (31 March 2014). http://newsoffice.mit.edu/2014/ancient-whodunit-may-be-solved-microbes-did-it.

Gillis, Justin. "U.N. Climate Panel Endorses Ceiling on Global Emissions." *New York Times* (September 27, 2013). www.nytimes.com/2013/09/28/science/global-climate-change-report.html?pagewanted=all.

Matthews, John A., and Keith R. Briffa, "The 'Little Ice Age': Re-Evaluation of an Evolving Concept," *Geografiska Annaler* Series A, Physical Geography, 87, 1 (2005): 17–36.

Shorto, Russell. "How to Think Like the Dutch in a Post-Sandy World," *NYT Magazine* (April 9, 2014): www.nytimes.com/2014/04/13/magazine/how-to-think-like-the-dutch-in-a-post-sandy-world.html.

Tollefson, Jeff. "The 8,000-year-old Climate Puzzle." *Nature* (25 March 2011): www.nature.com/news/2011/110325/full/news.2011.184.html.

UNESCO. *Global Change: Evidence from the Geological Record* (IGCP Reports 2013): www.unesco.org/new/fileadmin/MULTIMEDIA/HQ/SC/pdf/IGCP_THEME2_Global_Change_2013.pdf.

United Nations, Intergovernmental Panel on Climate Change (IPCC) Working Group II. *Climate Change 2014: Impacts, Adaptation, and Vulnerability.* http://ipcc-wg2.gov/AR5/.

Smits, Willie. "How to Restore a Rainforest." www.ted.com/talks/willie_smits_restores_a_rainforest.

Wimp.com. "This Guy's Creation Is Absolutely Astounding." www.wimp.com/creationastounding/.

Zimmer, Carl. "Seeking a Break in a 252-Million-Year-Old Mass Killing: A Geologist Investigates a Mass Extinction at the End of the Permian Period." *New York Times* (20 Feb 2014): www.nytimes.com/2014/02/21/science/earth/Mass-Extinction-Permian-Period.html?ref=science.

Additional Resources

"Climate Change Research in Partnership with Thoreau." http://primacklab.blogspot.com/.

"El Niño: Making Sense of the Weather." http://kids.earth.nasa.gov/archive/nino/intro.html.

The Journey North: A Global Study of Wildlife Migration and Seasonal Change. www.journeynorth.org/.

United States Environmental Protection Agency. "Causes of Climate Change." www.epa.gov/climatechange/science/causes.html (accessed 9 June 2014).

United States National Oceanic and Atmospheric Administration (NOAA), Climate.gov. Science and Information for a Climate-Smart Nation. www.climate.gov/.

World Meteorological Organization (WMO). www.wmo.int/pages/index_en.html.

WMO Youth Pages. www.wmo.int/youth/.

ENDNOTES

Introduction

1. Nicholas N. Ambraseys, "The 12th Century Seismic Paroxysm in the Middle East: A Historical Perspective," *Annals of Geophysics* 47 (April/June 2004): 733–58.

2. Republic of the Philippines National Disaster Risk Reduction and Management Council, "SitRep No. 104 Effects of Typhoon 'Yolanda' (Haiyan)," ndrrmc.gov.ph/attachments/article/1125/Update%20Sitrep%20No.%20104%20Effects%20of%20TY%20YOLANDA.pdf.

Chapter 1

1. Kathryn E. Fitzsimmons *et al.*, "The Campanian Ignimbrite Eruption: New Data on Volcanic Ash Dispersal and Its Potential Impact on Human Evolution," *PLoS ONE* 8 (6): e65839, plosone. org/article/info%3Adoi%2F10.1371%2Fjournal. pone.0065839.

2. Alwyn Scarth, *Vesuvius: A Biography* (Princeton, NJ: Princeton University Press, 2009), 16–17.

3. Scarth.

4. Fitzsimmons, *et al.*

5. Fitzsimmons, *et al.*

6. Fitzsimmons, *et al.*

7. Liubov Vitaliena Golovanova *et al.*, "Significance of Ecological Factors in the Middle to Upper Paleolithic Transition," *Current Anthropology* 51, 5 (October 2010): 655–91.

8. Pierre Sepulchre *et al.*, "H4 Abrupt Event and Late Neanderthal Presence in Iberia," *Earth and Planetary Science Letters* 258 (2007): 283–92.

9. B. A. Black, R.R. Neely, and M. Manga, "Testing Connections between Campanian Ignimbrite Volcanism, Climate, and the Decline of the Neanderthals," GSA Annual Meeting, Vancouver, BC, October 2014. Abstract, https://gsa.confex.com/gsa/2014AM/webprogram/Paper250287.html.

10. Siwan Davies and Peter Abbott, "Volcanic Secrets in the Ice," *Planet Earth Online*, March 19, 2010.

http://planetearth.nerc.ac.uk/features/story. aspx?id=674.

11. Haraldur Sigurdsson, *Melting the Earth: The History of Ideas on Volcanic Eruptions* (New York: Oxford University Press, 1999).

12. Michael R. Rampino and Stanley H. Ambrose, "Volcanic Winter in the Garden of Eden: The Toba Supereruption and the Late Pleistocene Human Population Crash," In *Volcanic Hazards and Disasters in Human Antiquity*, ed. Floyd W. McCoy and Grant Heiken, 71-82 (Boulder, CA: Geological Society of America, 2000).

13. Jonathan Amos, "Toba Super-Volcano Catastrophe Idea 'Dismissed,'" *BBC News* (30 April 2013): http://www.bbc.co.uk/news/science-environment-22355515.

14. Wikipedia, "Human Evolution," http://en.wikipedia.org/wiki/Human_evolution.

15. Wikipedia, "Anatomically Modern Humans," http://en.wikipedia.org/wiki/Anatomically_modern_humans.

16. "Kissing Cousins," *The Economist* (February 1, 2014): http://www.economist.com/news/science-and-technology/21595403-genetic-contribution-neanderthal-man-made-modern-humanity.

17. Sriram Sankararaman *et al.*, "The genomic landscape of Neanderthal ancestry in present-day humans," *Nature* (January 29, 2014): http://sriramsankararaman.com/publications/sankararaman.nature.2014.pdf

18. Benjamin Vernot and Joshua M. Akey, "Resurrecting Surviving Neandertal Lineages from Modern Human Genomes," *Science* 343, 6174 (28 February 2014): 1017-21.

Chapter 2.

1. Carl Knappett, Ray Rivers, and Tim Evans, "The Theran Eruption and Minoan Palatial Collapse: New Interpretations Gained from Modelling the Maritime Network," *Antiquity* 85 (2011): 1008–23.

2. Haraldur Sigurdsson, *Melting the Earth: The History of Ideas on Volcanic Eruptions* (New York: Oxford University Press, 1999).

3. Sigurdsson, 26.

4. Sigurdsson, 27–28.

5. Sigurdsson, p. 25.

6. Felix Höflmayer, "The Date of the Minoan Santorini Eruption: Quantifying the 'Offset,'" *Radiocarbon* 54 (2012): 435–48.

7. Malcolm H. Wiener, "Cold Fusion: The Uneasy Alliance of History and Science," in *Tree-Rings, Kings, and Old World Archaeology and Environment*, ed. Sturt W. Manning & Mary Jaye Bruce (Oxford: Oxbow Books, 2009), 279.

8. Knappett *et al.*

9. Hendrik J. Bruins *et al.*, "Geoarchaeological Tsunami Deposits at Palaikastro (Crete) and the Late Minoan IA Eruption of Santorini," *Journal of Archaeological Science* 35, 1 (January 2008): 191-212.

10. Floyd W. McCoy and Grant Heiken, "The Late-Bronze Age Explosive Eruption of Thera (Santorini), Greece: Regional and Local Effects," in *Volcanic Hazards and Disasters in Human Antiquity*, ed. by F. McCoy and G. Heiken (Boulder, CO: Geological Society of America Special Paper 345, 2000), 43–70.

Chapter 3

1. Stephen Dando-Collins, *The Great Fire of Rome: The Fall of the Emperor Nero and His City* (Cambridge, MA: Da Capo Press, 2010).

2. Wikipedia, "Firestorm," http://en.wikipedia.org/wiki/Firestorm.

3. Dando-Collins, *Great Fire of Rome* 10–14, 107–10.

Chapter 4

1. Haraldur Sigurdsson, *Melting the Earth: The History of Ideas on Volcanic Eruptions* (New York: Oxford University Press, 1999), 57.

2. John Clarke, *Physical Science in the Time of Nero: Being a Translation of the* Quaestiones Naturales *by* Seneca (London: Macmillan and Company, 1910), 221-25.

3. Sigurdsson, 60.

4. Alwyn Scarth, *Vesuvius: A Biography* (Princeton, NJ:

Princeton University Press, 2009), 48–53.

5. Natasha Sheldon, "Human Remains in Pompeii: The Body Casts," DecodedPast.com (March 23, 2014): http://decodedpast.com/human-remains-pompeii-body-casts/7532.

6. Pliny the Younger, *Letters of Pliny*, Ed. F. C. T. Bosanquet; Trans. William Melmoth. Project Gutenberg release date September, 2001 (Etext #2811). http://www.gutenberg.org/files/2811/2811-h/2811-h.htm.

7. Sigurdsson, 70.

8. Wikipedia, "Lake Nyos," http://en.wikipedia.org/wiki/Lake_Nyos.

9. USGS, "Invisible CO_2 Gas Killing Trees at Mammoth Mountain, California," U.S. Geological Survey Fact Sheet 172–96, Online Version 2.0, http://pubs.usgs.gov/dds/dds-81/Intro/facts-sheet/GasKillingTrees.html.

Chapter 5

1. Antti Arjava, "The Mystery Cloud of 536 CE in the Mediterranean Sources," *Dumbarton Oaks Papers* 59 (2005): 73–94.

2. David Keys, *Catastrophe: An Investigation into the Origins of the Modern World* (New York: Ballantine Books, 1999).

3. Arjava, "Mystery Cloud of 536 CE," 73–94.

4. Keys.

5. K. H. Wohletz, "Were the Dark Ages Triggered by Volcano-related Climate Changes in the 6th Century?" *EOS Transactions American Geophysical Union* 48, 81 (2000): F1305. http://www.ees.lanl.gov/geodynamics/Wohletz/Krakatau.htm.

6. Keys.

7. John Southon, Mahyar Mohtadi, and Ricardo De Pol-Holz, "Planktonic Foram Dates from the Indonesian Arc: Marine ^{14}C Reservoir Ages and a Mythical AD 535 Eruption of Krakatau," *Radiocarbon* 55, 2 (2013): 1164–72.

8. "*Catastrophe. An Investigation into the Origins of the Modern World*, by D. Keys." Review by Michael Whitby, *The Classical Review, New Series*, 50, No. 1 (2000), 350.

9. Franck Lavigne *et al.*, "Source of the Great A.D. 1257 Mystery Eruption Unveiled, Samalas Volcano, Rinjani Volcanic Complex, Indonesia," *PNAS* 110, 42 (15 October 2013): 16742–47.

Chapter 6.

1. John of Ephesus quoted in David Keys, *Catastrophe*, 11.

2. Evagrius Scholasticus quoted in Keys, *Catastrophe*, 9.

3. Antti Arjava, "The Mystery Cloud of 536 CE in the Mediterranean Sources," *Dumbarton Oaks Papers* 59 (2005): 73–94.

4. Peter Tyson, "A Short History of Quarantine," *NOVA* (12 October 2004), http://www.pbs.org/wgbh/nova/body/short-history-of-quarantine.html.

5. M. Drancourt *et al.*, "*Yersinia pestis* Orientalis in Remains of Ancient Plague Patients," *Emerging Infectious Diseases* 13, 2 (February 2007), http://wwwnc.cdc.gov/eid/article/13/2/06-0197.htm.

6. David M. Wagner *et al.*, "*Yersinia pestis* and the Plague of Justinian 541-543 AD: A Genomic Analysis," *The Lancet* (January 28, 2014): http://eeid.cornell.edu/files/2012/12/Wagner-1te9if4.pdf.

7. Hermann Kinder and Werner Kilgemann, *The Anchor Atlas of World History*, trans. Ernest A. Menze (New York: Anchor Press/Doubleday, 1974); Wikipedia, Byzantine Empire (http://en.wikipedia.org/wiki/Byzantine_Empire), Heraclius (http://en.wikipedia.org/wiki/Heraclius), List of Sieges of Constantinople (http://en.wikipedia.org/wiki/List_of_sieges_of_Constantinople), and Timeline of the Roman Empire (http://en.wikipedia.org/wiki/Timeline_of_the_Roman_Empire).

Chapter 7

1. Information Britain, "Deadly Storm Changes UK Coastline," http://www.information-britain.co.uk/famdates.php?id=1205.

2. Wikipedia, St. Lucia's Flood, http://en.wikipedia.org/wiki/St._Lucia%27s_flood

3. Medieval Sourcebook: Tables on Population in Medieval Europe. http://www.fordham.edu/halsall/source/pop-in-eur.asp.

4. Hub Zwart, "Aquaphobia, Tulipmania, Biophilia: A Moral Geography of the Dutch Landscape," *Environmental Values* 12, 1 (February 2003): 107–128.

5. Petra J. E. M. van Dam, "Sinking Peat Bogs: Enviornmental Change Holland, 1350–1550," *Environmental History* 6, 1 (Jan., 2001): 32–45.

6. van Dam, "Sinking Peat Bogs."

7. van Dam, "Sinking Peat Bogs."

8. Zwart, "Aquaphobia."

9. van Dam, "Sinking Peat Bogs."

10. William H. TeBrake, "Taming the Waterwolf: Hydraulic Engineering and Water Management in the Netherlands during the Middle Ages," *Technology and Culture* 43, 3 (July 2002): 477.

11. Russell Shorto, "How to Think Like the Dutch in a Post-Sandy World," *NYT Magazine* (April 9, 2014): http://www.nytimes.com/2014/04/13/magazine/how-to-think-like-the-dutch-in-a-post-sandy-world.html

12. USGS, "Peat," http://minerals.usgs.gov/minerals/pubs/commodity/peat/.

13. USGS, Energy Resources Program, "Peat," http://energy.usgs.gov/Coal/Peat.aspx#378846-overview.

14. Kentucky Geological Survey, "How Is Coal Formed?" http://www.uky.edu/KGS/coal/coalform.htm

15. Roger Harrabin, "Careless Farming Adding to Floods," *BBC News* (6 March 2014): http://www.bbc.com/news/science-environment-26466653

Chapter 8

1. Brian Fagan, *The Little Ice Age: How Climate Made History, 1300–1850* (New York: Basic Books, 2000), Chapter 2, "The Great Famine," 23–42.

2. William Rosen, *The Third Horseman: Climate Change and the Great Famine of the 14th Century* (New York: Viking, 2014).

3. Rosen, *Third Horseman*, 138.

4. Rosen, *Third Horseman*, 151.

5. Fagan, *Little Ice Age*.

6. Fagan, *Little Ice Age*, Chapter 2, "The Great Famine," 23–42.

7. Kirk A. Maasch, "What Triggers Ice Ages?" *PBS Nova* (1 January 1997): http://www.pbs.org/wgbh/nova/earth/cause-ice-age.html

8. Wikipedia, "Holocene," http://en.wikipedia.org/wiki/Holocene

9. H.J. de Blij, "*The Little Ice Age: How Climate Made History, 1300–1850* by Brian Fagan" [Review], *Annals of the Association of American Geographers* 92, No. 2 (June 2002): 377–379

10. Wallace S. Broecker, "Was the Medieval Warm Period Global?" *Science*, New Series, 291, No. 5508 (Feb. 23, 2001): 1497–1499.

11. Jeff Tollefson, "The 8,000-year-old Climate Puzzle," *Nature* (25 March 2011): http://www.nature.com/news/2011/110325/full/news.2011.184.html.

12. Broecker, "Was the Medieval Warm Period Global?"

13. Thomas J. Crowley and Thomas S. Lowery, "How Warm Was the Medieval Warm Period?" *Ambio* 29, 1 (February, 2000): 51-54

14. John A. Matthews and Keith R. Briffa, "The 'Little Ice Age': Re-Evaluation of an Evolving Concept," *Geografiska Annaler* Series A, Physical Geography, 87, 1 (2005): 17–36

15. Broecker, "Was the Medieval Warm Period Global?"; Matthews and Briffa, "Little Ice Age."

Chapter 9

1. M. Wheelis, "Biological Warfare at the 1346 Siege of Caffa," *Emerging Infectious Diseases* 8, 9 (September 2002), http://wwwnc.cdc.gov/eid/article/8/9/01-0536.htm.

2. Medieval Sourcebook: Tables on Population in Medieval Europe. http://www.fordham.edu/halsall/source/pop-in-eur.asp.

3. Joseph P. Byrne, *Daily Life during the Black Death* (Westport, CT: Greenwood Press, 2006), 22.

4. David Herlihy, *The Black Death and the Transformation of the West* (Cambridge: Harvard University Press, 1997), 64–66.

5. David M. Wagner et al., "*Yersinia pestis* and the Plague of Justinian 541-543 AD: A Genomic Analysis," *The Lancet* (January 28, 2014): http://eeid.cornell.edu/files/2012/12/Wagner-1te9if4.pdf.

6. Joan Thirsk, *Alternative Agriculture: A History from the Black Death to the Present Day* (New York: Oxford University Press, 1997).

7. Herlihy, *Black Death and Transformation*, 44–45.

8. Stephen Porter, *The Great Plague* (Stroud, Gloucestershire: Sutton Publishing, 1999), 11.

9. Kip Wheeler, "The Black Death: Did It Save English?" web.cn.edu/Kwheeler/ppt/Black_Death_Language.ppt.

10. Wikipedia, Black Death, http://en.wikipedia.org/wiki/Black_Death.

11. Porter, *Great Plague*, 10–15.

Chapter 10

1. Mario di Bacco et al., "The Effect of an Unbalanced Demographic Structure on Marriage and Fertility Patterns in Isolated Populations: The Case of Norse Settlements in Greenland," *Genus* 62, 1 (2006): 97–119.

2. Brian Fagan, *The Little Ice Age: How Climate Made History, 1300–1850* (New York: Basic Books, 2000).

3. Di Bacco et al., "Effect of Unbalanced Demographic," 99.

4. Di Bacco et al., "Effect of Unbalanced Demographic," 100.

5. Eva Panagiotakopulu, Peter Skidmore, and Paul Buckland, "Fossil Insect Evidence for the End of the Western Settlement in Norse Greenland." *Naturwissenschaften* 94 (2007): 300–306

6. Martin B. Hebsgaard et al., "'The Farm Beneath the Sand' – an Archaeological Case Study on Ancient 'Dirt' DNA," *Antiquity* 83 (2009): 430–44.

7. Jared Diamond, *Collapse: How Societies Choose to Fail or Succeed* (New York: Penguin, 2011): 245–46.

8. Hebsgaard et al., "Farm Beneath the Sand."

9. Elizabeth Kolbert, *The Sixth Extinction: An Unnatural History* (New York: Henry Holt, 2014): 151.

10. Günther Stockinger, "Abandoned Colony in Greenland: Archaeologists Find Clues to Viking Mystery," translated by Christopher Sultan, *Der Spiegel*, 10 January 2013, http://www.spiegel.de/international/zeitgeist/archaeologists-uncover-clues-to-why-vikings-abandoned-greenland-a-876626.html.

11. Thomas H. McGovern, "Climate, Correlation, and Causation in Norse Greenland," *Arctic Anthropology* 28, 2 (1991): 77–100.

12. Di Bacco et al., "Effect of Unbalanced Demographic."

13. Stockinger, "Abandoned Colony."

14. McGovern, "Climate, Correlation, and Causation," 94.

15. Jared Diamond, *Collapse: How Societies Choose to Fail or Succeed* (New York: Penguin, 2011).

Chapter 11

1. Charles C. Mann, *1491: New Revelations of the Americas before Columbus*, 2nd ed. (New York: Vantage Books, 2011), 147.

2. Mann, *1491*, 143.

3. D. A. Henderson, *Smallpox: The Death of a Disease* (Amherst, NY: Prometheus Books, 2009), 41.

4. Mann, *1491*, 100.

5. Michael B. A. Oldstone, *Viruses, Plagues, and History* (New York: Oxford University Press, 1998).

6. Wikipedia, "Bartolomé de las Casas," http://en.wikipedia.org/wiki/Bartolom%C3%A9_de_las_Casas.

7. Oldstone, *Viruses, Plagues, and History*.

Chapter 12

1. Britannica, "Shaanxi Province Earthquake of 1556": http://www.britannica.com/EBchecked/topic/1483629/Shaanxi-province-earthquake-of-1556

2. United States Geological Survey, "Earthquakes with 50,000 or More Deaths," http://earthquake.usgs.gov/earthquakes/world/most_destructive.php; https://web.archive.org/web/20140820090633/http://earthquake.usgs.gov/earthquakes/world/most_destructive.php

3. Jian Wang, "Historical Earthquake Investigation and Research in China," Annals of Geophysics 47 (April/June 2004): 831-38.

4. Richard Stone, "China Grapples with Seismic Risk in Its Northern Heartland," *Science*, New Series, 313, No. 5787 (Aug. 4, 2006): 599.

5. Robert Yeats, *Active Faults of the World* (New York: Cambridge University Press, 2012), 372.

6. Hong-key Yoon, "Loess Cave-Dwellings in Shaanxi Province, China," *GeoJournal* 21, ½, IGU Regional Conference: Asian Pacific Countries (May/June 1990): 95–102.

7. Zhang Zhenzhong and Wang Lanmin, "Geological Disasters in Loess Areas during the 1920 Haiyuan Earthquake, China," *GeoJournal* 36, No. 2/3, Loess-Paleosol and Paleoclimatic Investigations: Principles, Methods and Criteria (June/July 1995), 269–74.

8. Zhang and Wang, "Geological Disasters in Loess Areas."

9. USGS Earthquake Hazards Program, "The Modified Mercalli Intensity Scale," http://earthquake.usgs.gov/learn/topics/mercalli.php

10. Robert Yeats, *Active Faults of the World* (New York: Cambridge University Press, 2012), 7.

11. USGS Earthquake Hazards Program, "Measuring the Size of an Earthquake," http://earthquake.usgs.gov/learn/topics/measure.php

12. Robert Yeats, *Active Faults of the World* (New York: Cambridge University Press, 2012), 7–8.

13. USGS Earthquake Hazards Program, Seismic Glossary, "seismic moment," http://earthquake.usgs.gov/learn/glossary/?term=seismic%20moment

14. Roff Smith, "The Biggest One," *Nature* 465, 6 (May 6 2010): 24–25.

Chapter 13

1. Charles Mann, *1491: New Revelations of the Americas before Columbus*, 2d ed. (New York: Vintage, 2011), 76–77.

2. Jean-Claude Thouret and Jasmine Davila, "Large-Scale Explosive Eruption at Huaynaputina Volcano, 1600 AD, Southern Peru," *Fourth ISAG, Goettingen (Germany)*, 04-06/10/1999, 758–760.

3. Shanaka de Silva, Jorge Alzueta, and Guido Salas, "The Socioeconomic Consequences of the A.D. 1600 Eruption of Huaynaputina, Southern Peru," in *Volcanic Hazards and Disasters in Human Antiquity*, ed. Floyd W. McCoy and Grant Heiken, 15–24 (Boulder, CA: Geological Society of America, 2000), 17.

4. de Silva *et al.*, "Socioeconomic Consequences of the A.D. 1600 Eruption of Huaynaputina."

5. Thouret and Davila, "Large-Scale Explosive Eruption."

6. de Silva *et al.*, "Socioeconomic Consequences of the A.D. 1600 Eruption of Huaynaputina," 20.

7. de Silva *et al.*, "Socioeconomic Consequences of the A.D. 1600 Eruption of Huaynaputina."

8. de Silva *et al.*, "Socioeconomic Consequences of the A.D. 1600 Eruption of Huaynaputina."

9. Alexandra Witze, "The Volcano That Changed the World: Eruption in 1600 May Have Plunged the Globe into Cold Climate Chaos," *Nature* (11 April 2008): nature.com/news/2008/080411/full/news.2008.747.html.

10. Mary Bagley, "Mt. Etna: Facts about Volcano's Eruptions," *LiveScience* (25 February 2013), http://www.livescience.com/27421-mount-etna.html; "Etna," *Italy's Volcanoes*, http://www.italysvolcanoes.com/ETNA_1669.html.

Chapter 14

1. J. S. Marr and J. T. Cathey, "New Hypothesis for Cause of an Epidemic among Native Americans, New England, 1616–1619," *Emerging Infectious Diseases* 16, 2 (2010 Feb): http://wwwnc.cdc.gov/eid/article/16/2/09-0276.htm

2. D. A. Henderson, *Smallpox: The Death of a Disease* (Amherst, NY: Prometheus Books, 2009), 42.

3. Marr and Cathey, "New Hypothesis."

4. James Cross Giblin, *When Plague Strikes: The Black Death, Smallpox, AIDS* (New York: HarperCollins, 1995), 75–76.

5. Peter d'Errico, "Jeffrey Amherst and Smallpox Blankets," 2010, http://people.umass.edu/derrico/amherst/lord_jeff.html; Harold B. Gill, Jr., "Colonial Germ Warfare," *Colonial Williamsburg Journal* (Spring 2004), http://www.history.org/foundation/journal/spring04/warfare.cfm.

6. Henderson, *Smallpox*, 45.

Chapter 15

1. Neil Hanson, *The Great Fire of London in That Apocalyptic Year, 1666* (New York: John Wiley & Sons, 2002), 33.

2. Michael Cooper, *'A More Beautiful City': Robert Hooke and the Rebuilding of London after the Great Fire* (London: Sutton Publishing, 2003), 97.

3. Hanson, *The Great Fire*, 198.

4. Hanson, *The Great Fire*, 49.

5. Hanson, *The Great Fire*, 153.

6. Hanson, *The Great Fire*, 167.

7. Hanson, *The Great Fire*.

8. Cooper, *A More Beautiful City*, 102.

Chapter 16

1. Nicholas Shrady, *The Last Day: Wrath, Ruin & Reason in the Great Lisbon Earthquake of 1755* (New York: Penguin, 2008).

2. Benigno E. Aguirre, "Better Disaster Statistics: The Lisbon Earthquake," *Journal of Interdisciplinary History*, 43,1 (Summer, 2012): 37.

3. Shrady, *Last Day*.

4. Shrady, *Last Day*, 14–18, 116.

5. Shrady, *Last Day*, 24.

6. Aguirre, "Better Disaster Statistics."

7. Shrady, *Last Day*.

8. David K. Chester and Olivia K. Chester, "The Impact of Eighteenth Century Earthquakes on the Algarve Region, Southern Portugal," *The Geographical Journal*, 176, 4 (December 2010): 354.

7. Susan Neiman, *Evil in Modern Thought: An Alternative History of Philosophy* (Princeton, NJ: Princeton University Press, 2002), 242.

8. Shrady, *Last Day*, 142.

9. Shrady, *Last Day*, 45.

10. Chester & Chester, 363.

Chapter 17

1. Shuji Cao, Yushang Li, and Bin Yang, "Mt. Tambora, Climatic Changes, and China's Decline in the Nineteenth Century." *Journal of World History*, 23, No. 3 (2012): 587–607; Clive Oppenheimer, "Climatic, Environmental and Human Consequences of the Largest Known Historic Eruption: Tambora Volcano (Indonesia) 1815," *Progress in Physical Geography* 27,2 (2003): 230–259.

2. William K. Klingaman and Nicholas P Klingaman, *The Year Without Summer: 1816 and the Volcano That Darkened the World and Changed History* (New York: St. Martin's Press, 2013), 11.

3. Klingaman and Klingaman, *Year without Summer*.

4. Oppenheimer, "Climatic Consequences."

5. Oppenheimer, "Climatic Consequences."

6. Cao, Li, and Yang, "Mt. Tambora."

7. Haraldur Sigurdsson, *Melting the Earth: The History of Ideas on Volcanic Eruptions* (New York: Oxford University Press, 1999), 7.

8. Cao, Li, and Yang, "Mt. Tambora," 599.

9. Openheimer, "Climatic Consequences."

10. Oppenheimer, "Climatic Consequences."

11. Cao, Li, and Yang, "Mt. Tambora."

12. Hans Von Storch and Nico Stehr, "Anthropogenic Climate Change: A Reason for Concern since the 18th Century and Earlier," *Geografiska Annaler* 88, 2 (2006): 107–13.

13. Sigurdsson, *Melting the Earth*, 177.

Chapter 18

1. Nicholas Wade, "Gene Sleuths Find How Some Naturally Resist Cholera," *New York Times* (3 July 2013): http://www.nytimes.com/2013/07/04/health/gene-sleuths-find-how-some-naturally-resist-cholera.html

2. David Arnold, "Cholera and Colonialism in British India," *Past & Present* 113 (Nov., 1986): 127.

3. Arnold, "Cholera and Colonialism," 128.

4. Stephen W. Lacey, "Cholera: Calamitous Past, Ominous Future," *Clinical Infectious Diseases* 20, 5 (May, 1995): 1409–19.

5. Richard J. Evans, "Epidemics and Revolutions: Cholera in Nineteenth-Century Europe," *Past & Present* 120 (Aug., 1988): 123–146.

6. Centers for Disease Control, "Cholera – *Vibrio cholerae* Infection," http://www.cdc.gov/cholera/illness.html.

7. Evans, "Epidemics and Revolutions."

8. Arnold, "Cholera and Colonialism," 140.

9. Jeff Sahadeo, "Epidemic and Empire: Ethnicity, Class, and "Civilization" in the 1892 Tashkent Cholera Riot," *Slavic Review* 64, 1 (Spring, 2005): 117–139.

10. Lacey, "Cholera: Calamitous, Ominous."

11. D. Greenberg, "Two Historic World-Pestilences Robbed of Their Terrors by Modern Sanitation," *The Scientific Monthly* 4, 6 (Jun., 1917): 554.

12. René J. Borroto, "Global warming, rising sea level, and growing risk of cholera incidence: a review of the literature and evidence," *GeoJournal*, 44, 2 (1998): 111-20.

13. Rita R. Colwell, "Cholera Outbreaks and Ocean Climate," *Social Research* 73, 3 (2006): 753–60.

13. Rita R. Colwell, "Global Climate and Infectious Disease: The Cholera Paradigm," *Science*, New Series, 274, 5295 (Dec. 20, 1996): 2025–31.

14. Colwell, "Cholera Outbreaks."

15. Robert Roos, "Cholera Has Struck More Than 6% of Haitians," Center for Infectious Disease Research and Policy (January 9, 2013), http://www.cidrap.umn.edu/news-perspective/2013/01/cholera-has-struck-more-6-haitians

16. Centers for Disease Control and Prevention, Travelers' Health, http://wwwnc.cdc.gov/travel/yellowbook/2014/chapter-3-infectious-diseases-related-to-travel/cholera

17. Evans, "Epidemics and Revolutions," 136.

18. Wikipedia, "Burke and Hare Murders," http://en.wikipedia.org/wiki/Burke_and_Hare_murders.

19. Gregory Clark, "Farm Wages and Living Standards in the Industrial Revolution: England, 1670–1850," www.econ.ucdavis.edu/gclark/papers/farm_wages_&_living_standards.pdf.

20. Evans, "Epidemics and Revolutions," 138.

Chapter 19

1. William H. McNeill, "How the Potato Changed the World's History," *Social Research* 66, 1 (1999): 67–83.

2. John Kelly, *The Graves Are Walking: The Great Famine and the Saga of the Irish People* (New York: Picador, 2012), 328.

3. Gray, Peter. "The Irish Poor Law and the Great Famine." IEHC 2006 Helsinki Session 123. www.academia.edu/419878/The_Irish_poor_law_and_the_Great_Famine.

4. Seamus P. Metress, "The History of Irish-American Care of the Aged," *Social Service Review* 59, 1 (March, 1985): 26.

5. Kelly, *The Graves Are Walking*, 46.

Chapter 20

1. U.S. Census

2. Jim Murphy, *The Great Fire* (New York: Scholastic, 1995), 18.

3. Murphy, *Great Fire*.

4. Madelyn Horton, *Mother Jones* (San Diego: Lucent, 1996).

5. Stephanie Hemphill, "Peshtigo: A Tornado of Fire Revisited," Minnesota Public Radio, 27 November 2002, http://news.minnesota.publicradio.org/features/200211/27_hemphills_peshtigofire/

Chapter 21

1. John H. Ellis, *Yellow Fever & Public Health in the New South* (Lexington: University of Kentucky, 1992), 43.

2. Centers for Disease Control and Prevention, "Yellow Fever," www.cdc.gov/yellowfever/symptoms/index.html.

3. CDC, "Yellow Fever."

4. Michael B. A. Oldstone, *Viruses, Plagues, and History* (New York: Oxford University Press, 1998).

5. Ellis, *Yellow Fever*, 4.

6. "The History of Vaccines, Timelines: Yellow Fever," www.historyofvaccines.org/content/timelines/yellow-fever.

7. Ellis, *Yellow Fever*, 166; John Schladweiler, *Tracking Down the Roots of Our Sanitary Sewers*, "Timelines" (2011), www.sewerhistory.org/chronos/design_choices.htm.

8. World Health Organization, "Yellow Fever Factsheet," www.who.int/mediacentre/factsheets/fs100/en/.

Chapter 22

1. Wikipedia, "Ethnic Groups in Indonesia," en.wikipedia.org/wiki/Ethnic_groups_in_Indonesia

2. Simon Winchester, *Krakatoa: The Day the World Exploded: August 27, 1883* (New York: Harper Perennial, 2005), 205–06.

3. R. A. van Sandick, "The Eruption of Krakatoa," in *The Indonesia Reader: History, Culture, Politics*, ed. Tineke Hellwig and Eric Tagliacozzo (Durham, NC: Duke University Press, 2009), 252–55.

4. van Sandick, "Eruption of Krakatoa," 252–55.

5. Winchester, *Krakatoa*.

Chapter 23

1. Ma Junya and Tim Wright, "Sacrificing Local Interests: Water control policies of the Ming and Qing governments and the local economy of Huaibei, 1495–1949," *Modern Asian Studies*, 47, 4 (July 2013): 1361.

2. Desmond E. Walling, "Water: provision and control," *Geography* 74, 4 (October 1989): 356.

3. Wikipedia, "1887 Yellow River Flood," http://en.wikipedia.org/wiki/1887_Yellow_River_flood.

4. Yunzhen Chen *et al.*, "Socio-economic Impacts on Flooding: A 4000-Year History of the Yellow River, China," *AMBIO* 41, (2012): 690.

5. Chen *et al.*, "Socio-economic Impacts," 690.

6. Ma and Wright, "Sacrificing," 1358.

7. Asia for Educators, http://afe.easia.columbia.edu/tps/1750.htm

8. Chen *et al.*, "Socio-economic Impacts," 691.

9. Chen *et al.*, "Socio-economic Impacts," 692–3.

10. Hui Fan, Haijun Huang and Thomas Zeng, "Impacts of Anthropogenic Activity on the Recent Evolution of the Huanghe (Yellow) River Delta," *Journal of Coastal Research* 22, 4 (Jul., 2006): 888+919–929.

11. Ma and Wright, "Sacrificing," 1360.

Chapter 24

1. D. A. Carmichael, "Hawaiian Islands: Further Concerning Plague," *Public Health Reports* 15, 7 (16 February 1900), 360–61.

2. James Duval Phelan, quoted in Myron Echenberg, *Plague Ports: The Global Urban Impact of Bubonic Plague, 1894–1901* (New York University Press, 2007), 225.

3. Jew Ho vs. Williamson, 103 F. 10, 1990, in Lawrence Gostin, *Public Health Law and Ethics: A Reader* (2002), http://www.publichealthlaw.net/Reader/docs/JewHo.pdf.

Chapter 25

1. Eugene Zebrowski, Jr, *The Last Days of St. Pierre: The Volcanic Disaster That Claimed Thirty Thousand Lives* (New Brunswick, NJ: Rutgers University Press, 2002), 53.

2. Tom Simkin, Lee Siebert and Russell Blong, "Volcano Fatalities: Lessons from the Historical Record," *Science*, New Series, Vol. 291, No. 5502 (Jan. 12, 2001), 255.

3. Zebrowski, *Last Days of St. Pierre*.

Chapter 26

1. Simon Winchester, *A Crack in the Edge of the World: America and the Great California Earthquake of 1906* (New York: Harper Perennial, 2006).

2. U. S. Census Bureau.

Chapter 27

1. Nigel Watson, "The Tunguska Event," *History Today* (July 2008), 7.

2. Bill Napier and David Asher, "The Tunguska Impact Event and Beyond," *Astronomy and Geophysics* 50 (Feb 2009): 1.18.

3. NASA, "The Tunguska Explosion – 100 Years Later," *Science News* (June 30 2008), science.nasa.gov/science-news/science-at-nasa/2008/30jun_tunguska/

4. Watson, "Tunguska Event."

5. Tunguska Explosion Conspiracy, Georgia Tech Conspiracy Wiki, web.archive.org/web/20131011013916/http://conspiracytheories.lmc.gatech.edu/index.php/Tunguska_Explosion_Conspiracy.

7. G. S. Collins, N. Artemieva, K. Wünnemann, P. A. Bland, W. U. Reimold, and C. Koeberl, "Evidence that Lake Cheko Is Not an Impact Crater," *Terra Nova* 20 (2008): 165–68.

8. Watson, "Tunguska Event."

9. Napier and Asher, "Tunguska Impact."

10. Jeffrey Kluger, "The Man Who Guards the Planet" [profile of astronomer Don Yeomans], *Time* (9 June 2014): 34–37.

11. NASA, Near Earth Object Program, NEO Basics, "Target Earth," neo.jpl.nasa.gov/neo/target.html

12. Wikipedia, "2014 AA," en.wikipedia.org/wiki/2014_AA.

13. Kelly Beatty, "New Chelyabinsk Results Yield Surprises," *Sky and Telescope* (7 November 2013): skyandtelescope.com/community/skyblog/newsblog/New-Chelyabinsk-Results-Surprising-Sobering-231008971.html

14. Kluger, "Man Who Guards."

15. NASA, Near Earth Object Program, NEO Basics, "Near-Earth Objects and Life on Earth," neo.jpl.nasa.gov/neo/life.html.

16. J. F. Lerbekmo, "The Chicxulub-Shiva Extraterrestrial One-two Kller Punches to Earth 65 Million Years Ago," *Marine and Petroleum Geology* 49 (January 2014): 203–207.

17. Lerbekmo, "Chicxulub-Shiva."

18. Elizabeth Kolbert, *The Sixth Extinction: An Unnatural History* (New York: Henry Holt, 2014), 70–91.

19. Peter Brannen, "The Death of the Dinosaurs," *The New York Times* (January 31, 2015), nytimes.com/2015/02/01/opinion/sunday/the-death-of-the-dinosaurs.html.

Chapter 28

1. PBS, *The Great War: WWI Casualty and Death Tables*, pbs.org/greatwar/resources/casdeath_pop.html.

2. John M. Barry, *The Great Influenza: The Story of the Deadliest Pandemic in History*. New York: Penguin, 2005.

3. J.K. Taubenberger and David M. Morens, "1918 Influenza: The Mother of All Pandemics," *Emerging Infectious Diseases* 12, 1 (2006): dx.doi.org/10.3201/eid1209.050979.

4. Donald R. Olson *et al.*, "Epidemiological Evidence of an Early Wave of the 1918 Influenza Pandemic in New York City," *Proceedings of the National Academy of Sciences of the United States of America* 102, 31 (Aug. 2, 2005): 11059–63.

5. Anton Erkora, "Origins of the Spanish Influenza Pandemic (1918–1920) and Its Relation to the First World War," *Journal of Molecular and Genetic Medicine* 3, 2 (2009 December): 190–194.

6. Barry, *Great Influenza*, 376–77.

7. Patricia J. Fanning, *Influenza and Inequality: One Town's Tragic Response to the Great Pandemic of 1918* (Amherst: University of Massachusetts Press, 2010), 121.

8. Barry, *Great Influenza*, 382–86.

9. Taubenberger and Morens, "1918 Influenza."

Chapter 29

1. Steve Puleo, *Dark Tide: The Great Boston Molasses Flood of 1919* (Boston: New Beacon Press, 2004), 112–13.

2. Sean Potter, "Retrospect: January 15, 1919: Boston Molasses Flood," *Weatherwise* 64, 1 (2011): 10–11.

3. Puleo, *Dark Tide*, 85.

4. Potter, "Retrospect."

5. Steve Puleo, "Death by Molasses," *American History* 35, 6 (2001): 60–66.

6. "233,000 Gallons of Molasses Spills into Honolulu Harbor Kausing Fish Kill," *Hawaii News Now* (September 10, 2013): hawaiinewsnow.com/story/23396971/faulty-pipe-caused-honolulu-harbor-molasses-spill.

7. Rick Daysog, "Molasses Spill Caused Massive Coral Die-off," *Hawaii News Now* (December 14, 2013): hawaiinewsnow.com/story/24189342/exclusive-molasses-spill-disastrous-for-coral.

8. Oskar Garcia, "Hawaii Lawmakers Call for Changes after Molasses Spill," *Huffington Post* (January 27, 2014), nbcnews.com/news/us-news/pipe-had-leak-months-hawaii-molasses-spill-v20615693.

Chapter 30

1. Yoshiaki Ishiguro, "A Japanese National Crime: The Korean Massacre after the Great Kanto Earthquake of 1923," *Korea Journal* 38, 4 (Winter 1998): 335.

2. J. Charles Schencking, "The Great Kanto Earthquake and the Culture of Catastrophe and Reconstruction in 1920s Japan," *Journal of Japanese Studies*, 34, 2 (Summer, 2008): 303.

3. Schencking, "Great Kanto Earthquake," 303.

4. U. S. Geologic Survey, Historic Earthquakes: Kanto (Kwanto), Japan, earthquake.usgs.gov/earthquakes/world/events/1923_09_01.php

5. Joshua Hammer, "Aftershocks," *Smithsonian* 42, 2 (May 2011): 50–53.

6. Sonia Ryang, "The Great Kanto Earthquake and the Massacre of Koreans in 1923: Notes on Japan's Modern National Sovereignty," *Anthropological Quarterly*, 76, 4 (Fall 2003): 733.

7. Wikipedia, "1923 Great Kantō Earthquake," http://en.wikipedia.org/wiki/1923_Great_Kant%C5%8D_earthquake#Postquake_violence.

8. Ishiguro, "Japanese National Crime."

9. Janet Borland, "Capitalising on Catastrophe: Reinvigorating the Japanese State with Moral Values through Education Following the 1923 Great Kantô Earthquake," *Modern Asian Studies*, 40, 4 (Oct., 2006): 887; quoting Yamamoto.

10. Borland, "Capitalising on Catastrophe," 895.

11. Hammer, "Aftershocks."

12. Schencking, "Great Kanto Earthquake," 296.

13. Schencking, "Great Kanto Earthquake," 329.

14. Schencking, "Great Kanto Earthquake," 306.

15. Hammer, "Aftershocks."

Chapter 31

1. University of Rhode Island Graduate School of Oceanography, Hurricanes: Science and Society, hurricanescience.org/history/timeline/#/?-decade=pre1900.

2. URI GSO, Hurricanes: Science and Society, hurricanescience.org/history/timeline/#/?-decade=pre1900.

3. Christine Gibson, "How the Hurricane Got Its Name," *American Heritage* 57, 4 (2006), americanheritage.com/content/how-hurricane-got-its-name.

4. R. A. Scott, *Sudden Sea: The Great Hurricane of 1938* (Boston: Back Bay Books, 2003): 113–14.

5. Scott, *Sudden Sea.*

6. Everett S. Allen, *A Wind to Shake the World: The Story of the 1938 Hurricane* (Beverly, MA: Commonwealth Editions, 1976): 81.

7. Christine Gibson, "Our 10 Greatest Natural Disasters," *American Heritage* 57, 4 (2006), americanheritage.com/content/our-10-greatest-natural-disasters.

8. Scott, *Sudden Sea,* 98.

9. National Weather Service, "The Great Hurricane of 1938," weather.gov/box/1938hurricane.

10. WGBH, American Experience, "The Hurricane of '38, Interview: Norman Caswell," pbs.org/wgbh/americanexperience/features/interview/hurricane-norman-caswell/.

11. Vaclav Smil, "The Next 50 Years: Fatal Discontinuities," *Population and Development Review* 31, 2 (June 2005): 201-36.

Chapter 32

1. William Wise, *Killer Smog: The World's Worst Air Pollution Disaster* (Rand McNally, 1968), 122.

2. Wise, *Killer Smog.*

3. Wise, *Killer Smog,* 19.

4. U.S. Environmental Protection Agency, Clean Energy, Coal, epa.gov/cleanenergy/energy-and-you/affect/coal.html.

5. Met Office, "The Great Smog of 1952," metoffice.gov.uk/education/teens/case-studies/great-smog.

6. Wikipedia, "1930 Meuse Valley Fog," en.wikipedia.org/wiki/1930_Meuse_Valley_fog.

7. United States Environmental Protection Agency, History of Air Pollution, epa.gov/airscience/air-historyofairpollution.htm.

8. U.S. EPA, Clean Air Research, "Science to Protect the Air We Breathe," epa.gov/research/video/ca/index.html.

9. Met Office, "Great Smog of 1952."

10. Wise, *Killer Smog,* 145.

11. Wise, *Killer Smog,* 157.

12. Wise, *Killer Smog*, 42.

13. Wise, *Killer Smog*, 174.

14. Mario Moretto, "Environmentalists decry proposal to loosen Maine smog rules; paper mill officials say change will spur job creation," *Bangor Daily News* September 10, 2013, bangordailynews. com/2013/09/10/politics/environmentalists-decry-proposal-to-loosen-maine-smog-rules-paper-mill-officials-say-change-will-spur-job-creation/

15. Thomas M. Parris, "Smog Season," *Environment* (May 2006), 3.

16. Coral Davenport, "Obama to Take Action to Slash Coal Pollution," *New York Times*, 1 June 2014, nytimes.com/2014/06/02/us/politics/epa-to-seek-30-percent-cut-in-carbon-emissions.html.

17. Wikipedia, "Coal," en.wikipedia.org/wiki/Coal.

18. U.S. Energy Information Administration, eia.gov/ tools/faqs/faq.cfm?id=427&t=3.

19. International Energy Agency, Coal, iea.org/topics/ coal/.

20. U.S. EPA, Clean Energy, Coal, epa.gov/cleanenergy/energy-and-you/affect/coal.html.

21. NASA, Earth Observatory, "How Is Today's Warming Different from the Past?" earthobservatory.nasa. gov/Features/GlobalWarming/page3.php.

22. Damocles, "Animation about the Greenhouse Effect," damocles-eu.org/education/Animation_ about_the_greenhouse_effect_182.shtml

Chapter 33

1. IRIN News and Analysis, "Sahel: Backgrounder on the Sahel, West Africa's Poorest Region" (2 June 2008), irinnews.org/report/78514/sahel-backgrounder-on-the-sahel-west-africa-s-poorest-region.

2. Environment and Society Portal, Sahel Drought and Famine, 1968–1985, environmentandsociety. org/tools/keywords#/id/1865; United Nations Environmental Programme, Africa Environment Outlook, "West Africa," unep.org/dewa/Africa/ publications/AEO-1/056.htm

3. Albert E. Sollod, "Rainfall Variability and Twareg Perceptions of Climate Impacts in Niger," *Human Ecology*, 18, 3 (September 1990): 267–281.

4. Ning Zeng, "Drought in the Sahel," *Science*, New Series 302, No. 5647 (Nov. 7, 2003): 999–1000.

5. K.W. Butzer, "Paleo-Environmental Perspectives on the Sahel Drought of 1968—73," *GeoJournal* 7, 4 (1983): 369–374.

6. Zeng, "Drought in the Sahel."

7. U.S., NOAA, Earth System Research Laboratory, "El Niño/Southern Oscillation (ENSO),"esrl.noaa. gov/psd/enso/.

8. Zeng, "Drought in the Sahel."

9. Simon Batterbury, "The Sahel Region: Assessing Progress 25 Years after the Great Drought,"simon-batterbury.net/pubs/geogmag.html.

10. I. M. Held *et al.*, "Simulation of Sahel Drought in the 20th and 21st Centuries," *Proceedings of the National Academy of Sciences of the United States of America* 102, 50 (December 13, 2005): 17891-96.

11. U.S., NOAA, Climate.gov, "January Precipitation Deficits Keep California Drought Outlook Grim" (February 7, 2014), climate.gov/news-features/ event-tracker/january-precipitation-deficits-keep-california-drought-outlook-grim

12. U.S. House of Representatives, Natural Resources Committee, "The Man-Made California Drought," naturalresources.house.gov/issues/issue/?IssueID=5921.

13. NOAA, "El Niño—And What Is the Southern Oscillation Anyway?!" kids.earth.nasa.gov/archive/ nino/intro.html.

14. NOAA, "What Is an El Niño?" pmel.noaa.gov/tao/ elnino/el-nino-story.html.

Chapter 34

1. D. A. Henderson, *Smallpox: The Death of a Disease* (Amherst, NY: Prometheus Books, 2009), 31.

2. Henderson, *Smallpox*, 223–24.

Chapter 35

1. Shaorong Zhao and Shuzo Takemoto, "Aseismic Fault Movement before the 1976 Tangshan Earthquake Detected by Levelling: Implications for Pre-seismic Stress Localization?" *Geophysical Journal International* 136 (1999): 68–82

2. Zhang, Hon-Can, and Zhang, Yi-Jong, "Psychological Consequences of Earthquake Disaster Survivors," *International Journal of Psychology* 26, 5 (November 1991): 613–621.

3. James Palmer, *Heaven Cracks, Earth Shakes: The Tangshan Earthquake and the Death of Mao's China* (New York: Basic Books, 2012), 134.

4. Arthur Waldron, "Starving in China," *The New Criterion* (May 2013): 4–8.

5. Palmer, *Heaven Cracks*.

6. Palmer, *Heaven Cracks*, 119.

7. Xiangming Chen; Kejing Dai; Parnell, Allan. "Disaster Tradition and Change: Remarriage and Family Reconstruction in a Post-Earthquake Community in the People's Republic of China," *Journal of Comparative Family Studies* 23, 1 (Spring 1992): 115–132

8. Palmer, *Heaven Cracks*, 189.

9. Palmer, *Heaven Cracks*, 65.

Chapter 36

1. Jonathan Engel, *The Epidemic: A Global History of Aids* (New York: HarperCollins, 2006), 16.

2. United States, Aids.gov, "U.S. Statistics," aids.gov/hiv-aids-basics/hiv-aids-101/statistics/.

3. Engel, *Epidemic*, 245.

4. Nicoli Nattrass, *The AIDS Conspiracy: Science Fights Back* (New York: Columbia University Press, 2012).

5. Nattrass, *AIDS Conspiracy*, 139.

6. U.S. Aids.gov, "U.S. Statistics."

7. World Health Organization, "HIV/AIDS: Data and Statistics," who.int/hiv/data/en/.

8. World Health Organization, "South Africa: Health Profile," who.int/gho/countries/zaf.pdf?ua=1.

9. Fraser G. McNeill, *AIDS, Politics, and Music in South Africa* (New York: Cambridge University Press, 2011), 2.

10. McNeill, *AIDS, Politics, and Music*, 250.

Chapter 37

1. Ward Morehouse and M. Arun Subramaniam, *The Bhopal Tragedy: What Really Happened and What It Means for American Workers and Communities at Risk* (New York: Council on International and Public Affairs, 1986).

2. R. Clayton Trotter, Susan G. Day and Amy E. Love, "Bhopal, India and Union Carbide: The Second Tragedy," *Journal of Business Ethics*, 8, 6 (Jun., 1989): pp. 439–454.

3. Radhika Iyengar and Monisha Bajaj, "After the Smoke Clears: Toward Education for Sustainable Development in Bhopal, India," *Comparative Education Review* 55, 3 (August 2011): 424–425.

4. U.S. Census Bureau, International Programs, Historical Estimates of World Population, census.gov/population/international/data/worldpop/table_history.php.

5. Organisation for Economic Co-operation and Development, oecd.org/newsroom/34992235.pdf.

6. International Food Policy Research Institute, *Green Revolution: Curse or Blessing?* ifpri.org/sites/default/files/pubs/pubs/ib/ib11.pdf.

7. Morehouse and Subramaniam, *Bhopal Tragedy*, 4–20.

8. Armin Rosencranz, "Bhopal, Transnational Corporations, and Hazardous Technologies," *Ambio* 17, 5 (1988): 336–341.

9. Morehouse and Subramaniam, *Bhopal Tragedy*, 20–21.

10. Rosencranz, "Bhopal, Transnational Corporations."

11. William Bogard, *The Bhopal Tragedy: Language, Logic, and Politics in the Production of a Hazard* (Boulder, CO: Westview Press, 1989).

12. Wikipedia, "Bhopal Disaster," en.wikipedia.org/wiki/Bhopal_disaster#Legal_action_against_Union_Carbide.

13. India Blooms News Service, "Bhopal Victims Protest for Clean Water," February 17, 2014, indiablooms.com/NewsDetailsPage/2014/newsDetails170214d1.php

14. Prasenjit Bhattacharyar, "Court Rules Union Carbide Not Liable in Bhopal Case," *Wall Street Journal* (June 28, 2012): online.wsj.com/news/articles/SB10001424052702303561504577493642502980690.

15. "NGOs want Modi to take up issues of Bhopal gas tragedy victims with Obama," *Hindustan Times* (25 January 2015): hindustantimes.com/bhopal/ngos-want-modi-to-take-up-issues-of-bhopal-gas-tragedy-victims-with-obama/article1-1310623.aspx.

Chapter 38

1. Hobart King, "Novarupta: The Most Powerful Volcanic Eruption of the Twentieth Century," geology.com/novarupta/.

2. Barry Voight, "The 1985 Nevado del Ruiz Volcano Catastrophe: Anatomy and Retrospection," *Journal of Volcanology and Geothermal Research* 44(1990): 349–386.

3. USGS, Hawaiian Volcano Observatory, "Lessons Learned from the Armero, Colombia Tragedy" (2009): hvo.wr.usgs.gov/volcanowatch/archive/2009/09_10_29.html.

4. M. Murray, "Scientists Predict Second Ruiz Blast," *Science News*, 129, 25 (Jun. 21, 1986): 390–391.

5. Voight, "1985 Nevado del Ruiz Volcano Catastrophe."

6. Voight, "1985 Nevado del Ruiz Volcano Catastrophe."

7. BBC, "Picture Power: Tragedy of Omayra Sanchez," news.bbc.co.uk/2/hi/4231020.stm

8. A. L. Hansell, C. J. Horwell and C. Oppenheimer, "Education: The Health Hazards of Volcanoes and Geothermal Areas," *Occupational and Environmental Medicine*, 63, 2 (Feb., 2006): 149–156.

9. Bruno R. Lima *et al.*, "Disasters and Mental Health: Experience in Colombia and Ecuador and Its Relevance for Primary Care in Mental Health in Latin America," *International Journal of Mental Health*, 19, 2, (Summer 1990): 3–20.

10. Hansell *et al.*, "Education."

11. Graham A. Tobin and Linda M. Whiteford, "Provisioning Capacity: A Critical Component of Vulnerability and Resilience under Chronic Volcanic Eruptions," Chapter 8 in *Forces of Nature and Cultural Responses*, ed. Katrin Pfeifer and Niki Pfeifer (New York: Springer, 2013), 139–166.

12. Jean-Christophe Gaillard, "Was it a *Cultural Disaster*? AETA Resilience Following the 1991 Mt. Pinatubo Eruption," *Philippine Quarterly of Culture and Society* 34, 4 (December 2006): 376–399.

13. Kirk Johnson, "After Mountain's Collapse, Uncertainty and Loss," *New York Times* (March 26, 2014): nytimes.com/2014/03/27/us/washington-mudslide-search.html?hp&_r=0

Chapter 39

1. L. L. Bennett & R. Skjoeldebrand, "Pages from the Past: Nuclear Power Redux," *IAEA Bulletin* 50, 2 (May 2009): iaea.org/Publications/Magazines/Bulletin/Bull502/50201215860.html, 58.

2. Victor Snell, "The Cause of the Chernobyl Accident,"

Introduction to David R. Marples, *The Social Impact of the Chernobyl Disaster* (New York: St. Martin's Press, 1988).

3. David R. Marples, *The Social Impact of the Chernobyl Disaster* (New York: St. Martin's Press, 1988), 28–29.

4. Harold M. Ginzburg and Eric Reis, "Consequences of the Nuclear Power Plant Accident at Chernobyl," *Public Health Reports* 106, 1 (Jan. - Feb., 1991): 32–40.

5. Marples, *Social Impact*, 36.

6. Keith Baverstock and Dillwyn Williams, "The Chernobyl Accident 20 Years on: An Assessment of the Health Consequences and the International Response," *Environmental Health Perspectives* 114, 9 (Sep., 2006): 1312–17.

7. Leonid Lomat *et al.*, "Incidence of Childhood Disease in Belarus Associated with the Chernobyl Accident," *Environmental Health Perspectives* 105, Supplement 6: Radiation and Human Health (Dec., 1997): 1529–32.

8. Hava-Shifra Weinberg *et al.*, "Molecular Changes in the Offspring of Liquidators Who Emigrated to Israel from the Chernobyl Disaster Area," *Environmental Health Perspectives* 105, Supplement 6: Radiation and Human Health (Dec., 1997), 1479–81.

9. Marples, *Social Impact*, 76–77; also 2012 abstract at ncbi.nlm.nih.gov/pubmed/22217593.

10. Sonja D. Schmid, "Transformation Discourse: Nuclear Risk as a Strategic Tool in Late Soviet Politics of Expertise," *Science, Technology, & Human Values* 29, No. 3 (Summer, 2004): 353–376.

11. NEI Knowledge Center, "World Statistics: Nuclear Energy Around the World," nei.org/Knowledge-Center/Nuclear-Statistics/World-Statistics.

12. Bonnie A. Osif, Anthony J. Baratta, and Thomas W. Conkling, *TMI 25 Years Later: The Three Mile Island Nuclear Power Plant Accident and Its Impact* (University Park: The Pennsylvania State University Press, 2004).

13. U.S. NRC Backgrounder on Three Mile Island, nrc.gov/reading-rm/doc-collections/fact-sheets/3mile-isle.html.

14. U.S. Energy Information Administration, *Monthly Energy Review* (February 2014), 115: eia.gov/totalenergy/data/monthly/pdf/sec8.pdf.

Chapter 40

1. Joseph D. Ayotte, Denise L. Montgomery, and Sarah M. Flanagan, "Arsenic in Groundwater in Eastern New England: Occurrence, Controls, and Human Health Implications," *Environmental Science & Technology* 37, 10 (2003): 2075–83.

2. James Salzman, *Drinking Water: A History* (New York: Overlook Duckworth, 2013), 115.

3. Salzman, *Drinking Water*, 115.

4. Allan H. Smith, Elena O. Lingas, and Mahfuzar Rahman, "Contamination of Drinking-Water by Arsenic in Bangladesh: A Public Health Emergency," *Bulletin of the World Health Organization* **78, 9 (Jan. 2000)**, 1093–1103.

5. "Luminous Water Technologies Licenses Berkeley Lab Invention for Arsenic Free Water in India, Bangladesh," *Business Standard* (March 28, 2014), business-standard.com/article/news-ani/luminous-water-technologies-licenses-berkeley-lab-invention-for-arsenic-free-water-in-india-bangladesh-114032100361_1.html.

6. Central Intelligence Agency, "Bangladesh," *The World Fact Book*, cia.gov/library/publications/the-world-factbook/geos/bg.html.

7. Salzman, *Drinking Water*, 76.

8. UNICEF, Bangladesh Overview, History, unicef.org/bangladesh/overview_4842.htm.

9. UNICEF, Bangladesh Overview, History.

10. UNICEF, Arsenic Mitigation in Bangladesh, unicef.org/bangladesh/Arsenic.pdf.

11. Salzman, *Drinking Water*, 117.

12. Gadgil Lab for Energy and Water Research, Arsenic Removal, gadgillab.berkeley.edu/research/water/arsenic_removal/.

13. Steven E. F. Brown, "Berkeley Lab Licenses Arsenic-Cleaning Technology to Indian Company," *San Francisco Business Times* (March 5, 2014), bizjournals.com/sanfrancisco/news/2014/03/05/berkeley-lab-licenses-arsenic-cleaning.html.

14. Evan Osnos, "Chemical Valley: The Coal Industry, the Politicians, and the Big Spill," *New Yorker* (April 7, 2014): http://www.newyorker.com/magazine/2014/04/07/chemical-valley.

Chapter 41

1. World Health Organization, Poliomyelitis Fact Sheet, who.int/mediacentre/factsheets/fs114/en/

2. David M. Oshinsky, *Polio: An American Story* (New York: Oxford University Press, 2005), 162.

3. Elisha P. Renne, *The Politics of Polio in Northern Nigeria* (Bloomington: Indiana University Press, 2010), 8.

4. Centers for Disease Control, "A Polio-Free U.S. Thanks to Vaccine Efforts," cdc.gov/features/poliofacts/.

5. WHO, "Nigeria: Health Profile," who.int/gho/countries/nga.pdf?ua=1.

6. Renne, *Politics of Polio*, 9.

7. Polio Global Eradication Initiative, "Circulating Vaccine-Derived Poliovirus 2000–2013," polioeradication.org/Dataandmonitoring/Poliothisweek/Circulatingvaccinederivedpoliovirus.aspx.

8. Renne, *Politics of Polio*, 18.

9. Renne, *Politics of Polio*, 44.

10. Renne, *Politics of Polio*, 47.

11. Renne, *Politics of Polio*, 49.

12. WHO, Poliomyelitis Fact Sheet, who.int/mediacentre/factsheets/fs114/en/.

Chapter 42

1. Narayan Sastry, "Forest Fires, Air Pollution, and Mortality in Southeast Asia," *Demography* 39, 1 (2002): 1-23.

2. Elizabeth Frankenberg, Douglas McKee and Duncan Thomas, "Health Consequences of Forest Fires in Indonesia," *Demography* 42, 1 (2005): 109–129.

3. Sastry, "Forest Fires."

4. Frankenberg *et al.*, "Health Consequences."

5. S. Robert Aiken, "Runaway Fires, Smoke-Haze Pollution, and Unnatural Disasters in Indonesia," *Geographical Review* 94, 1 (2004): 55–79.

6. US CIA, "Indonesia," *World Fact Book*, cia.gov/library/publications/the-world-factbook/geos/id.html.

7. David Rosenberg, "Environmental Pollution around the South China Sea: Developing a Regional Response," *Contemporary Southeast Asia* 21, 1 (1999): 119–145.

8. Aiken, "Runaway Fires."

9. Paul K. Gellert, "A Brief History and Analysis of Indonesia's Forest Fire Crisis," *Indonesia* 65 (Apr., 1998): 63–85.

10. Aiken, "Runaway Fires."

11. Ekoningtyas Margu Wardani, "A Nation of Fire: What Should We Learn from the 1997/1998 Haze?" *Jakarta Post* (June 25 2013), thejakartapost.com/news/2013/06/25/a-nation-fire-what-should-we-learn-19971998-haze.html.

12. Aiken, "Runaway Fires."

13. Aiken, "Runaway Fires."

14. Wardani, "Nation of Fire."

15. Yenni Kwok, "The Southeast Asian Haze Is Back and Worse May Follow," *Time Magazine* (July 30, 2013), http://world.time.com/2013/07/30/the-southeast-asian-haze-is-back-and-worse-may-follow/.

16. Kwok, "Southeast Asian Haze Is Back."

17. Jane Braxton Little, "Regrowing Borneo, Tree by Tree," *Scientific American* 18, 5 (December 2008).

18. Dennis Normile, "Restoring a 'Biological Desert' on Borneo," *Science* (New Series) 325, 5940 (31 June 2009): 557.

19. Little, "Regrowing Borneo."

Chapter 43

1. R. García-Herrera *et al.*, "A Review of the European Summer Heat Wave of 2003," *Critical Reviews in Environmental Science and Technology* 40, 4 (2010): 267–306.

2. García-Herrera *et al.*, "Review."

3. Laurent Toulemon and Magali Barbieri, "The Mortality Impact of the August 2003 Heat Wave in France: Investigating the 'Harvesting' Effect and Other Long-Term Consequences," *Population Studies* 62, 1 (Mar. 2008): 39–53.

4. Toulemon and Barbieri, "Mortality Impact."

5. Carme Borrell *et al.*, "Socioeconomic Position and Excess Mortality during the Heat Wave of 2003 in Barcelona," *European Journal of Epidemiology* 21, 9 (2006): 633–40.

6. Grégoire Rey *et al.*, "Heat Exposure and Socio-Economic Vulnerability as Synergistic Factors in Heat-Wave-Related Mortality," *European Journal of Epidemiology* 24, 9 (2009): 495–502.

7. United States Environmental Protection Agency, Heat Island Effect, epa.gov/heatisland/.

8. García-Herrera *et al.*, "Review."

9. Gerald A. Meehl and Claudia Tebaldi, "More Intense, More Frequent, and Longer Lasting Heat Waves in the 21st Century," *Science*, New Series 305, 5686 (Aug. 13, 2004): 994–97.

10. Wenhong Li *et al.*, "Changes to the North Atlantic Subtropical High and Its Role in the Intensification of Summer Rainfall Variability in the Southeastern United States," *J. Climate* 24 (2011), 1499–1506, journals.ametsoc.org/doi/abs/10.1175/2010J-CLI3829.1.

11. LuAnn Dahlman, "Climate Change: Global Temperature" (August 30, 2009), NOAA, Climate.gov, climate.gov/news-features/understanding-climate/climate-change-global-temperature.

12. Environmental Protection Agency, Heat Island Effect, epa.gov/heatisland/

13. E. Klinenberg, *Heat Wave: A Social Autopsy of Disaster in Chicago* (Chicago: University Chicago Press, 2002).

Chapter 44

1. Abigail A. Baird, "Sifting Myths for Truths about Our World: *When They Severed Earth from Sky: How the Human Mind Shapes Myth* by Elizabeth Wayland Barber; Paul T. Barber" [review], *Science*, New Series, 308, 5726 (May 27, 2005): 1261.

2. Bruce Jaffe, Eric Geist, and Helen Gibbons, "Indian Ocean Earthquake Triggers Deadly Tsunami," *Sound Waves* (USGS Newsletter), soundwaves.usgs.gov/2005/01/.

3. "Girl, 10, Used Geography Lesson to Save Lives," *The Telegraph* (January 1, 2005), telegraph.co.uk/news/1480192/Girl-10-used-geography-lesson-to-save-lives.html.

4. Ilan Kelman *et al.*, "Tourists and Disasters: Lessons from the 26 December 2004 Tsunamis," *Journal of Coastal Conservation* 12, 3 (Sep., 2008): 105–13.

5. California Institute of Technology Tectonics Observatory, "What Happened During the 2004 Sumatra Earthquake," tectonics.caltech.edu/outreach/highlights/sumatra/what.html.

6. United States Geological Survey, "Earthquakes with 50,000 or More Deaths," archive.org/web/20140820090633/http://earthquake.usgs.gov/earthquakes/world/most_destructive.php.

7. E. N. Bernard *et al.* "Tsunami: Scientific Frontiers, Mitigation, Forecasting and Policy Implications." *Philosophical Transactions: Mathematical, Physical*

and Engineering Sciences 364, 1845 (Aug. 15, 2006): 1989–2007.

8. Sonali Deraniyagala, *Wave* (New York: Knopf, 2013).

9. Jin Sato, "Matching Goods and People: Aid and Human Security after the 2004 Tsunami," *Development in Practice* 20, 1 (Feb., 2010): 70–84.

10. Kyle Beardsley and Brian McQuinn, "Rebel Groups as Predatory Organizations: The Political Effects of the 2004 Tsunami in Indonesia and Sri Lanka," *The Journal of Conflict Resolution* 53, 4 (August 2009): 624–45.

11. Hutanuwatr, Khanin, Bolin, Bob, & Pijawka, David. "Vulnerability and Disaster in Thailand: Scale, Power, and Collaboration in Post-tsunami Recovery." Chapter 5 in *Forces of Nature and Cultural Responses*, edited by Katrin Pfeifer and Niki Pfeifer, 69–92. Dordrecht: Springer, 2005.

12. Bernard et al., "Tsunami."

13. Sato, "Matching Goods."

14. United Nations Office for Disaster Risk Reduction, Hyogo Framework for Action, unisdr.org/we/coordinate/hfa.

15. Mary-Laure Martin, "Child Participation in Disaster Risk Reduction: The Case of Flood-Affected Children in Bangladesh," *Third World Quarterly* 31, 8 (2011): 1357–75.

Chapter 45

1. Dr. William W. Locke, "Understanding Katrina," Laurie Cantwell, *Teaching with Hurricane Katrina: The Physiography, Climate, Storm, and Impact*, Science Education Resource Center, Carleton College, serc.carleton.edu/research_education/katrina/understanding.html.

2. Richard D. Knabb, Jamie R. Rhome, and Daniel P. Brown, "Tropical Cyclone Report: Hurricane Katrina, 23–30 gust 2005," National Hurricane Center, 20 December 2005; updated 14 September 2011 and 10 August 2006. nhc.noaa.gov/pdf/TCR-AL122005_Katrina.pdf.

3. Lise Olsen, "5 Years after Katrina, Storm's Death Toll Remains a Mystery," *Houston Chronicle* (Aug. 30, 2010), chron.com/news/nation-world/article/5-years-after-Katrina-storm-s-death-toll-remains-1589464.php.

4. Ewen McCallum and Julian Heming, "Hurricane Katrina: An Environmental Perspective," *Philo-sophical Transactions: Mathematical, Physical and Engineering Sciences* 364, 1845 (Aug. 15, 2006): 2099–2115.

5. Hurricane Katrina, History.com, history.com/topics/hurricane-katrina.

6. Jennifer A. Reich and Martha Wadsworth, "Out of the Floodwaters, But Not Yet on Dry Ground: Experiences of Displacement and Adjustment in Adolescents and Their Parents Following Hurricane Katrina," *Children, Youth and Environments* 18, 1 (2008): 358.

7. Elizabeth Fussell, Narayan Sastry and Mark Van Landingham, "Race, Socioeconomic Status, and Return Migration to New Orleans after Hurricane Katrina," *Population and Environment* 31, 1/3 (January 2010): 20–42.

8. John S. Petterson, Laura D. Stanley, Edward Glazier and James Philipp, "A Preliminary Assessment of Social and Economic Impacts Associated with Hurricane Katrina," *American Anthropologist*, New Series 108, 4 (Dec., 2006): 643–70.

9. Reich and Wadsworth, "Out of the Floodwaters."

10. Diana B. Elliott, "Understanding Changes in Families and Households Pre- and Post-Katrina," U.S. Census Bureau, (San Francisco: American Sociological Association Meeting, August 10, 2009).

11. Fussell *et al.*, "Race, Socioeconomic Status, and Return."

12. Elliott, "Understanding Changes."

13. Danielle Dreilinger, "7,000 New Orleans Teachers, Laid Off after Katrina, Win Court Ruling," *The Times-Picayune* (January 17, 2014): nola.com/crime/index.ssf/2014/01/7000_new_orleans_teachers_laid.html.

14. Ismail K. White *et al.*, "Feeling the Pain of My People: Hurricane Katrina, Racial Inequality, and the Psyche of Black America," *Journal of Black Studies* 37, 4 (Mar., 2007) 523–38.

15. Douglas A. Kysar and Thomas O. McGarity, "Did NEPA Drown New Orleans? The Levees, the Blame Game, and the Hazards of Hindsight," *Duke Law Journal* 56, 1 (Oct.,2006): 179–235.

16. Petterson *et al.*, "Preliminary Assessment."

17. Mike Brunker, "Class-Action Suit Against FEMA Trailer Manufacturers Settled for $42.6 Million," investigations.nbcnews.com/_news/2012/09/28/14140222-class-ac-

tion-suit-against-fema-trailer-manufacturers-set-
tled-for-426-million.

18. U.S. Environmental Protection Agency, "Formaldehyde Emissions from Composite Wood Products,"
epa.gov/opptintr/chemtest/formaldehyde/.

Chapter 46

1. Google Earth, Satellite View and Map of the City of
Port-au-Prince (Pòtoprens), Haiti, nationsonline.
org/oneworld/map/google_map_Port-au-Prince.
htm.

2. USGS, Earthquake Hazards Program, Haiti Region
Magnitude 7.0, earthquake.usgs.gov/earthquakes/
eqinthenews/2010/us2010rja6/#summary.

3. Mark Schuller and Pablo Morales, "Introduction," in
Tectonic Shifts: Haiti Since the Earthquake, ed. Mark
Schuller and Pablo Morales, 1-8 (Sterling, VA:
Kumarian Press, 2012).

4. UN Development Programme, 2013 Human Development Report, Haiti, hdr.undp.org/sites/default/
files/Country-Profiles/HTI.pdf.

5. Haiti Partners, Haiti Statistics, haitipartners.org/
who-we-are/haiti-statistics/.

6. Myron M. Beasley, "Women, *Sabotaj*, and Underground Food Economies in Haiti," *Gastronomica:
The Journal of Food and Culture* 12, 2 (Summer
2012).

7. CIA, World Fact Book, cia.gov/library/publica-
tions/the-world-factbook/geos/ha.html.

8. UN Development Programme, 2013 Human Development Report, Haiti, hdr.undp.org/sites/default/
files/Country-Profiles/HTI.pdf.

9. Carol Presutti, "Haiti Struggles to Begin Free Public
Education," *Voice of America* (October 31, 2011):
voanews.com/content/haiti-struggles-to-be-
gin-free-public-education-133018688/164638.
html.

10. Beasley, "Women, *Sabotaj*, and Underground
Food," 33.

11. CIA, World Fact Book.

12. Mats Lundahl, *Poverty in Haiti: Essays on Underdevelopment and Post Disaster Projects* (New York:
Palgrave Macmillan, 2011).

13. Lundahl, *Poverty in Haiti*.

14. Beasley, "Women, *Sabotaj*, and Underground
Food," 37.

15. Elizabeth McAlister, "Humanitarian Adhocracy,
Transnational New Apostolic Missions, and
Evangelical Anti-Dependency in a Haitian Refugee
Camp," *Nova Religio: The Journal of Alternative and
Emergent Religions* 16, 4 (May 2013).

16. Global Research, Haiti Grassroots Watch, "Haiti:
Reconstruction's Housing Projects Still Plagued
with Problems Four Years after the Earthquake"
(January 8, 2014): globalresearch.ca/haiti-recon-
structions-housing-projects-still-plagued-with-
problems-four-years-after-the-earthquake/5364749

17. Robert Roos, "Cholera Has Struck More Than 6%
of Haitians," Center for Infectious Disease Research
and Policy, January 9, 2013, cidrap.umn.edu/
news-perspective/2013/01/cholera-has-struck-
more-6-haitians.

18. Randal C. Archimbold and Samini Sangupta,
"U.N. Struggles to Stem Haiti Cholera Epidemic,"
New York Times (19 April 2014): nytimes.
com/2014/04/20/world/americas/un-strug-
gles-to-stem-haiti-cholera-epidemic.html?hp.

Chapter 47

1. NOAA Fisheries, Office of Science & Technology,
Fisheries Economics of the U.S., 2011, st.nmfs.noaa.
gov/Assets/economics/documents/feus/2011/
FEUS2011%20-%20Gulf%20of%20Mexico.pdf.

2. U.S. Environmental Protection Agency, Gulf of Mexico Program, General Facts about the Gulf of Mexico, epa.gov/gmpo/about/facts.html#resources.

3. U.S. Energy Information Administration, Gulf of
Mexico Fact Sheet, eia.gov/special/gulf_of_mex-
ico/data.cfm.

4. Edward Klump, "Wildcatter Hunch Unlocks $1.5
Trillion Oil Offshore U.S.," *Bloomberg* (September
13, 2013), bloomberg.com/news/2013-09-12/
wildcatter-hunch-unlocks-1-5-trillion-oil-offshore-
u-s-.html.

5. David Barstow, David Rohde, and Stephanie Saul,
"Deepwater Horizon's Final Hours," December
12, 2010, nytimes.com/2010/12/26/us/26spill.
html?pagewanted=all.

6. Barstow *et al.*, "Deepwater Horizon's Final Hours."

7. U.S. Environmental Protection Agency, BP Oil Spill
(Deepwater Horizon), Description of the Event
and EPA's Response/Role, epa.gov/aed/html/
research/bpspill.html.

8. Charles H. Peterson *et al.*, "A Tale of Two Spills: Novel Science and Policy Implications of an Emerging New Oil Spill Model," *BioScience* 62, No. 5 (May 2012): 461–69.

9. Julia M Gohlke *et al.*, "A Review of Seafood Safety after the "Deepwater Horizon" Blowout," *Environmental Health Perspectives* 119, No. 8 (AUGUST 2011): 1062–69.

10. Reuters, "BP Loses Bid to Cut Maximum $13.7 Billion Gulf Spill Fine," *New York Times* (February 19, 2015): nytimes.com/reuters/2015/02/19/business/19reuters-bp-spill.html?_r=0.

11. David Wethe, "U. S. Oil Profits Lure $16 Billion More Rigs by 2015," *Bloomberg* (July 17, 2013), bloomberg.com/news/2013-07-16/u-s-gulf-oil-profits-lure-16-billion-more-rigs-by-2015.html.

12. Coral Davenport, "Obama's Plan: Allow Drilling in Atlantic, but Limit It in Arctic," *New York Times* (January 27, 2015): nytimes.com/2015/01/28/us/obama-plan-calls-for-oil-and-gas-drilling-in-the-atlantic.html.

Chapter 48

1. Ian Stimson, "Japan's Tohoku Earthquake and Tsunami," *Geology Today* 27, 3 (May–June 2011): 96–98.

2. Nobohito Mori, Tomoyuki Takahashi, and the 2011 Tohoku Earthquake Tsunami Joint Survey Group, "Nationwide Post Event Survey and Analysis of the 2011 Tohoku Earthquake Tsunami," *Coastal Engineering Journal* 54, 1 (2012): 1250001-1 – 1250001-27.

3. Lucy Birmingham and David McNeill, *Strong in the Rain: Surviving Japan's Earthquake, Tsunami, and Fukushima Nuclear Disaster* (New York: Palgrave MacMillan, 2012), 50–51.

4. NOAA, "Japan's 'Harbor Wave': The Tsunami One Year Later," noaa.gov/features/03_protecting/japantsunami_oneyearlater.html.

5. World Nuclear Association, "Nuclear Energy in Japan," (Updated February 2014), world-nuclear.org/info/Country-Profiles/Countries-G-N/Japan/.

6. Birmingham and McNeill, *Strong in the Rain*, 63.

7. Mori and Takahashi, "Nationwide Post Event Survey."

8. Birmingham and McNeill, *Strong in the Rain*, 64.

9. Rupert Wingfield-Hayes, "Fukushima: Is Fear of Radiation the Real Killer?" *BBC Asia* (11 March 2014), bbc.com/news/world-asia-26483945.

10. Ben Sharples and Tsuyoshi Inujima, "Uranium Poised for Bull Market as Japan Reviews Reactors: Energy," *Bloomberg* (January 22, 2014), bloomberg.com/news/2014-01-21/uranium-poised-for-bull-market-as-japan-reviews-reactors-energy.html.

11. Martin Fackler, "Nuclear Issue in Limbo as Indecision Grips Japan," *New York Times* (February 11, 2014): nytimes.com/2014/02/12/world/asia/nuclear-issue-in-limbo-as-indecision-grips-japan.html.

12. Reuters, "Japan Aims to Restart Nuclear Reactor in June," *New York Times* (February 6, 2015): nytimes.com/reuters/2015/02/06/world/asia/06reuters-japan-nuclear-restart.html.

13. Birmingham and McNeill, *Strong in the Rain*, 78.

14. Birmingham and McNeill, *Strong in the Rain*, 199.

Chapter 49

1. WHO, *One Year into the Ebola Epidemic: A Deadly, Tenacious, and Unforgiving Virus* (January 2015): who.int/csr/disease/ebola/one-year-report/ebola-report-1-year.pdf?ua=1.

2. Angus J. Dawson, "Ebola: What It Tells Us about Medical Ethics," *J Med Ethics* 41 (2015):107–110.

3. CDC, "How to Talk with Your Children about Ebola," cdc.gov/vhf/ebola/pdf/how-talk-children-about-ebola-factsheet.pdf.

4. WHO, *One Year into the Ebola Epidemic.*

5. CDC, "Ebola: Ebola Virus Disease," cdc.gov/vhf/ebola/

6. WHO, *One Year into the Ebola Epidemic.*

7. WHO, *One Year into the Ebola Epidemic.*

8. WHO, "Ebola Virus Disease Fact Sheet," who.int/mediacentre/factsheets/fs103/en/.

9. Elhadj Ibrahima Bah *et al.*, "Clinical Presentation of Patients with Ebola Virus Disease in Conakry, Guinea," *New England Journal of Medicine* 2015; 372:40-47 (January 1, 2015): nejm.org/doi/full/10.1056/NEJMoa1411249.

10. WHO, *One Year into the Ebola Epidemic.*

11. U.S. National Weather Service, "Lightning Safety," lightningsafety.noaa.gov/fatalities.htm.

12. "The Latest: Ebola in the United States," *The Atlantic* (November 20, 2014): theatlantic.com/health/archive/2014/11/ebola-in-the-us/381575/.

13. "The Latest: Ebola in the United States."

14. Dawson, "Ebola: What It Tells Us about Medical Ethics," 109.

Chapter 50

1. Wikipedia, "Quaternary Glaciation," en.wikipedia.org/wiki/Quaternary_glaciation.

2. Wikipedia, "Human Evolution," en.wikipedia.org/wiki/Human_evolution.

3. IPCC Working Group I, "Headline Statements from the Summary for Policy Makers," from *Climate Change 2013: The Physical Science Basis*: climatechange2013.org/images/uploads/WG1AR5_Headlines.pdf.

4. NOAA, "Changes in Wind Shear Accompany Shift in Latitude Where Hurricanes Reach Maximum Intensity," *ClimateWatch Magazine* (10 June 2014), climate.gov/news-features/featured-images/changes-wind-shear-accompany-shift-latitude-where-hurricanes-reach.

5. CIA, *World Fact Book*, "Marshall Islands," cia.gov/library/publications/the-world-factbook/geos/rm.html.

6. IPCC Working Group II, "Summary for Policymakers," from *Climate Change 2014: Impacts, Adaptation, and Vulnerability*: ipcc-wg2.gov/AR5/press-events/press-kit/.

7. Willie Smits, "How to Restore a Rainforest," ted.com/talks/willie_smits_restores_a_rainforest

8. Wimp.com, "This Guy's Creation Is Absolutely Astounding," wimp.com/creationastounding/.

9. Russell Shorto, "How to Think Like the Dutch in a Post-Sandy World," *NYT Magazine* (April 9, 2014): nytimes.com/2014/04/13/magazine/how-to-think-like-the-dutch-in-a-post-sandy-world.html.

10. United Nations, Framework Convention on Climate Change, unfccc.int/kyoto_protocol/items/2830.php.

11. United Nations, Framework Convention on Climate Change,

12. IPCC Working Group III, "Summary for Policymakers," from *Climate Change 2014: Mitigation of Climate Change*: ipcc-wg3.de/.

13. *New York Times* Editorial Board, "Running Out of Time," *New York Times* (20 April 2014): nytimes.com/2014/04/21/opinion/running-out-of-time.html?hp&rref=opinion.

14. Wikipedia, "Permian-Triassic Extinction Event," en.wikipedia.org/wiki/Permian%E2%80%93Triassic_extinction_event.

15. David L. Chandler, "Ancient whodunit may be solved: The microbes did it!: Methane-producing microbes may be responsible for the largest mass extinction in Earth's history," *MIT News* (31 March 2014), newsoffice.mit.edu/2014/ancient-whodunit-may-be-solved-microbes-did-it.

Sources

1. For a codified introduction to information literacy, see the Big6 Skills Overview, developed by Mike Eisenberg and Bob Berkowitz: big6.com/pages/about/big6-skills-overview.php.

INDEX

Page numbers followed by *ph* indicate illustrations or their captions.

ABOUT THE AUTHOR

Gale Eaton has spent a lifetime with books for children and young adults, first as a children's librarian at the Boston Public Library and the Berkshire Athenaeum, and later as a professor of children's literature at the University of Rhode Island Graduate School of Library and Information Studies. She is the author of two previous books (*Well-Dressed Role Models: The Portrayal of Women in Biographies for Children* and *The Education of Alice M. Jordan: Navigating a Career in Children's Librarianship*) and numerous journal articles and is presently at work on *A History of Ambition in 50 Hoaxes*. Raised in Maine, Gale lives in Wakefield, Rhode Island. (Photo by Tony Balko, the Harrington School of Communication and Media, University of Rhode Island)

ABOUT THE HISTORY IN 50 SERIES EDITOR

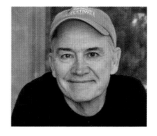

Phillip Hoose is the widely acclaimed author of books, essays, stories, songs, and articles, including the National Book Award and Newbery Honor winning book *Claudette Colvin: Twice toward Justice* and the Boston Globe–Horn Book Honor winner *The Boys Who Challenged Hitler: Knud Pedersen and the Churchill Club*. A graduate of Indiana University and the Yale School of Forestry and Environmental Sciences, Hoose was for 37 years a staff member of The Nature Conservancy, dedicated to preserving the plants, animals, and natural communities of the Earth. Find out more at www.philliphoose.com. (Photo by Gordon Chibrowski, Maine Newspapers)